John Gilmary Shea

Hierarchy of the Catholic Church in the United States

embracing sketches of all the archbishops and bishops from the establishment of

the See of Baltimore to the present time

John Gilmary Shea

Hierarchy of the Catholic Church in the United States
embracing sketches of all the archbishops and bishops from the establishment of the See of Baltimore to the present time

ISBN/EAN: 9783337302146

Printed in Europe, USA, Canada, Australia, Japan

Cover: Foto ©Lupo / pixelio.de

More available books at **www.hansebooks.com**

THE HIERARCHY

OF THE

CATHOLIC CHURCH

IN THE

UNITED STATES,

EMBRACING SKETCHES OF ALL THE

ARCHBISHOPS AND BISHOPS

FROM THE ESTABLISHMENT OF THE SEE OF BALTIMORE TO THE PRESENT TIME.

ALSO,

AN ACCOUNT OF THE PLENARY COUNCILS OF BALTIMORE, AND A BRIEF
HISTORY OF THE CHURCH IN THE UNITED STATES.

BY

JOHN GILMARY SHEA, LL.D.

Profusely Illustrated with Portraits.

TO WHICH ARE ADDED

*NUMEROUS PORTRAITS WITH BRIEF BIOGRAPHICAL NOTES OF CANADIAN BISHOPS
OF OUR OWN TIME.*

NEW YORK:
THE OFFICE OF CATHOLIC PUBLICATIONS,
14 BARCLAY STREET.

 MICHAEL A. CORRIGAN,

SEPTEMBER 14, 1886.

PREFACE.

THE Roman Catholic Church, Papal in its head, is eminently Episcopal in its general working. It is diffused, maintained, continued by the action of its Bishops, and it is in them, their lives and career, that we can most easily study the development of the Church, especially in a country like ours.

This work, without pretending to give elaborate or exhaustive biographies, which would require a series of expensive volumes, affords the reader, however, in a convenient compass the life of every Archbishop and Bishop connected with the Church in the United States from the appointment of the Most Rev. John Carroll as Bishop of Baltimore, in 1789, to the present time, as also a brief history of the Church from its beginning in this country to our own day, and an account of the Plenary Councils of the United States. It thus pictures the life and expansion of the Church in this Republic during a century, and will be a useful work of reference to all classes, and to the Catholic a source of religious pleasure, by affording all some notice of the Bishops under whom they live, and of those who have gone to their reward, of whose zeal and labors they have heard their elders expatiate, or whom it has been their own privilege to know.

As no work of such a character has ever been presented, it will prove as acceptable as it was surely necessary. Every effort has been made to secure authentic portraits to accompany the text.

J. G. S.

CONTENTS.

	PAGE
THE PLENARY COUNCILS OF THE CATHOLIC CHURCH IN THE UNITED STATES,	43
THE CATHOLIC CHURCH IN THE UNITED STATES,	49
VICARS-APOSTOLIC OF ENGLAND AND THE LONDON DISTRICT,	59

DIOCESE OF BALTIMORE:
- Most Rev. John Carroll, ... 61
- Leonard Neale, ... 65
- Ambrose Maréchal, ... 67
- James Whitfield, ... 69
- Samuel Eccleston, ... 72
- Francis P. Kenrick, ... 74
- Martin John Spalding, ... 77
- James Roosevelt Bayley, ... 81
- His Eminence James Cardinal Gibbons, ... 82

DIOCESE OF BOSTON:
- Right Rev. John Cheverus, ... 85
- Benedict J. Fenwick, ... 87
- John B. Fitzpatrick, ... 89
- Most Rev. John J. Williams, ... 91

DIOCESE OF CHICAGO:
- Right Rev. William Quarter, ... 95
- James Oliver Van de Velde, ... 96
- Anthony O'Regan, ... 97
- James Duggan, ... 98
- Thomas Foley, ... 99
- Most Rev. Patrick A. Feehan, ... 100

DIOCESE OF CINCINNATI:
- Right Rev. Edward Fenwick, ... 103
- Most Rev. John Baptist Purcell, ... 105
- William Henry Elder, ... 109

DIOCESE OF MILWAUKEE:
- Most Rev. John Martin Henni, ... 111
- Michael Heiss, ... 114

DIOCESE OF NEW ORLEANS:
- Most Rev. Louis Ignatius Peñalver y Cardenas, ... 118
- William Louis Dubourg, ... 120
- Right Rev. Leo Raymond de Neckere, ... 122
- Most Rev. Anthony Blanc, ... 123
- John Mary Odin, ... 125
- Napoleon J. Perché, ... 127
- Francis X. Leray, ... 129

DIOCESE OF NEW YORK :   PAGE
 Right Rev. Richard Luke Concanen, O.S.D., ... 132
    John Connolly, O.S.D., ... 133
    John Du Bois, ... 134
 Most Rev. John Hughes, ... 136
 His Eminence John Cardinal McCloskey, ... 142
 Most Rev. Michael A. Corrigan, ... 148
DIOCESE OF OREGON :
 Most Rev. Francis N. Blanchet, ... 150
    Charles John Seghers, ... 152
    William H. Gross, ... 153
DIOCESE OF PHILADELPHIA :
 Right Rev. Michael Egan, ... 155
    Henry Conwell, ... 156
    John N. Neumann, ... 157
 Most Rev. James Frederic Wood, ... 158
    Patrick John Ryan, ... 160
DIOCESE OF ST. LOUIS :
 Right Rev. Joseph Rosati, ... 162
 Most Rev. Peter Richard Kenrick, ... 164
DIOCESE OF SAN FRANCISCO :
 Right Rev. Francis Garcia Diego y Moreno, ... 169
 Most Rev. Joseph Sadoc Alemany, ... 170
    Patrick W. Riordan, ... 172
DIOCESE OF SANTA FE :
 Most Rev. John B. Lamy, ... 174
    John B. Salpointe, ... 178
DIOCESE OF ALBANY :
 Right Rev. John Joseph Conroy, ... 179
    Francis S. McNeirny, ... 180
DIOCESE OF ALTON :
 Right Rev. Henry Damian Juncker, ... 184
    Peter Joseph Baltes, ... 185
DIOCESE OF BROOKLYN :
 Right Rev. John Loughlin, ... 187
DIOCESE OF BUFFALO :
 Right Rev. John Timon, C.M., ... 189
    Stephen Vincent Ryan, C.M., ... 193
DIOCESE OF BURLINGTON :
 Right Rev. Louis de Goesbriand, ... 195
DIOCESE OF CHARLESTON :
 Right Rev. John England, ... 197
    William Clancy, Coadjutor, ... 200
    Ignatius Aloysius Reynolds, ... 201
    Patrick Niesen Lynch, ... 202
    Henry P. Northrop, ... 204
DIOCESE OF CLEVELAND :
 Right Rev. Amadeus Rappe, ... 205
    Richard Gilmour, ... 206
DIOCESE OF COLUMBUS :
 Right Rev. Sylvester H. Rosecrans, ... 209
    John Ambrose Watterson, ... 213

CONTENTS.

	PAGE
DIOCESE OF COVINGTON:	
Right Rev. George A. Carrell,	214
Augustus M. Toebbe,	215
Camillus Paul Maes,	216
DIOCESE OF DAVENPORT:	
Right Rev. John McMullen,	218
Henry Cosgrove,	219
DIOCESE OF DETROIT:	
Right Rev. Frederick Résé,	221
Peter Paul Lefevre, Administrator,	222
Caspar H. Borgess,	224
DIOCESE OF DUBUQUE:	
Right Rev. Matthias Loras,	227
Clement Smyth,	229
John Hennessy,	230
DIOCESE OF ERIE:	
Right Rev. Josue M. Young,	232
Tobias Mullen,	233
DIOCESE OF FORT WAYNE:	
Right Rev. John Henry Luers,	235
Joseph Dwenger,	236
DIOCESE OF GALVESTON:	
Right Rev. Claude Mary Dubuis,	238
Nicholas A. Gallagher,	239
DIOCESE OF GRAND RAPIDS:	
Right Rev. Henry Joseph Richter,	243
DIOCESE OF GRASS VALLEY:	
Right Rev. Eugene O'Connell,	245
Patrick Manogue,	246
DIOCESE OF GREEN BAY:	
Right Rev. Joseph Melcher,	248
Francis X. Krautbauer,	249
DIOCESE OF HARRISBURG:	
Right Rev. Jeremiah F. Shanahan,	251
DIOCESE OF HARTFORD:	
Right Rev. William Tyler,	253
Bernard O'Reilly,	254
Francis Patrick McFarland,	255
Thomas Galberry, O.S.A.,	256
Lawrence S. McMahon,	258
DIOCESE OF HELENA:	
Right Rev. John B. Brondel,	261
DIOCESES OF KANSAS CITY AND ST. JOSEPH:	
Right Rev. John Joseph Hogan,	263
DIOCESE OF LA CROSSE:	
Right Rev. Kilian Flasch,	266
DIOCESE OF LEAVENWORTH:	
Right Rev. John B. Miége, S.J., Vicar Apostolic,	268
Louis Maria Fink, O.S.B.,	270
DIOCESE OF LITTLE ROCK:	
Right Rev. Andrew Byrne,	274
Edward Fitzgerald,	275

CONTENTS.

	PAGE
DIOCESE OF LOUISVILLE:	
Right Rev. Benedict Joseph Flaget,	277
John Baptist David,	280
Guy Ignatius Chabrat, Coadjutor,	282
Peter Joseph Lavialle,	283
William G. McCloskey,	285
DIOCESE OF MANCHESTER:	
Right Rev. Denis M. Bradley,	286
DIOCESE OF MARQUETTE:	
Right Rev. Frederic Baraga,	288
Ignatius Mrak,	291
John Vertin,	292
DIOCESE OF MOBILE:	
Right Rev. Michael Portier,	293
John Quinlan,	296
Dominic Manucy,	298
Jeremiah O'Sullivan,	300
DIOCESE OF MONTEREY AND LOS ANGELES:	
Right Rev. Thaddeus Amat,	301
Francis Mora,	303
DIOCESE OF NASHVILLE:	
Right Rev. Richard Pius Miles, O.S.D.,	305
James Whelan, O.S.D.,	307
Joseph Rademacher,	308
DIOCESE OF NATCHEZ:	
Right Rev. John Joseph Chanche,	311
Francis Janssens,	313
DIOCESE OF NATCHITOCHES:	
Right Rev. Augustus M. Martin,	318
Anthony Durier,	319
DIOCESE OF NESQUALLY:	
Right Rev. Augustine M. Blanchet,	320
Ægidius Junger,	322
DIOCESE OF NEWARK:	
Right Rev. Winand M. Wigger,	324
DIOCESE OF OGDENSBURG:	
Right Rev Edgar P. Wadhams,	326
DIOCESE OF OMAHA:	
Right Rev. James O'Gorman,	331
James O'Connor,	332
DIOCESE OF PEORIA:	
Right Rev. John L. Spalding,	334
DIOCESE OF PITTSBURGH:	
Right Rev. Michael O'Connor,	336
Michael Domenec,	338
John Tuigg,	339
Richard Phelan, Coadjutor,	343
DIOCESE OF PORTLAND:	
Right Rev. David W. Bacon,	344
James Augustine Healy,	345
DIOCESE OF PROVIDENCE:	
Right Rev. Thomas F. Hendricken,	347

CONTENTS.

	PAGE
DIOCESE OF RICHMOND:	
Right Rev. Patrick Kelly,	349
Richard V. Whelan,	350
John McGill,	352
John J. Keane,	353
DIOCESE OF ROCHESTER:	
Right Rev. Bernard J. McQuaid,	357
DIOCESE OF SAN ANTONIO:	
Right Rev. Anthony D. Pellicer,	359
J. C. Neraz,	360
DIOCESE OF SAVANNAH:	
Right Rev. Francis X. Gartland,	362
John Barry,	363
Augustine Verot,	364
Ignatius Persico,	366
DIOCESE OF SCRANTON:	
Right Rev. William O'Hara,	369
DIOCESE OF SPRINGFIELD:	
Right Rev. P. T. O'Reilly,	371
DIOCESE OF ST. AUGUSTINE:	
Right Rev. John Moore,	375
DIOCESE OF ST. PAUL:	
Right Rev. Joseph Crétin,	377
Thomas L. Grace, O.S.D.,	378
John Ireland,	379
DIOCESE OF TRENTON:	
Right Rev. Michael J. O'Farrell,	381
DIOCESE OF VINCENNES:	
Right Rev. Simon Gabriel Bruté,	383
Celestine R. L. G. de la Hailandière,	385
John Stephen Bazin,	386
James M. M. de St. Palais,	387
Francis Silas Chatard,	388
DIOCESE OF WHEELING:	
Right Rev. John J. Kain,	391
DIOCESE OF WILMINGTON:	
Right Rev. Thomas A. Becker,	392
VICARIATE-APOSTOLIC OF ARIZONA:	
Right Rev. P. Bourgade,	402
VICARIATE-APOSTOLIC OF COLORADO:	
Right Rev. Joseph P. Machebœuf,	394
VICARIATE APOSTOLIC OF DAKOTA:	
Right Rev. Martin Marty, O.S.B.,	396
VICARIATE-APOSTOLIC OF IDAHO:	
Right Rev. Louis Lootens,	399
A. J. Glorieux,	400
VICARIATE-APOSTOLIC OF NORTHERN MINNESOTA:	
Right Rev. Rupert Seidenbush, O.S.B.,	401

THE PLENARY COUNCILS

OF THE

CATHOLIC CHURCH IN THE UNITED STATES.

FROM the moment that the Sovereign Pontiff, dividing the diocese of Baltimore into those of Baltimore, Boston, New York, Philadelphia, and Bardstown, founded a hierarchy, it was the wish of the venerable Archbishop Carroll to assemble his suffragans in council and concert measures for the good of the Church. The delays caused by the arrest of Bishop Concanen in Italy, and finally his death, defeated this project, and the proto-bishop and archbishop gathered his newly-consecrated suffragans, and in an informal assembly adopted some regulations in order to maintain uniform discipline.

Louisiana and the Floridas, which had been formed into a diocese in 1793, had long been deprived of the supervision of a bishop, and in part were for a time under the administratorship of Archbishop Carroll, so that no concurrence from those parts of the country was possible.

Under the successors of Archbishop Carroll steps were taken here and at Rome to effect the holding of a provincial council, but this was not carried into effect till the year 1829, when the First Provincial Council of Baltimore was held by Archbishop Whitfield. Though not styled a Plenary Council, it was in a certain sense really one, for not only were the Archbishop of Baltimore and his suffragans present, but also the Bishop of St. Louis, who was also Administrator of the diocese of New Orleans; and the Bishop of Mobile, who was a suffragan of the Archbishop of Santiago de Cuba, had been invited, but did not return from Europe in time to take part in the sessions. It was intended to be a council of all the Catholic bishops having jurisdiction in the United States. The First Provincial Council of Baltimore, convened under authority from the Pope in 1828, assembled on the 1st of October, 1829, the Most Rev. James Whitfield, Archbishop of Baltimore, presiding, and Bishops Benedict Joseph Flaget, of Bardstown; John England, of Charleston; Edward Fenwick, of Cincinnati; Benedict Fenwick, of Boston; Joseph Rosati, of St. Louis; and the Very Rev. William Matthews, Vicar-General Apostolic of Philadelphia, attending. The council was succeeded by other Provincial Councils held at Baltimore under the presidency of the archbishops of that city; but when other sees were raised to the archiepiscopal dignity, and there seemed to be a probability that, as councils were held in the new provinces, divergences would arise in discipline on many essential points, it was deemed highly conducive to the general good of the Church that the several metropolitans of the United States and their suffragans should assemble together in a Plenary Council, and adopt, where possible, uniform rules to be observed in all parts of the country. The mischiefs and miseries which had arisen elsewhere, leading at times to schism, where a national character was sought to be imposed on the Church, cutting it away from the Holy See and from the Church in other countries, were too well known not to be avoided.

Pope Pius IX., approving of the desire of the American bishops by his Apostolic Brief, *In Apostolicæ Sedis fastigio*, August 19, 1851, appointed the Most Rev. Francis Patrick Kenrick, Archbishop of Baltimore, Delegate Apostolic to preside over the assembled prelates, recognizing "his remarkable knowledge of ecclesiastical discipline, zeal for the Catholic faith, and eminent fidelity to the Holy See."

The Council met on the 8th of May, 1852, in the Cathedral of Baltimore. Besides the Most Reverend Delegate Apostolic, there were present the Most Reverend Archbishops Blanchet, of Oregon; Kenrick, of St. Louis; Blanc, of New Orleans; Hughes, of New York; Purcell, of Cincinnati; the Right Rev. Bishops Portier, of Mobile; Loras, of Dubuque; Miles, of Nashville; Chanche, of Natchez; Whelan, of Wheeling; Lefevre, (Administrator) of Detroit; Odin, of Galveston; O'Connor, of Pittsburgh; Byrne, of Little Rock; McCloskey, of Albany; Reynolds, of

Charleston; Henni, of Milwaukee; Fitzpatrick, of Boston; Rappe, of Cleveland; Timon, of Buffalo; Spalding, of Louisville; Van de Velde, of Chicago; Blanchet, of Nesqually; Alemany, of Monterey; O'Reilly, of Hartford; Gartland, of Savannah; McGill, of Richmond; Lamy (Vicar-Apostolic), of New Mexico; Cretin, of St. Paul; Miège (Vicar-Apostolic), of Indian Territory; and Neumann, of Philadelphia. Each bishop and archbishop was attended by theologians, and there were also summoned to the Council the Abbot of La Trappe, the Commissary-General of the Augustinians, the Visitor-General of the Dominicans, the Superiors of the Benedictine and Franciscan orders, the Provincial of the Society of Jesus in Maryland, the Vice-Provincial of Missouri, and the Superiors at New York and New Orleans, the Provincial of the Redemptorists, the Rector of the Sulpitian Seminary, and the Lazarist Director of the Sisters of Charity. The sessions closed on the 20th of May, and issued twenty-five decrees, which were approved by a decree of the Congregation *de Propaganda Fide*, Sept. 26, 1852. The acts and decrees of this First Plenary Council were published at Baltimore in 1853.

The decrees of this Council were also promulgated in almost all the provinces, and the beneficial results soon led to a desire for another general assemblage of the archbishops and bishops of the country, who had grown in number by the erection of new sees and the establishment of new metropolitan jurisdictions.

The Letters Apostolic of Pius IX. *Apostolici ministerii munus*, Feb. 16, 1866, appointed the Most Reverend Martin John Spalding to preside in a Second Plenary Council at Baltimore. It opened on the 7th and closed on the 21st of October. The Fathers of the Council comprised the Archbishops of Baltimore, Oregon, St. Louis, San Francisco, New Orleans, New York, the Bishop Administrator of Detroit, the Bishops of Milwaukee, Nesqually, Cleveland, Buffalo, Vincennes, Richmond, Santa Fé, Brooklyn, Newark, Burlington, Covington, Monterey and Los Angeles, Natchitoches, Portland, Alton, Chicago, Natchez, Fort Wayne, Charleston, Hartford, the Vicar-Apostolic of Nebraska, the Bishops of St. Paul, Mobile, Philadelphia, Pittsburgh, the Vicar-Apostolic of Marysville, the Bishops of Savannah, Galveston, Louisville, Albany, Nashville, Boston, Dubuque, the Auxiliar Bishop of Cincinnati, the Administrator of the diocese of Erie, and a representative of the Vicar-Apostolic of Indian Territory,* as well as the Abbots of La Trappe and St. Benedict. The Bishop of Galveston was absent from the country.

There were also Provincials or Superiors of the Dominicans, Reformed, Conventual, and Observantine Franciscans, the Capuchins, the Society of Jesus, Lazarists, Sulpitians, Redemptorists, Passionists, Oblates, Most Precious Blood, Paulists, and Brothers of Mary.

The decrees passed, instead of being confined to mere points of discipline adapted to this country, cover the whole field of the doctrines and discipline of the Church. The decrees, comprising 532 sections, divided under fourteen titles, were approved by Pope Pius IX., through the Propaganda, on the 24th of January, 1868, and were published in 1868, comprising a volume of 554 pages. It was at once adopted in the theological seminaries as a comprehensive manual of the doctrinal and disciplinary law of the Catholic Church in the United States. A volume of Notes explaining many of the provisions was prepared by the Rev. S. Smith, D.D., and published in 1874.

The gathering of all the Catholic bishops of the world in an Oecumenical Council at the Vatican led to the discussion of many points of Church government and discipline which could not be passed upon by the Council, its sessions having been interrupted by the sacrilegious seizure of the Capital of the Catholic world.

A third Plenary Council was accordingly convened in pursuance of Letters Apostolic of His Holiness Pope Leo XIII., who appointed the Most Rev. James Gibbons, Archbishop of Baltimore, to preside over its deliberations as Delegate Apostolic. The matters to be treated of in the Council were on this occasion first discussed at Rome by the Most Reverend Archbishops or their delegates, and a commission of theologians appointed by the Holy See.

The Third Plenary Council was opened in the Cathedral at

---

* The Bishop of Vancouver's Island attended as a suffragan of the Archbishop of Oregon, although his diocese was not within the limits of the United States.

Baltimore on the 9th of November, 1884, and closed on the 7th of the following month, its deliberations having been extended far beyond the time of the previous gatherings of the American prelates. It was attended by fourteen archbishops, sixty bishops, four bishops from Canada and one from Japan as visitors, one prefect-apostolic, seven abbots, and twenty-three superiors of religious orders, with vicars-general, superiors of seminaries, and theologians.

THE CATHOLIC CHURCH

IN THE

UNITED STATES.

EVEN in the territory now embraced in the United States this ancient Church preceded all other Christian denominations.

As early as 1521 Ponce de Leon, seeking to plant civilization and Christianity on our shores, landed in Florida with Catholic priests and religious, and the liturgy of the Catholic Church was offered amid the evergreen glades. But while the Spaniards were building their houses and chapel, the Indians kept up such constant war that the settlement was abandoned by the wounded commander. In 1526 Vasquez de Ayllon commenced a settlement on one of the rivers flowing into the Chesapeake, and the Dominican friars who attended him reared a chapel on the James, where for months the rites of the Church were offered; but the commander died and the settlement was abandoned.

The expeditions of Narvaez and De Soto had clergymen with them, but no settlements were formed, and the pioneer ministers of religion who accompanied the conquistadores perished amid the hardships of the march. Impelled by the account of a survivor of one of these ill-fated expeditions, the Franciscan Father Mark, of Nice, in Italy, penetrated in 1539 to New Mexico. Others followed and began missions, only to be murdered by the Indians. In 1595 the Spaniards occupied the country and founded San Gabriel. The Catholic worship was established, and has continued almost uninterruptedly in that territory for nearly three centuries. In an outbreak against the

Spaniards at the close of the seventeenth century many of the missionaries perished. Some Dominican priests were slain in Florida in 1549 while trying to convert the natives; and Tristan de Luna, in 1559, had a Christian shrine at Pensacola. When St. Augustine was begun, in 1565, a Catholic chapel was erected, and from that time the services of the Church were regularly offered. At St. Helena, on Port Royal Sound, and later on the banks of the Rappahannock, there were Catholic chapels as early as 1571. For many years St. Augustine had its Franciscan convent and chapels within and without the walls. Missions were established among the Indian tribes by the Jesuits and then by the Franciscans, and the Timuquans, Apalaches, and other tribes embraced Christianity. In 1699 Pensacola was founded and a Catholic church erected there; but the Indian missions were finally almost extirpated by the English colonists of Carolina and Georgia. Many devoted missionaries were slain amid their pious labors to regenerate the aborigines.

Texas was settled by the Spaniards, and a town grew up at San Antonio, with church and convent, while missionaries planted the cross among the Indian tribes from the Rio Grande to the Sabine. The Catholic Church was the only Christian body here for a century and a quarter.

Upper California was settled about the time of our Revolution, and the Franciscans established a series of Indian missions whose names are still retained. They were finally destroyed by the greed of the Mexican government, just before our conquest of the country. The Catholic Church in New Mexico, Texas, and California, like that in Florida, has its lists of missionaries who held life less precious than the cause of Christ.

North of our territory lie Canada and Nova Scotia, settled at an early day by Catholic France. The worship of the Church of Rome was celebrated beneath rude temporary structures at Boone Island, in Maine, and subsequently at Mount Desert, early in the seventeenth century. And soon after the Capuchin Fathers had missions from the Kennebec to Gaspé. The very year the Pilgrim Fathers landed at Plymouth Rock a Franciscan priest in sandalled feet crossed the Niagara River from Canada, and preached Christ, and him crucified, to the Indians of Western New York. A few years later two Jesuits met the Chippewas at Sault St. Mary's, by the outlet of the most remote of the Western lakes, and one of them, the gentle yet intrepid Father Jogues, returned to die by the tomahawk while endeavoring to imbue the minds of the Mohawks with the sweet spirit of Christ. In the latter part of the seventeenth century there were Catholic chapels on the Kennebec and coast of Maine, from the Mohawk to the Niagara, at Mackinaw, Sault St. Mary's, Green Bay, and Kaskaskia. Early in the last century Detroit had a church. Kaskaskia, Cahokia, and Vincennes were the next seats of Catholicity. At the South New Orleans and Mobile were founded and Catholic churches were established, Capuchins laboring in the settlements, and Jesuits and missionary priests among the Indian tribes. The Ursuline nuns at New Orleans began to labor as teachers and nurses. These churches and institutions, from Maine to Louisiana, were subject to the bishops of Quebec.

In the English colonies Catholicity began its life in Maryland coeval with the settlement, two Jesuit priests having formed part of the first body of colonists, taking up lands and bringing over men to cultivate them. By the leader of this mission, Father Andrew White, Catholic worship was first offered on St. Clement's Isle, in the Potomac, on the 25th of March, 1634. Catholic clergymen were for many years the only ministers of religion in Maryland, and most of the settlers attended their church. The conversion of the Indians was immediately undertaken, and the Piscataways and Potopacos, with their rulers, became Christians.

Maryland was founded on the broad principles of religious freedom, and Puritans expelled from Virginia found shelter there. During the period of the Commonwealth, however, the very men who had sought an asylum in Maryland overthrew the authority of Lord Baltimore and passed severe penal laws against the Catholics, sending all the priests as prisoners to England. In a few years they returned and resumed their labors under great disadvantages. Though a law of toleration was passed in 1649, it was of brief duration. In 1654 Catholics were deprived of civil rights, and, though there was a lull during the reigns of Charles II. and James II., the storm broke out with renewed fury on the accession of William III. The Catholic worship was forbidden by law, and could be offered only in secrecy; Catholics were loaded with double taxes, deprived of all power of voting or bearing arms. Yet most of the Catholics persevered, the Jesuits and Franciscans having chapels in houses, which were attended by the people. A school was even established where boys were fitted for a college training in Europe.

During the control of James as duke and king over New York liberty of conscience prevailed and Catholics began to settle there. Several clergymen of that faith came over, and the settlers who adhered to it were thus enabled to enjoy the consolations of religion. A Latin school was also opened, the first one in the colony. Leisler, on the fall of James, drove nearly all Catholics out of New York, and penal laws were passed to punish any Catholic priest who entered the colony.

When Pennsylvania began to be settled under the liberal policy of Penn, Catholics gradually entered, and as the German immigration began a considerable number adhered to the faith planted in their fatherland by St. Boniface. As early as 1708 the Mass was regularly offered in Philadelphia, and after a time St. Joseph's Church, on Willing's Alley, was begun by the Jesuit Fathers when they assumed the care of the mission. A church was erected at an early period at Lancaster, and there were mission-houses at Conewago and Goshenhoppen.

In other colonies there were a few scattered Catholics, but nowhere in numbers sufficient to establish a church. The Acadians, carried off by the British government from Nova Scotia in 1755 and scattered on the coast, were Catholics, but only at Baltimore and Philadelphia did they find a welcome. At Baltimore they were attended by a priest and founded the first Catholic church.

The Catholics in the British colonies were subject to a bishop in England, known as the Vicar-Apostolic of the London District.

At the beginning of the Revolution there was a strong feeling against the adherents of the Church of Rome. Catholics, however, without exception, rallied to the cause of freedom.

The Catholic Indians in Maine, under their chief, Orono, took up the cause of the colonies; the St. Regis Indians, on the New York border, did the same; and the French settlers in Illinois, with the Indians around them, joined Colonel Clarke and gained the West for the United States. Two regiments of Canadian Catholics fought on the American side during the whole war, attended by their chaplain, a priest commissioned by the Continental Congress.

The Continental Congress itself and the Constitutional Convention had Catholic members, who were honored by all.

After the close of the Revolution the Catholics in the United States could no longer be subject to the London vicar-apostolic. Some desired a bishop; others thought that the time had not yet come. Pope Pius VI., in 1784, appointed as prefect-apostolic the Rev. John Carroll, a Maryland patriot-priest, who had, at the desire of Congress, gone to Canada during the Revolution to try and win over the inhabitants of that province.

The new prefect set to work to ascertain what scattered Catholics there were in the country. More were found in all parts than had been anticipated. The priests in Pennsylvania had before the war visited Catholics at the Iron-Works and at Macopin, in New Jersey, and the Rev. F. Steenmeier (Farmer), a Fellow of the Royal Society and a distinguished mathematician, quietly visited New York and gathered a little congregation.

These flocks had now increased. There were a few Catholics even in Boston, at points on the Hudson and Mohawk, near Pittsburgh, and in Kentucky. Other priests came over from Europe, and these scattered bodies began to organize and assemble for worship. The total number of Catholics in the United States at this time could not have been much under forty thousand, including the French and Indians.

The reports of Very Rev. Mr. Carroll to the Pope satisfied him that a bishop was needed, and he left to the clergy in the country the nomination of a suitable candidate and the selection of his see. The choice fell on Dr. Carroll, who was appointed Bishop of Baltimore November 6, 1789, and his diocese embraced the whole United States.

Bishop Carroll proceeded to England, and was consecrated in the chapel of Lulworth Castle, August 15, 1790. The founder of the American hierarchy is a grand figure worthy of his time. His wisdom, learning, ability, and moderation were all required to build up the Church. Soon after his return to the United States the Revolution in France drove into exile many worthy and learned priests, not a few of whom came to America and aided Bishop Carroll in his work. Churches were begun or completed at Boston, New York, Albany, Charleston, Greensburg, and other points. Carmelite nuns came to found a convent of their order in Maryland; the Sulpitians established a seminary in Baltimore; a college was begun at Georgetown, soon followed by one at Emmittsburg.

In 1791 Bishop Carroll gathered twenty priests in a synod at Baltimore, and rules were adopted suited to the exigencies of the situation; but the duties of bishop were too heavy for one man. The Rev. Leonard Neale was appointed his coadjutor and consecrated bishop in 1800.

This was, however, but a temporary relief, and in 1808 bishops were appointed for Boston, Philadelphia, New York, and Bardstown, Ky. At this time his diocese contained sixty-eight priests and eighty churches. Bishop Cheverus, appointed Bishop of Boston, a man of zeal, charity, and gentleness, had all New England as his diocese, and won the affection of persons of every creed. As the Bishop of New York died at Naples, his diocese languished, and many important works, a college, and a convent-academy were abandoned. Bishop Egan, of Philadelphia, had as his diocese the State of Pennsylvania and part of New Jersey. He met with difficulties in Philadelphia, which increased under his successor and were detrimental to all real religious life; but in other parts of the diocese religion progressed. The diocese of Bardstown embraced Kentucky, with Ohio and all the Northwest. Here much was to be done; but the saintly Flaget, with coadjutors like Nerinckx, Badin, Richard, Salmon, and the English Dominicans, soon revived religion in places where it seemed dying out.

The United States were then bounded by the Mississippi. Louisiana, which embraced the country west of that river, had, at the request of the Spanish government, been formed into a diocese by Pope Pius VI., who in 1793 appointed a learned and charitable Cuban, Rev. Dr. Peñalver, Bishop of Louisiana. When Louisiana was ceded to the United States, in 1803, the bishopric was vacant, and the administration of the Church in that vast province was also confided to Bishop Carroll. The Church there was in a peculiar condition, organized originally under the Spanish system, but long neglected. Great troubles ensued, but the elevation of Rt. Rev. William Louis Dubourg to the episcopate, and the establishing of sees at New Orleans and St. Louis, gave a new impulse to religion.

The rapidly-increasing immigration after the fall of Napoleon added greatly to the number of Catholics, and priests were called for at many points. The first effort of the Catholic priest is to erect a church or churches in the district assigned to him, and in time to add schools. As a diocese is formed the bishop aids his clergy in this work, and endeavors to establish seminaries for young ladies, orphan asylums, hospitals under the care of Sisters belonging to some religious order fitted to the work, and colleges, high-schools, and a theological seminary. The religious orders of men come as auxiliaries to the secular clergy and conduct many of the colleges. Each diocese thus becomes a centre of such institutions. The rapid increase of Catholics and their comparative poverty have made this work difficult and onerous, and aid has been derived from organizations like the Association for the Propagation of the Faith in France, which was organized originally to aid the struggling churches in America.

The original dioceses, with the growth of the country, soon required division. Out of that of Baltimore have grown those of Richmond (1821), Charleston (1820), Savannah (1850), Wheeling (1850), and Wilmington (1868), and North Carolina has been formed into a vicariate. The original diocese of Philadelphia has been divided into those of Philadelphia, Scranton (1868), Harrisburg (1868), Pittsburgh and Allegheny (1843–76), and Erie (1853). The diocese of Newark has been formed to embrace New Jersey (1853), and Trenton (1881) has since been set off from it. New York contains the dioceses of New York, Albany (1847), Brooklyn (1853), Buffalo (1847), Rochester (1868), Ogdensburg (1872). Besides the see of Boston there are in New England sees at Portland (1855), Manchester (1884), Burlington (1853), Springfield (1870), Providence (1872), and Hartford (1844). In the West, Kentucky has bishops at Louisville and Covington (1853); Ohio an archbishop at Cincinnati (1822), and bishops at Cleveland (1847) and Columbus (1868); Indiana comprises two dioceses, Vincennes (1834) and Fort Wayne (1857); Michigan those of Detroit (1832), Marquette (1857), and Grand Rapids (1882); Illinois has an archbishop at Chicago (1844), and bishops at Alton (1857) and Peoria (1877); Wisconsin an archbishop at Milwaukee (1844), and bishops at La Crosse and Green Bay (1868); in Missouri there is an archbishop at St. Louis, and bishop at Kansas City and St. Joseph (1868–80); in Arkansas a bishop at Little Rock (1843); in Iowa bishops at Dubuque (1837) and Davenport (1881), in Minnesota at St. Paul (1850) and St. Cloud (1875), in Kansas at Leavenworth (1877), in Montana at Helena (1884); Nebraska, Idaho, Dakota, and Colorado are vicariates-apostolic, each under a bishop. In the South there is an archbishop at New Orleans; bishops at Nashville (1837), at Natchitoches (1853), Natchez (1837), Mobile (1824), St. Augustine (1870), Galveston (1847), San Antonio (1874), and a vicar-apostolic on the Rio Grande. Ancient New Mexico has its archbishop at Santa Fé (1850); Arizona a vicar apostolic. California has an archbishop at San Francisco (1853), and bishops at Monterey (1850) and Grass Valley (1868). Oregon has its archbishop (1846), Washington Territory a bishop (1850), and Indian Territory a prefect-apostolic.

The diocese of an archbishop and those of his suffragans form a province. In each province from time to time Provincial Councils are held, in which the archbishop presides and his suffragans take part, with their theologians and the heads of the religious orders. In these assemblies decrees are adopted for the better government of the Church in the province. The first council was that of Baltimore in 1829, held by Archbishop Whitfield; a number of councils were subsequently held there, and when other archbishoprics were erected councils were held at New York, Cincinnati, New Orleans, St. Louis, San Francisco, and in Oregon. Besides these there have been three Plenary

Councils, imposing assemblages held at Baltimore, attended by all the archbishops and bishops of the country.

The wonderful growth of the Catholic Church has not been without opposition. Many saw in it a danger to republican institutions, and violence has not been confined merely to words or publications. Catholic institutions and churches have been destroyed by mobs.

To advocate and defend their doctrines and polity the Catholics have a quarterly review, several monthlies, and a large number of weekly papers in English, German, French, and Spanish. Their publishing houses issue in great numbers Bibles, Testaments, Prayer-books, doctrinal and controversial as well as devotional works, and books of a lighter character chiefly for the young.

The Catholic body is composed of the descendants of the colonial settlers and more recent immigrants and their offspring, with members joining them from other religious bodies; but they have no missionary societies and no direct machinery for extending their doctrine among those unacquainted with it. Many of its prominent men have, however, been converts—Archbishops Whitfield, Eccleston, Bayley, Wood; Bishops Tyler, Wadhams, Young, Gilmour, Rosecrans; Orestes A. Brownson, the philosopher; Haldeman, the philologist; Dr. L. Silliman Ives, formerly bishop in the Protestant Episcopal Church; Father Hecker, founder of the Paulists; Mother Seton, founder of the Sisters of Charity.

Among other distinguished men of the Catholic body must be named Cardinal McCloskey, the first American member of the Sacred College; Archbishop Hughes; Archbishop Kenrick, of Baltimore, a great theologian and Biblical scholar; Bishop England, of Charleston; Bishop Baraga, Father De Smet; the Abbé Rouquette and Rev. A. J. Ryan, gifted poets; Bishop Du Bois, founder of Mount St. Mary's; Bishop Bruté, of Vincennes; Prince Galitzin, Carroll of Carrollton, Commodore Barry, Colonels Moylan and Vigo, Generals Rosecrans, Stone, and Newton.

Religious orders are numerous: the ancient Benedictine and Cistercian monks; the Franciscan, Dominican, Carmelite, and Augustinian friars; Jesuits, Redemptorists, Servites, Oblates;

Priests of the Holy Cross, of the Holy Ghost, of the Resurrection; Sulpitians, Brothers of the Christian Schools, Brothers of Mary; Xaverian, Alexian, and Franciscan Brothers; Benedictine, Carmelite, Ursuline, Visitation, Dominican nuns; Ladies of the Sacred Heart; Sisters of Charity, of Mercy, and many others.

At the close of the year 1885 the Catholic Church in the United States comprised 12 archbishops, 62 bishops, 7,296 priests; more than 1,600 young men studying for the priesthood; 6,755 churches, some of them, like the cathedrals of New York and Philadelphia, magnificent structures; nearly 3,000 chapels and stations, 36 ecclesiastical seminaries, 87 colleges, 618 academies for young ladies, 2,621 parochial schools with 500,000 pupils, 449 asylums and hospitals, and nearly eight million adherents.

RT. REV. INNOCENT WOLF.
Born April 13, 1843.

Entered St. Vincent's College, Pa., 1854; made vows of the Benedictine Order, 1861; Ordained May 26, 1866; Professor of Theology in St. Vincent's, 1870; elected Abbot of St. Benedict's Abbey at Atchison, Kansas, 1876.

VERY REV. I. T. HECKER.
Born in New York City, Dec. 18, 1819.

Became a Roman Catholic, 1845; joined the Redemptorists in Belgium, 1847; Ordained 1849; released from the Order, 1857; founded the Congregation of St. Paul the Apostle, in New York City, 1858.

RT. REV. B. WIMMER.
Born in Thalmassing, Bavaria, Jan. 14, 1809.

Ordained Aug. 1, 1831; joined the Order of St. Benedict, Sept. 13, 1842; came to U. S., 1846; Superior of the monastery of St. Vincent, Pa., May 21, 1852; Abbot *ad triennium*, Sept. 17, 1855; Abbot for life and President of American Congregation, July 27, 1866.

VERY REV. E. SORIN.
Born in Ahuillé, France, Feb. 6, 1814.

Ordained 1838; entered Congregation of the Holy Cross, 1839; landed in U. S., May 2, 1842; founded University of Notre Dame, Ind., also Institution of Sisters of the Holy Cross; Superior-General of the Congregation for life, 1868.

THE VICARS-APOSTOLIC OF LONDON.

THE Catholic Church throughout the world is, under the Sovereign Pontiff, governed by bishops or archbishops, so that almost every part of the earth is under the spiritual care of one of the consecrated successors of the Apostles. There are dioceses, governed by archbishops and bishops; vicariates-apostolic, under the charge of bishops assigned to the task; some places where the faith has developed less are committed to prefects-apostolic till the number of Catholics requires a bishop's care.

The British colonies which were formed on the Atlantic coast of North America in the seventeenth and eighteenth centuries, extending from New Hampshire to Georgia, were, in regard to the Catholics dwelling in them, under the charge of the vicars-apostolic in England. The first of these was Right Rev. William Bishop, Bishop of Chalcedon, Vicar-Apostolic of England and Scotland, consecrated in 1623. His successor, Right Rev. Richard Smith, a native of Lincolnshire, who had studied at Oxford, Rome, and Valladolid, was consecrated Bishop of Chalcedon and vicar-apostolic January 12, 1625. He was in office when a community of Catholics settled in Maryland, but he was a fugitive in France and seems to have taken no part in regulating the discipline of the Church in America. After his death no appointment of a bishop as vicar-apostolic for England was made till 1685, when the Right Rev. John Leyburne was consecrated Bishop of Adrumetum and Vicar-Apostolic of England on September 9, 1685. He had been president of Douay College and vicar-general to Bishop Smith. He suffered imprisonment under William III., and died piously June 9, 1702.

In 1688 England was divided into four vicariates, and Bishop Leyburne retained that of the London District. He was succeeded by Right Rev. Bonaventure Giffard, consecrated April 22, 1688, Bishop of Madaura and Vicar-Apostolic of the Midland District. He was a native of Wolverhampton. Under William III. he, too, was imprisoned for a year in Newgate. He took an active interest in the American mission, where the superior of the Jesuit missions was his vicar-general. His regulations in regard to the holidays and fast-days of obligation to be observed in the colonies were followed till the erection of the see of Baltimore. Bishop Giffard died at Hammersmith March 12, 1734. He was succeeded by Right Rev. Benjamin Petre, Bishop of Prusa, who governed the vicariate till 1758. For many years, however, the great burden fell on his coadjutor, the zealous Dr. Richard Challoner, Bishop of Debra, consecrated January 29, 1741. This great prelate, who prepared a new translation of the Bible for English Catholics, gave them the "Catholic Christian Instructed," "Meditations," and other works still prized, presided as vicar-apostolic for forty years, and his care extended to this country down to the Revolution. In his later years he had as coadjutor Right Rev. James Talbot, consecrated Bishop of Birtha August 24, 1759. Bishop Challoner died in January, 1781, aged nearly ninety.

When the Revolution broke out Bishop Talbot ceased to hold intercourse with the Catholic priests and people in the thirteen colonies. Accordingly, when peace was made and the independence of the United States acknowledged, the clergy in America applied to the Pope for the appointment of a prefect-apostolic. The attempt of the Anglicans to obtain a bishop in colonial days had made the very name so objectionable that Catholics were afraid to ask that one should be appointed for America.

The Rev. John Carroll was appointed prefect-apostolic in 1784. His jurisdiction did not extend over the whole territory of the United States, the settlements in Michigan, Indiana, Illinois, as well as Indian missions in Maine, Ohio, and New York, being still under the charge of the Bishop of Quebec. At this time Florida and Louisiana, embracing all west of the Mississippi, belonged to the diocese of Santiago de Cuba. Texas was part of the diocese of Guadalajara, New Mexico of that of Durango, while California was governed by a prefect-apostolic. In 1789 Pope Pius VI. erected the see of Baltimore, and appointed as its first bishop the Right Rev. John Carroll, who had been selected by the American clergy, his diocese embracing the whole territory of the republic at that time—that is to say, the portion of the United States of our day lying east of the Mississippi, with the exception of Florida.

THE CATHOLIC HIERARCHY
IN
THE UNITED STATES.

DIOCESE OF BALTIMORE.

MOST REV. JOHN CARROLL, D.D.,
First Bishop and first Archbishop of Baltimore.

THE Most Rev. John Carroll is the origin of the American episcopate, as first bishop and subsequently first archbishop of Baltimore, all dioceses east of the Mississippi having been formed from that confided to his care, and all archbishops and bishops succeeding to some part of his authority. He was eminently worthy of the high position, and stands in history as a noble character, maintaining in all his acts the greatest episcopal dignity.

John Carroll was born at Upper Marlborough, Maryland, January 8, 1735, son of Daniel Carroll, a native of Ireland, and Eleanor Darnall. He began his studies at a school established at Bohemia, in Maryland, but was sent ere long to the great college at St. Omer, in Flanders. During his stay at that seat of learning he resolved to devote himself to a religious life, and entered the Society of Jesus at Watton September 17, 1753. After passing some years as professor he made his divinity course and was ordained in 1769. While at the College of Bruges in 1773 the establishment was seized by the Austro-Belgian government and the Fathers expelled. On becoming a professed Father he had given up all his property to his brother, and was now thrown on the world in a foreign land. He returned to America in June, 1774, and began his labors as a secular priest among the Catholics in Maryland and Virginia. The claims of the colonists for their just rights were ignored by the English king and parliament, and war was imminent. Carroll had from the outset supported the rights of America, and when Congress sent delegates to Canada to win the co-operation, or at least neutrality, of the Catholic people of that province, the Rev. John Carroll accompanied Franklin, Chase, and Carroll to aid their mission by his influence as a priest. Bigotry in Congress defeated the mission, and the Rev. Mr. Carroll resumed his labors at Rock Creek.

At the close of the war the clergy in Maryland and Pennsylvania were anxious to be independent of the authorities of England, fearing to give offence to their fellow-citizens. Accordingly in 1783 they addressed a memorial to the Holy Father, not asking for a bishop, but for a superior independent of the Vicar-Apostolic of London. Benjamin Franklin at Paris strongly recommended to the Nuncio the reverend gentleman whom he knew so well, and, as he was the choice of the American clergy, Pope Pius VI. in June, 1784, appointed the Rev. John Carroll prefect-apostolic in the United States. Before the tidings of the appointment or the documents imparting authority had reached him, the Rev. Mr. Carroll stood forth as the champion of the Catholic cause in America by a convincing and learned reply to the pamphlet of an apostate priest which was widely circulated.

As prefect-apostolic he had all to organize and supply; Catholics were beginning to arrive and settle in the country, who were anxious for priests to offer the Holy Sacrifice for them. Churches were to be erected, but the prefect had no clergymen and no funds at his disposal. The old missionaries in the country were sinking under age and infirmities. Rev. Dr. Carroll visited the missions, laboring earnestly himself and doing all in his power to supply the wants of a flock scattered over the country. He began the erection of a college at Georgetown, now the oldest Catholic institution of learning. A Jubilee was for the first time proclaimed and the sacrament of Confirmation administered. After visiting Maryland, Pennsylvania, New Jersey, and New York he made a report to the Congregation *de Propaganda Fide* on the condition of the Church in the United States. It was soon evident that a bishop with full powers was needed, and in 1788 the clergy again addressed the Pope and solicited the erection of an episcopal see, asking to be permitted to propose a candidate. The Holy See, guided by the Spirit of God, looked far into the future; the see of Baltimore was erected by the bull of Pope Pius VI., dated November 6, 1789, and the Sovereign Pontiff with great joy confirmed the choice of the American clergy and appointed as first bishop the Rev. John Carroll, whose virtue, wisdom, and prudence had become so well known.

On receiving his bulls the Rev. Mr. Carroll proceeded to England and was consecrated bishop by the learned Benedictine, the Right Rev. Charles Walmesley, then Vicar-Apostolic of the London District. The ceremony took place in the chapel of Lulworth Castle, August 15, 1790. Before he returned to America he was gladdened by a proposal from the superior of the Sulpitians, a body devoted to educating young men for the priesthood, to send some of their members to America. On his return he visited the cities and towns where Catholic congregations had risen up, extending his episcopal journey as far as Boston, where he received an appeal from the Catholic Indians of Maine. His bulls made his diocese co-extensive with the United States, and the French settlements in the West, heretofore dependent on the Bishop of Quebec, now appealed to him for aid. Yet in all his vast diocese he had few priests and not a single institution of learning or charity. God, who in his providence allowed vice and irreligion to scourge France, made the time of trial beneficial to England and the United States. Bishop Carroll received a body of Sulpitians, many pious and devoted secular priests from France, a colony of English Dominican Fathers, a community of Carmelite nuns, another of Poor Clares. He was thus enabled to give priests to New England, Kentucky, Indiana, and Illinois. A seminary was opened, and one of the first ordained from it was the Russian Prince Dmitri Galitzin, who became the apostle of the Alleghanies. On the 7th of November, 1791, he convened his clergy in a diocesan synod at Baltimore. Twenty-two priests, American, English, French, Irish, German, met to concert plans for a uniform discipline in the services of religion, for the support of the clergy, and the establishment of new churches.

The statutes drawn up by Bishop Carroll and adopted in this synod have ever since won admiration. The impulse given to religion by the appointment of a bishop was marked; but in the rapid growth of the Church came some sore trials to Right Rev. Dr. Carroll. At Philadelphia and Baltimore German congregations defied his authority; in other parts priests without faculties usurped churches, and some gave scandal instead of edification. It was evident that so vast a diocese was beyond the power of any one. Bishop Carroll soon solicited the appointment of a coadjutor and the division of the diocese; but the priest first selected as coadjutor died in Philadelphia of yellow-fever, a victim to charity, and Bishop Carroll received new responsibilities in the charge of some West India islands, and a few years later in the administration of the diocese of Louisiana. In 1800 the Right Rev. Leonard Neale was consecrated coadjutor-bishop, to the great joy of the founder of the American hierarchy. Guided by this pious director, Miss Alice Lalor soon after founded at Georgetown the first monastery in the United States of Visitation Nuns. In 1809 Mrs. Eliza A. Seton, a convert to the faith, founded at Emmittsburg the first American house of Sisters of Charity. The religious communities thus begun under the auspices of the great Bishop Carroll flourish to this day, the Sisters of Charity numbering more than a thousand. In 1809 the Rev. John Du Bois began in a log-cabin at Emmittsburg a new institution of learning, Mount St. Mary's, which as a theological seminary and a college has sent forth for more than three-quarters of a century well-trained priests and accomplished laymen. In 1806 Bishop Carroll was so encouraged that he laid the foundations of the cathedral of Baltimore.

Great as was the assistance rendered by Bishop Neale, Bishop Carroll was sensible that the interest of religion demanded a division of his diocese. Wherever a priest could be sent Catholics before unheard of gathered around the altar he reared. On his appointment as prefect Dr. Carroll estimated the Catholics in the country at 24,500, with twenty-four priests, some of them superannuated. In 1808 he could count sixty-eight priests, eighty churches, several religious orders, and three colleges. Pope Pius VII., by his brief of April 8, 1808, raised Baltimore to the rank of a metropolitan see, and, dividing the diocese, founded new sees at Boston, New York, Philadelphia, and Bardstown, appointing to New York Father Richard Luke Concanen, a Dominican highly esteemed at Rome, and to the other sees priests already known by their zealous labors in America. Unable at once to hold a provincial council, Archbishop Carroll with his suffragans adopted a series of wise regulations which for years guided the bishops of the United States.

The diocese of Baltimore, as reduced, embraced Maryland, Virginia, and the Southern States to the Gulf and the Mississippi. Devoting his remaining strength and energy to build up the house of the Lord in this field, Archbishop Carroll lived to see consoling fruits. He beheld, too, the Society of Jesus in Maryland reorganized with the approval of the Holy See, and the mission increased by a number of learned fathers from Europe, and had the joy of living to see Pope Pius VII. formally restore the Society, to which he had so long belonged, by his bull of August 7, 1814. Towards the close of the year 1815 the aged patriarch of the Church in America showed by his failing health that death was approaching. He calmly awaited the last struggle, fortified by the sacraments, and expired Sunday, December 3, 1815. His pastoral letters show the bishop caring for his flock; his controversies with Wharton and others his ability in defending the faith against assaults.

MOST REV. LEONARD NEALE,

Second Archbishop of Baltimore.

LEONARD NEALE was born at Port Tobacco, in Maryland, on the 15th of October, 1746, of a family which had for more than a century maintained the faith in that province. His pious mother sent her children to Europe to obtain an education, and Leonard, after his course at St. Omer's, resolved to embrace the religious life, as his brothers and sister had done. After studying at Bruges and Liege he was ordained, and exercised the ministry till the suppression of the Society of Jesus. He then went to England, but, hearing that priests were needed in Demerara, sailed to that province and labored there as a missionary among whites, negroes, and Indians. Returning to Maryland in 1783, he took charge of a mission at Port Tobacco; but when the yellow-fever in 1793 carried off two priests in Philadelphia—Rev. Mr. Gressel, who had been named coadjutor-bishop, and the able controversialist, the Rev. Father Fleming, of the order of St. Dominic, died amid their apostolic labors—Rev. Mr. Neale hastened to the spot, and during that and subsequent visitations of the terrible disease labored with zeal and courage. He was not only pastor in Pennsylvania, but also vicar-general for that and the other Northern States. At Philadelphia Miss Alice Lalor became his penitent, and, under his direction and advice, in time founded the first community of Visitation Nuns in America. In 1798 Bishop Carroll appointed the Rev. Mr. Neale president of Georgetown College. His experience in colleges of the Society of Jesus in Europe enabled him to give the new institution a solid and tried system. He was at last selected as the coadjutor of Bishop Carroll, and was consecrated Bishop of Gortyna, December 7, 1800. Retaining the position of president of Georgetown College, he was also director of the Visitation Nuns and of the Poor Clares.

He took part in the meeting of the suffragans after the division of the diocese, and in the wise statutes framed on that occasion. On the death of Archbishop Carroll, December 3, 1815, he succeeded to the metropolitan see of Baltimore, and received the pallium from Pope Pius VII. in the following year. One of his first steps was to solicit from the Holy See a formal approval of the Visitation community founded under his direction.

The aged archbishop was not free from trials. The condition of the Church in Philadelphia and in South Carolina involved him in troubles that weighed heavily on him. Anxious to secure a successor, who might be better able to bear the burden of the archiepiscopate, he earnestly besought Bishop Cheverus, of Boston, to become his coadjutor; but, yielding to the advice of that great bishop, finally selected a Sulpitian of learning and ability, the Rev. Ambrose Maréchal, who was appointed Bishop of Stauropolis, July 24, 1817. Before the bulls arrived from

Rome the venerable archbishop had expired in his residence adjoining the Visitation Convent at Georgetown, June 15, 1817. The Sisters claimed his body as a sacred deposit, and it was interred beneath the altar of their convent chapel, where it remains to this day.

MOST REV. AMBROSE MARÉCHAL,

Third Archbishop of Baltimore.

AMBROSE MARÉCHAL was born in 1768 at a place called Ingre, near Orleans, France. His family were able to give him the highest education, but, while all was tending to irreligion and impiety, young Maréchal resolved to enter the ecclesiastical state. He had studied his theology under the Sulpitians and was ready for ordination when the blow fell on the Church. He, however, contrived to be ordained secretly at Bordeaux, and the same day embarked for America, reaching Baltimore June 24, 1792. He entered on his priestly career by missionary labors in St. Mary's County and on the Eastern Shore, but on the organization of St. Mary's College in 1799 became professor of theology. In 1803 the superior of St. Sulpice recalled him to France, where he filled the chair of theology in several seminaries. In 1812, to his own joy, he was assigned to his old position in Baltimore. He refused the see of Philadelphia, to which he had been nominated; but when, at the urgent request of Archbishop Neale and Bishop Cheverus, he was appointed coadjutor of Baltimore, he yielded. The bulls arrived after the death of the venerable Doctor Neale, and the Rev. Dr. Maréchal was consecrated Archbishop of Baltimore by Bishop Cheverus, December 14, 1817.

His great predecessors had suffered much from unworthy priests, accepted from abroad without full knowledge of their character. Archbishop Maréchal had a body of priests many of whom had been trained for the American mission, but he encountered opposition from lay trustees, who in not a few places, misled by intriguing men, claimed the right to appoint priests, and who wished to make the pastors of God's Church their hired servants. The adjusting of questions as to the legal title of property belonging to the old Jesuit missions also involved difficulties of no slight moment.

In 1820 the diocese of Baltimore was again divided, and an episcopal see was erected at Charleston, the diocese embracing the Carolinas and Georgia, and another see at Richmond, with Virginia for its diocese. The newly-appointed Bishop of Richmond found such scanty resources in Virginia that, after a year's struggle, he was translated to a see in Ireland. Archbishop Maréchal then governed the diocese of Richmond as administrator-apostolic.

He completed and dedicated his cathedral in May, 1821, the fine altar being a gift from priests who had been his pupils in French seminaries. One of his great objects was to convene a Provincial Council in the United States, that by united counsel the bishops might give stability to the house of God. He drew up the plans for one, and, proceeding to Rome in 1821, took steps to secure so desirable a synod. Briefs regarding the future council were issued by Pope Pius VII. in 1823 and by Pope Leo XII. in 1828, but Archbishop Maréchal did not live to see the council assemble.

A community of colored Sisters had been founded by the Rev. Mr. Joubert, known as Sisters of Providence, and in 1825 their association was approved by Archbishop Maréchal. In 1826 he visited Canada in the interest of religion, and on his return, while at Emmittsburg, began to disclose symptoms of dropsy of the chest. He at once forwarded to Rome the names of three whom he recommended for the position of coadjutor. The Pope, by bulls of January 8, 1828, appointed the Rev. James Whitfield Bishop of Apollonia and coadjutor with the right of succession.

Archbishop Maréchal, feeling that the work of the diocese would be ably continued, dismissed all care and prepared for death. Fortified by all the consolations of religion, he expired calmly on the 29th of January, 1828.

MOST REV. JAMES WHITFIELD,

Fourth Archbishop of Baltimore.

James Whitfield was born in Liverpool November 3, 1770, and on the death of his father set out with his mother for Italy, in hope that the climate would benefit her health. While returning to England they were detained at Lyons by one of Napoleon's decrees against the English government. Here he formed the acquaintance of the Rev. Ambrose Maréchal, and, entering the seminary, was ordained priest in 1809, his good mother living to see her son minister at the altar. Returning to England, he served for some years as parish priest at Crosby, but, on the pressing invitation of Archbishop Maréchal, came to America in the autumn of 1817. As one of the pastors of the cathedral he showed great zeal, prudence, and ability. In the care of the negroes he was especially interested.

He was appointed, by bull of January 8, 1828, Bishop of Apollonia and coadjutor of Baltimore; but as the document did not arrive during the lifetime of Archbishop Maréchal, he was consecrated Archbishop of Baltimore by succession on Whitsunday, May 25, 1828, the venerable Bishop Flaget officiating. The pallium reached him the next year.

Archbishop Whitfield made a careful and strict visitation in the diocese of Baltimore and in that of Richmond, of which he was administrator. He submitted to the Holy See his learned predecessor's plan for a Provincial Council, and, on its approval, proceeded, in compliance with the instructions, to summon his suffragans to meet him in the cathedral of Baltimore.

The first Provincial Council of Baltimore forms an epoch in the history of the Catholic Church in the United States. It was held a little more than half a century after the day which, by declaring the colonies free and independent States, liberated the Catholics and their Church from the oppressive laws of England. During that half-century the Church, which, after the Peace of Paris, was represented by Dr. Carroll as having some twenty-five thousand members and twenty-five priests, had risen to a body of half a million in a population of twelve millions. In the limits of the original diocese of Baltimore there were seven bishops, one hundred and sixty priests, nearly as many churches, three colleges, eight convents, and three hundred and fifty thousand Catholics; while the dioceses of New Orleans, St. Louis, and Mobile gave two more bishops, more than eighty priests, some ten convents, and one hundred and fifty thousand of the faithful. It was essential to adopt uniform regulations for the spiritual government of this large and rapidly increasing body, which had seminaries, colleges, schools, but could not obtain churches and priests for all who desired them.

The council opened in the cathedral of Baltimore on Sunday, October 4, 1829. Beside Archbishop Whitfield, who presided, there sat in this memorable synod the venerable Bishop Flaget of Bardstown; the able and eloquent Bishop England, of Charleston; Bishop Edward Fenwick, of Cincinnati; Bishop Rosati, of St. Louis, administrator of New Orleans; and Bishop Benedict Fenwick, of Boston. Bishop Du Bois and Bishop Portier, of Mobile, were in Europe, and Bishop David, coadjutor of Bardstown, was unable from ill health to attend. Philadelphia was represented by the administrator, Very Rev. William Mathews. The superior of the Jesuits, the visitor of St. Sulpice, and several theologians attended. Eminent lawyers, called in to consult in regard to the tenure of church property in the eye of the civil law, were struck by the grave and venerable assembly of the superiors of the Catholic Church, while to the people at large the pomp and ceremonial seemed to revive the ages of faith and give earnest of future triumphs for the Church. Thirty-eight decrees were adopted regulating the appointment of pastors and other priests, the administration of the sacraments, the holidays and fasts of obligation, the tenure of Church property, the establishment of schools, and the diffusion of Catholic books and periodicals. The decrees were transmitted to his Holiness Pope Pius VIII. and formally approved — the basis of the law for the Church in the United States.

The council was followed by consoling results. Archbishop Whitfield wrote in 1832: "The wonders, if I dare so express myself, that have been operated and are daily operated in my diocese are a source of consolation to me amid the difficulties against which I have still often to struggle." "A truly Catholic spirit distinguishes Maryland and the District of Columbia. . . . Conversions of Protestants in health are also numerous, and not a week, in some seasons not a day, passes without our priests being called to the bedside of some invalid who wishes to abjure error and die in the bosom of the Church."

The terrible Asiatic cholera in that year visited the United States. Archbishop Whitfield, with his priests and Sisters, was untiring in devotion to the afflicted. The diocese lost two priests by death, and two Sisters died of cholera while attending the sick in the hospital, and a colored Oblate Sister of Providence was another victim of charity.

The next year the archbishop obtained of the Holy See a dispensation for the United States from the usual abstinence on Saturdays and Rogation Days, many of the poorer Catholics at service finding it difficult to obtain necessary food on those days.

On the 20th of October, 1833, Archbishop Whitfield opened the Second Provincial Council of Baltimore, which was attended by Bishop David, coadjutor of Bardstown, representing the aged Bishop Flaget; and also by Bishops England of Charleston, Rosati of St. Louis, Du Bois of New York, Portier of Mobile, Kenrick, administrator of Philadelphia, Résé of Detroit, and Purcell of Cincinnati. The two last were consecrated a few days before the session of the council, Dr. Purcell succeeding Bishop Fenwick, who had died of cholera while visiting his diocese. The see of New Orleans was vacant, Bishop de Neckere having died in September. In this council a plan was adopted for the future appointments to the episcopate, and the boundaries of the dioceses definitely fixed. The council also took steps in regard to missions among the Indian tribes and among the negroes in Liberia. The establishment of a theological seminary in each diocese was advised, and a committee appointed to revise books used in Catholic schools. The decrees of the council were duly approved at Rome, and a see established at Vincennes, as requested by the fathers of the council.

Archbishop Whitfield devoted his large private fortune to the good of his diocese, completing the tower of the cathedral and the archiepiscopal residence. He built at his own cost the church of St. James, laying the corner-stone May 1, 1833, and consecrating it on the first of May, 1834. His health was then rapidly failing. Visits to medicinal springs proved of no avail, and he returned to his episcopal city to prepare for the close of his well-spent life. Fortified by the sacraments and surrounded by his coadjutor and clergy, to whom he had been a father and a model, he died piously October 19, 1834.

At the time of his death the dioceses of Baltimore and Richmond contained sixty-eight priests, about sixty-four churches or chapels, three colleges, four academies or boarding-schools for girls, an orphan asylum, an infirmary, and several schools.

MOST REV. SAMUEL ECCLESTON,

Fifth Archbishop of Baltimore.

SAMUEL ECCLESTON was born in Kent County, Maryland, on the 27th of June, 1801, of parents belonging to the Episcopal Church, but, his widowed mother marrying a Catholic, he was led by the examples he saw to embrace the faith while a pupil of St. Mary's College. He resolved, too, to devote his life to the ministry, and, having made his divinity studies in the seminary, was ordained April 24, 1825. To ground himself still more in sacred learning he spent some time at Issy, and, after visiting England and Ireland, returned to his native country. He was appointed vice-president and soon became president of St. Mary's College, and in 1834 was elected Bishop of Thermia and coadjutor to Archbishop Whitfield, by whom he was consecrated on the 14th day of September. In little more than a month he had the sad task of chanting the requiem for his metropolitan. Archbishop Eccleston came to his high duties in the vigor of early manhood, and gave them the energy of his life. Under his encouragement the Visitation nuns increased the number of their academies, Brothers of St. Patrick came to direct parochial schools for boys, and the German Catholics were confided to the care of the sons of St. Alphonsus, the Redemptorist Fathers; the preparatory college of St. Charles for young levites was founded; soon after the Lazarists, in 1850, began their labors in the diocese of Baltimore, and the Brothers of the Christian Schools established a novitiate of their order; so that the diocese has ever since been the hive for the great missionary body of Redemptorists and that excellent teaching body, the sons of the Venerable La Salle.

Nor was it only in his own diocese that his influence was felt. It was the privilege of Archbishop Eccleston to preside in no fewer than five provincial councils as metropolitan of the Church in the United States. In the third council, which met April 16, 1837, eight bishops sat with the metropolitan; in the fourth, which opened May 17, 1840, the number, by the increase of sees, had risen to twelve. This council addressed letters of sympathy to the Bishop of Cologne and the Archbishop of Posen, who were suffering under the merciless iron hand of Prussian intolerance. This council provided for the transmission of property held by a bishop to his successor, the laws of the several States not recognizing the bishop as a corporation sole. One of the important decrees of the fifth council, which opened May 14, 1843, was that which cut off from the sacraments any Catholic who dared remarry after obtaining a divorce under State laws. The memorable act of the sixth council was the decree by which the twenty-three bishops of the Catholic Church in this country chose "The Blessed Virgin conceived without sin" as the patroness of the United States.

When the revolutionary storms drove Pope Pius IX. from his sacred city, Archbishop Eccleston, in January, 1849, invited him to Baltimore to preside in the Seventh Provincial Council. That synod met May 6, 1849, and was attended by twenty-five bishops. It urged the definition of the dogma of the Immaculate Conception of the Blessed Virgin Mary. By this time the number of sees made a division of the province desirable. Archbishoprics were created at New York and Cincinnati.

Archbishop Eccleston was stricken with a fatal illness in

April, 1851, while residing at Georgetown, in a house adjoining the monastery of the Visitation. Here he died piously April 22, 1851. His body was removed to his episcopal city, honored by obsequies of an imposing character, at which even the President of the United States attended.

MOST REV. FRANCIS PATRICK KENRICK,

Third Bishop of Philadelphia, Sixth Archbishop of Baltimore.

THE successor of Archbishop Eccleston was a bishop already world-renowned for learning and ability. Francis Patrick Kenrick, born in Dublin, Ireland, December 3, 1796, received a sound and pious education under the care of a learned uncle, a clergyman, and completed his studies in the College of the Propaganda at Rome, where he spent seven years. He was sent to Kentucky in 1821 on the request of Bishop Flaget for a priest fitted to occupy a chair in a theological seminary. He was already remarked for the depth and accuracy of his mind, and the extent of his studies in dogmatic and patristic theology and in Holy Scriptures. As professor at St. Thomas' Seminary, Bardstown, he trained many excellent priests, and, untiring in his labors, acted as professor in the college and discharged parochial duties. His health was really injured by his devotion to the multiform work before him. Ready in disputation, he became an acknowledged champion of the faith. A Presbyterian clergyman assailed the doctrine of the Holy Eucharist under the title of Omega. Kenrick's "Letters from Omicron to Omega" were an overwhelming reply that silenced the impugner of the words of Christ; other discussions ensued, in all which the learned professor acquired new fame. While attending the first Provincial Council of Baltimore as theologian of Bishop Flaget, Rev. Mr. Kenrick was selected for the difficult post of Bishop-administrator of Philadelphia. He was consecrated Bishop of Arath, June 6, 1830, in the cathedral at Bardstown. On assuming the charge of the diocese he found the trustees of St. Mary's Church defiant when he declared himself pastor of that church; but, interdicting it, he rented a house and began within its walls a theological seminary. Then he entered the pulpit of St. Mary's and broke the power of the trustees, permitting only the exercise of functions recognized by the Church. The trustees soon attempted to renew their rebellion; but he repressed their turbulence and made it a rule to allow no church to be organized in the diocese under the trustee system. Having overcome that great obstacle to Catholic progress and piety, Bishop Kenrick, by constant visitations of his diocese, made himself acquainted with his flock. Few of the parishes at first had resident pastors, but his little seminary in his own house developed into the noble theological seminary of St. Charles Borromeo, which has given Pennsylvania so many excellent priests. The cholera called forth all the zeal of the bishop and his clergy, and the Sisters of Charity of the Blessed Virgin, a community instituted in Philadelphia, were especially devoted. In 1834 Philadelphia had five churches and twenty-five thousand Catholics, and another church, St John's, was soon erected by Rev. John Hughes.

In the ensuing years schools and charitable institutions were multiplied; but a new storm of persecution arose against the Catholics, and in 1844 a blood-thirsty mob took possession of Philadelphia. St. Michael's and St. Augustine's churches, with a library of very great value, houses of devoted Sisters, and many residences of humble Catholics, were given to the flames, the city authorities offering no protection. Many Catholics were butchered. The State authorities at last quelled the riot, but it was renewed again in July and repressed only by decisive measures.

In 1843 the diocese of Philadelphia was divided, that of Pittsburgh having been set off. Bishop Kenrick retained eastern Pennsylvania, Delaware, and western New Jersey. In this part had arisen the Jesuit college of St. Joseph and the Augustinian college of St. Thomas of Villanova, the academies of the Ladies of the Sacred Heart, Visitation nuns, and Sisters of St. Joseph, while Sisters of the Good Shepherd began their holy work. The Redemptorists and School Sisters of Notre Dame began to labor among the Germans. When in 1851 Bishop Kenrick was promoted to the see of Baltimore the diocese of Philadelphia contained one hundred and two churches and chapels, one hundred and one priests, and forty-six seminarians preparing to reinforce them. While Bishop of Philadelphia Dr. Kenrick published two works which rendered great service to the seminarians and clergy—his "Theologia Dogmatica" and his "Theologia Moralis." His "Primacy of the Apostolic See," "Vindication of the Catholic Church," and works on baptism and justification were able and timely.

On the 3d of August, 1851, Bishop Kenrick was promoted to the see of Baltimore, and was soon after appointed apostolic delegate to preside at a Plenary Council. It was opened May 9, 1852, and was attended by six archbishops and twenty-six bishops of the United States. Its decrees aimed to give uniformity to discipline throughout the whole country. They recognized the infallibility of the Sovereign Pontiff, re-enacted the decrees of the Provincial Councils, regulated the Ritual and Manual of Ceremonies, the absence of bishops, the establishment of consultors and a chancery in each diocese, the fixing of limits to parishes, publication of banns, marriage and baptism, catechetical instructions, the maintenance of theological seminaries and parochial schools, took steps to prevent the reception of wandering priests, the usurpation of lay trustees, encouraged the Associations for the Propagation of the Faith and for the conversion of non-Catholics.

In 1853 Archbishop Kenrick convened a diocesan synod, promulgating statutes in harmony with the council, and a year later attended the gathering of the episcopate at Rome when Pope Pius IX. solemnly defined the dogma of the Immaculate Conception. On his return he held a Provincial Council and encouraged the establishment of several needed asylums in his diocese. Ever anxious to uphold the discipline of the Church, he convened another synod in 1857 and a Provincial Council in 1858. He took an active part in placing on a firm foundation the American College at Rome, founded by Pope Pius IX.

His life of active zeal and study had gradually undermined his health, and in 1863 general anxiety was felt, although there was no indication of immediate danger. Bishop O'Connor spent the evening of the 5th of July with him, leaving him in apparently his usual condition; but during the night he expired calmly by a sudden but not unprovided death.

The last work of this studious prelate was a revision of the Catholic version of the Bible, which, translated originally by Rev. Gregory Martin, of Douay College, had been revised by Bishop Challoner, and had undergone so many changes at the hands of others as to be no longer creditable to the Catholic body or safe as a translation. His epitaph says that "he adorned the archiepiscopal chair with the greatest piety and learning, as well as with equal modesty and poverty."

MOST REV. MARTIN JOHN SPALDING,

Second Bishop of Louisville, Seventh Archbishop of Baltimore.

MARTIN JOHN SPALDING was born May 23, 1810, on the Rolling Fork, Kentucky, where his grandfather, Benedict Spalding, had settled in 1790 when he came from St. Mary's County, Maryland. Both his parents, Richard Spalding and Henrietta Hamilton, were natives of that old Catholic county. After studying the rudiments in the nearest log school he entered St. Mary's College as soon as it opened in 1821, and so distinguished himself that at the age of fourteen he was the professor of mathematics. On being graduated in 1826 he resolved to become a priest, and entered the seminary at Bardstown. At the age of twenty he was sent to Rome, and, though stricken down by a dangerous illness, won his doctor's cap by an able defence of his theses against some of the greatest men in the Catholic capital. Returning to his own diocese, he became pastor of the cathedral and professor of philosophy in the diocesan seminary. He aided in establishing the Minerva, and contributed to periodical literature. The college journal soon gave way to the *Catholic Advocate*, of which he was chief editor, as he soon became of the *United States Catholic Magazine*. He was also a contributor to the Catholic magazines, his collected articles forming a valuable volume. In 1838 he became president of St. Joseph's College, but was placed again at Bardstown when the bishop removed his see to Louisville, but soon, as vicar-general, followed Dr. Flaget. Averse to controversy, he gave lectures in defence of Catholic doctrines when a knot of Protestant ministers misrepresented and assailed them. On the resignation of Bishop Chabrat, Doctor Spalding was appointed Bishop of Lengone and coadjutor of Louisville, and was consecrated by Bishop Flaget, September 10, 1848. From this time the administration really devolved upon him, and on the death of the venerable bishop, February 11, 1850, he became Bishop of Louisville. He wrote the early history of the diocese in his "Sketches of Kentucky," and the life of his predecessor apart in a special work. He recalled the Jesuits to his diocese, and welcomed a colony of Cistercians who founded the Trappist abbey at Gethsemane. In 1842 the Sisters of the Good Shepherd began their redeeming work in Louisville. By visitations of his diocese, retreats of the clergy, and missions among the people Bishop Spalding labored to keep alive the spirit of Catholic faith. He established orphan asylums, attended to the spiritual wants of those who did not speak English, establishing churches for the Germans. He completed the cathedral, the corner-stone of which he had laid while coadjutor, and erected many new churches; but he felt that the diocese ought to be divided. The Plenary Council accordingly asked the Holy See to establish the see of Covington. After joining in the deliberations of the council he visited Europe, obtained a colony of Xaverian Brothers in Belgium, and took steps towards establishing a missionary college at Louvain—a project which he afterwards, with the aid of Bishop Lefevre, carried out successfully.

In August, 1855, Louisville was given up to a Know-Nothing mob, who butchered or burned nearly one hundred Catholics and gave some twenty houses to the flames. The cathedral was menaced, but, by the providence of God, escaped. Bishop Spalding took an important part in the councils held at Cincinnati in 1855, 1858, and 1861, the pastoral letters all emanating from his pen.

While constant in the care of his diocese, he was always engaged in some literary work. He exposed the fallacy of Morse's pretended Lafayette motto, silenced Prentiss in regard to Catholic education, and gave a noble refutation of D'Aubigné's "History of the Reformation." When the civil war began his diocese became a scene of military operations; colleges closed and churches were exposed to destruction. "I must attend to souls," he wrote, "without entering into angry political discussion." His priests and sisters of various orders were untiring in their devotion to the sick and wounded on the battle-field and in the hospital, several dying martyrs to charity. Amid all the turmoil of war, however, Bishop Spalding assembled his priests in synod to renew their fervor in such dread times.

On the 11th of June, 1864, he received the Papal Rescript which promoted him to the archiepiscopal see of Baltimore as successor to Archbishop Kenrick. He took possession of his new see on the 31st of July. One of his earliest acts was to found a House of the Good Shepherd in Baltimore, a colony of sisters coming from Louisville at his request. He then made a visitation of his diocese, urging the faithful to profit by the jubilee then granted by Pope Pius IX. In his pastoral on that occasion he explained and justified the famous Syllabus. In 1865 he convened the sixth synod of the diocese. As the war went on he was charged with the administration of the diocese of Charleston, to which the bishop was unable to return, and he made a successful appeal to Northern Catholics to aid their war-stricken brethren in the faith. His own diocese was not neglected; in 1866 he began a boys' protectory, confiding it to the Xaverian Brothers. A Plenary Council was again required, and Pope Pius IX., approving the plan, by letters of February 16, 1866, appointed Archbishop Spalding to preside. He immediately set to work to plan out its whole work, and when, years after, a third council was called it was found that there was little to be done except to carry out such parts of his plan as had not been acted upon at the time. The great ecclesiastical assembly met in his cathedral on the 7th of October, seven archbishops, thirty-eight bishops, three mitred abbots, and more than a hundred theologians taking part in its deliberations. It was the largest council since the general one held at Trent. Its decrees covered the whole field of dogma and discipline.

The great archbishop then devoted himself to his own diocese, and gave especial attention to extending the ministry to Catholic colored people and all who sought to enter the Church. He visited Europe, but even there was laboring for the good of the Church in this country.

On the 20th of October, 1869, he took leave of his diocese in order to attend the General Council of the Vatican, summoned by Pope Pius IX. At first he was one who deemed the definition of the Pope's infallibility when teaching *ex cathedra* inopportune; but when he found the rationalistic governments of France, Spain, Bavaria, Austria, and Italy intriguing to prevent it, he declared that the definition was necessary. With the bishops from countries where Catholicity was free, he insisted upon it. He labored incessantly during the eight months that the sessions lasted, and remained in Rome till the fourth and last general congregation, July 18, 1870. After the Constitution issued, Archbishop Spalding addressed a pastoral to his flock on the Papal Infallibility, treating the subject in the plain and simple style that carries light and conviction to the mind. He then visited Switzerland and Savoy, intending to return to the council when it reassembled, but the wicked course of Victor Emmanuel in seizing Rome made its reassembling impossible. Archbishop Spalding returned to his diocese. There he resumed his labors, though recurring illness made all exertion at times impossible; he built fine parochial schools near his cathedral, and began a church in honor of St. Pius V. A visit to New York on matters relating to the Church in the whole country brought on acute bronchitis. On Christmas day he said Mass at a temporary altar in the hall near his bedroom, and it was the last time he was to offer the Holy Sacrifice. His sufferings became intense, and the remedies employed to relieve him were extremely painful, but he bore all with cheerfulness and resignation. He expired on the 7th of February, 1872,[2] Bishop Becker giving him the last blessing, and on the 12th his body was laid beside that of Archbishop Kenrick.

MOST REV. JAMES ROOSEVELT BAYLEY,

First Bishop of Newark and Eighth Archbishop of Baltimore.

JAMES ROOSEVELT BAYLEY was the son of Dr. Guy Carleton Bayley and Grace Roosevelt, his father being a brother of the holy Eliza Seton, who founded the Sisters of Charity in the United States. He was brought up in the Episcopalian creed, to which the family belonged, and early evinced a love of literature and books. After an early course at Mount Pleasant Academy he entered Trinity College, Hartford, and became a pupil of Rev. Dr. Samuel Farmer Jarvis, whose love of the Fathers and clear, logical mind drew himself and his pupils irresistibly towards Catholic truth. Under him he prepared for admission to the ministry of the Episcopal Church, and in time became rector of a church at Harlem. But his soul felt cramped in the cold formalities of that sect. Visiting the poor and often suffering Catholic huts in his district, he was impressed by the lively faith, piety, and resignation which he witnessed. He resolved to become a Catholic. An uncle, whose favorite he was, endeavored to dissuade him and sent him abroad, certain that if young Bayley saw Catholicity as it was in Rome he would be cured of all such ideas. Renouncing the worldly prospects before him, he was received into the Church in Rome in April, 1842. Proceeding to Paris, he entered the seminary of St. Sulpice, and, to gratify the wish of Archbishop Hughes, returned to New York to be ordained by him in 1844. Attached to the cathedral, he was zealous on the mission; and, as secretary of the archbishop, organized the chancery of the diocese, collecting and arranging all records of the past and insuring future regularity. When New Jersey, which had been part of the dioceses of New York and Philadelphia, was formed into a bishopric the Rev. Mr. Bayley was selected as the first Bishop of Newark, and was consecrated on the 30th of October, 1853, in St. Patrick's Cathedral, New York, by Archbishop Bedini. In his new diocese he established Seton Hall, a theological seminary and college of a high order, introduced several religious communities, encouraged the building of churches, and above all of schools, formed associations to keep young men together and give them innocent enjoyment. For nineteen years his influence was felt throughout the State, the bitterest enemies of the faith acknowledging that it was ever exerted in the cause of morality and good citizenship. His pastoral letters were read with reverence by his flock and with respect by all, and in the three councils of New York and the Second Plenary Council of Baltimore his learning, wisdom, and practical methods carried great weight. He visited Rome in 1862 at the time of the canonization of the Japanese martyrs, and some years later to attend the centenary of the Apostles St. Peter and St. Paul. In 1872 he was, to his own regret, transferred by a brief of July 10 to the see of Baltimore as successor of Archbishop Spalding. His health was already impaired, but he twice visited his diocese and began a third visitation. He freed the cathedral from debt and consecrated it. In 1877 he was advised to visit Vichy for the benefit of his health, but, finding his disease increase, he sought only to die among his flock. He reached New York in a dying condition, and expired at Newark, among the clergy and people who loved him so devotedly, October 3, 1877. After funeral services in the cathedral of that city his remains were conveyed to Baltimore for similar honors, and were finally laid beside those of his venerated aunt, Mother Seton, at Emmittsburg.

Beside his pastorals he published a "Sketch of the Catholic Church on the Island of New York" and "Memoirs of Bishop Bruté, of Vincennes."

HIS EMINENCE JAMES CARDINAL GIBBONS,

First Vicar-Apostolic of North Carolina, Fourth Bishop of Richmond, Ninth Archbishop of Baltimore.

JAMES GIBBONS was born in the cathedral parish, Baltimore, and baptized in that venerable church by the Rev. Charles I. White. He was taken to Ireland at the age of ten, and made his earliest studies there, attracting the attention of Archbishop Mc-

Hale by his piety and diligence. Returning to his native country, he entered the preparatory seminary, St. Charles' College, and after his course there entered St. Mary's College, Baltimore. He was ordained in March, 1861, and assigned to St. Patrick's Church, but in a few months received charge of St. Bridget's Church, Canton, with the care of St. Lawrence's at Locust Point, as well as of the Catholic soldiers at Fort McHenry. The zeal of the young priest in this laborious duty showed his merit, and Archbishop Spalding made him his secretary and assistant at the cathedral. The peculiar charm of his manner, the influence his piety exercised, made him a marked man, and at the Second Plenary Council of Baltimore he was selected as the priest best fitted to organize the new vicariate-apostolic in North Carolina, a State where Catholicity had made least impression. He did not shrink from the difficult task. Everything was to be created; the scattered Catholics were fewer in the whole State than would be found in a Maryland parish. He was consecrated Bishop of Adramyttum in the cathedral of Baltimore, August 16, 1868, and proceeded to Wilmington, North Carolina, making St. Thomas' Church his residence. He found one or two priests in the State, and seven hundred Catholics scattered in a population of a million. He drew devoted priests to him, and labored in person with the gentle zeal of a St. Francis of Sales, winning a way to hearts that the profoundest erudition or the highest eloquence failed to reach. He visited every part of the State, preaching and lecturing in court-houses, meeting-houses, any hall that could be had, and everywhere presenting the unknown truth with irresistible power. His method can be best understood by his wonderful little book, "The Faith of our Fathers," a work that has been more effective than any other since Milner published his "End of Controversy." Little communities of converts began to form, and the ministers of God began to feel courage. Churches sprang up in the larger cities, the Sisters of Mercy came to open an academy, and the ancient order of St. Benedict prepared to found a monastery. On the death of Bishop McGill, Doctor Gibbons was transferred to the see of Richmond, July 30, 1872, retaining, however, the charge of his vicariate. His labors in the larger field were even more fruitful, and the influence was gradually extending, when Archbishop Bayley, finding his health precarious, asked that he should be appointed coadjutor of Baltimore. On the 29th of May, 1877, he was made Bishop of Janopolis and proceeded to Maryland. He left with reluctance the flocks in Virginia and North Carolina to assume the charge of the ancient diocese of Baltimore, of which he became archbishop on the death of Archbishop Bayley in the following October. The pallium was conferred upon him on the 10th of February, 1878. His venerable mother, who had lived to see her son enthroned in the cathedral where he had been baptized, died soon after at the age of eighty. Raised thus to the highest position in the American hierarchy, he enjoys the respect of all, and was chosen by Pope Leo XIII. to preside in the Third Plenary Council of Baltimore in November, 1884, having been invited to Rome with other archbishops and bishops in the previous year in order to deliberate on the most urgent matters to be considered in that assembly.

In the Consistory held by Pope Leo XIII. in June, 1886, the Archbishop of Baltimore was created a cardinal priest, and the insignia of his new dignity were soon after borne to him across the Atlantic.

DIOCESE OF BOSTON.

RIGHT REV. JOHN CHEVERUS,

First Bishop of Boston, then Bishop of Montauban, Archbishop of Bordeaux, and Cardinal.

JOHN LOUIS LEFEBVRE CHEVERUS was born at Mayenne, France, January 28, 1768, where his family held a high position. Trained by a pious mother, he received the tonsure at the age of twelve, and studied at college only to prepare himself for the altar. He completed his studies at the college of Louis le Grand and the seminary of St. Magloire, and was ordained priest December 8, 1790. He became curate of his uncle, a parish priest in Mayenne, whom he soon succeeded, and was made canon of Mans. Refusing the constitutional oath, he was cast into prison, but escaped in June, 1792, and reached England. He had begun to labor as a missionary there when his old friend, the Abbé Matignon, then the only priest in New England, implored him to come to his aid. He landed at Boston in April, 1796, and, receiving faculties from Bishop Carroll, set to work with Dr. Matignon to attend the scattered Catholics, from the Penobscot Indians in Maine to the poor emigrants in Connecticut. So bitter was the feeling against Catholicity that he was soon arrested in Maine and tried with criminals for marrying a couple in that district, and narrowly escaped imprisonment with thieves and drunkards. But his charity, learning, and piety soon made a deep impression on all, and the Catholic body found some of the still oppressive laws modified out of respect to him. The original church of the Holy Cross was rebuilt by him and dedicated by Archbishop Carroll in 1803. Other churches were soon erected by his zeal. When the see of Boston was erected he was selected as bishop, though he sought to have the honor conferred on Dr. Matignon. From his consecration in Baltimore,

November 1, 1810, his whole thought was devoted to his diocese. He soon lost his friend and coadjutor, but gathered other priests around him, laboring more abundantly than any of them in enduring all the hardships of a missionary priest, relieving the poor in his unbounded charity, and winning Protestants to the faith by the example of his virtue as well as the clearness and force of his arguments. His health began to sink under his arduous duties, but when Louis XVIII. named him for the see of Montauban, and urged him to return to France, he declined to abandon the poor diocese which had so long been the scene of his priestly and episcopal labors. He yielded only when physicians declared that he could not live if he spent another winter in Boston. After giving away all he possessed to the clergy and the poor he embarked for Europe in October, 1823. When Matignon and Cheverus began their labors there was one poor church in all New England. Bishop Cheverus left a cathedral in Boston, St. Augustine's in South Boston, a church in Maine, and one in New Hampshire.

He had, too, seen many embrace the faith—the Barbers of New Hampshire, Dr. Green in Boston, Rev. Dr. Kewley, of Connecticut. He could feel that the Church he had done so much to found was destined, with God's blessing, to thrive and prosper.

As Bishop of Montauban Dr. Cheverus was soon known throughout France. Eloquent in the pulpit, full of learning, charitable and benevolent to the suffering and poor without distinction, impressing all by the sanctity of his life, the fiercest of the old revolutionists acknowledged his power. A higher sphere was evidently soon to be his. On the death of the Archbishop of Bordeaux in 1826 he was promoted to that see and made a Peer of France. Other honors flowed upon him: he was chosen to the Royal Council, created Knight Commander of the Order of the Holy Ghost. The fall of Charles X. and the accession of Louis Philippe did not alter the general esteem for Archbishop Cheverus, and all hailed his elevation to the cardinalate in 1836. He did not long survive this exaltation, dying in the midst of his labors on the 19th of July.

Each diocese that he had directed had some institution, some good work, as a monument of his zeal. All the early churches in New England were to some extent his work, as was the Ursuline convent at Charlestown.

RIGHT REV. BENEDICT JOSEPH FENWICK,

Second Bishop of Boston.

BISHOP FENWICK was a native of Maryland, born near Leonardtown, in St. Mary's County, the cradle of Catholicity, September 3, 1782, descended from one of the earliest settlers under Lord Baltimore. No sooner was Georgetown College opened in 1792 than he and his brother were prepared for admission to it. His course there confirmed his vocation, and he was soon enrolled as a student in the Sulpitian seminary at Baltimore. When the members of the Society of Jesus were permitted in 1806 to reorganize under the superiors in Russia the two brothers sought admission. Benedict was ordained by Bishop Neale at Georgetown, March 12, 1808. The difficult mission of New York was his first mission, and there, as assistant to the venerable Father Kohlman, he rendered the greatest service not only in the parochial work, but in establishing and directing "The New York Literary Institution." He was in time administrator of the diocese in the absence and after the death of Bishop Concanen, and began the erection of St. Patrick's Cathedral from his own designs. After becoming vicar-general of Bishop Connolly he was made president of Georgetown College in 1817, but was sent the next year to Charleston by Bishop Neale to restore peace to the Church. Having successfully carried out his mission, he returned to the college and soon after resumed the presidency. On the 10th of May, 1825, he was appointed Bishop of Boston, and was consecrated on All Saints' Day by Archbishop Maréchal, assisted by Bishops England and Conwell. His diocese, comprising all the New England States, contained four churches, but on his arrival he found only two priests remaining. He at once assumed the parochial duty at the cathedral, opened a school, and taught the catechism on Sunday. One of his first cares was to secure for the Ursuline nuns a considerable property in Charlestown, which received the name of Mount Benedict, and where a fine convent and academy were soon erected. Priests were obtained and new missions opened, while his house became a seminary where young men were prepared to increase the clergy of the diocese. He made a visitation of his diocese and learned by personal observation the number and condition of the Catholics, and selected spots for churches. He rebuilt that at Charlestown, and had the gratification of seeing others begun at Eastport, Orono, Saco, and Portland, Me., at Dover, N. H., Hartford, Newport, and Pawtucket. One of his earliest cares was to mark by a suitable monument the spot at Norridgewalk, Me., where Rev. Sebastian Rale had been killed in 1724.

There was much to encourage Bishop Fenwick, especially after the first and second councils of Baltimore; but unprincipled men stimulated prejudice and hatred against Catholics, and a book appeared full of calumnies against the Ursuline nuns. On the 11th of August, 1834, a mob attacked that house of defenceless ladies, drove them from it, and burned it to the ground, by the apathy if not the connivance of the authorities. It was a terrible blow to the bishop, who saw courts acquit the guilty. In 1842 he held the first synod in his diocese, and formally put in force the decrees of the Baltimore councils. The next year he obtained the erection of a see of Hartford, with Connecticut and Rhode Island as the diocese. In 1843 he founded the college of the Holy Cross at Worcester, confiding it to the Society of Jesus, but was never able to obtain a charter for it. The next year, finding his strength and health decline, he obtained a coadjutor in the person of the Rt. Rev. John B. Fitzpatrick. In the same year he received into the Church the distinguished philosopher, O. A. Brownson. Bishop Fenwick continued in the constant discharge of his duties, but in the summer of 1846 disease manifested itself in a fatal form, and he expired on the 11th of August.

Bishop Fenwick was one of the great bishops of the Church, learned and prudent in the council, eloquent in the pulpit, energetic and active in his episcopal duties, a father to his clergy and people. The diocese he found with two priests he left with forty-five, and with a corresponding increase in churches and institutions.

RIGHT REV. JOHN BERNARD FITZPATRICK,

Third Bishop of Boston.

JOHN BERNARD FITZPATRICK was born in Boston, November 1, 1812, his parents having emigrated seven years before from Tullamore, Ireland. Their son received his early training in the best city schools, and in the famous Boston Latin School he won several medals. Bishop Fenwick, who knew his piety and talents, saw and encouraged his vocation for the priesthood, and in 1829 he was sent to the Sulpitian college in Montreal. Here he so thoroughly mastered the French language in all its niceties that he was made professor of rhetoric and belles-lettres. His studies for the priesthood were made at St. Sulpice, Paris, and he was ordained priest June 13, 1840. Returning home, he was assistant at the cathedral, and afterwards at St. Mary's Church, Boston. Having been appointed to East Cambridge, he erected a substantial stone church. When the health of Bishop Fenwick required aid he chose Rev. Mr. Fitzpatrick as his coadjutor, aware of his sound theological learning, his zeal, and his administrative ability. On being appointed Bishop of Gallipolis in 1844, he was consecrated at Georgetown on the 24th of March. He at once took up his residence with the bishop, laboring with his wonted zeal. In less than two years the whole burden of the diocese devolved upon him, and he overtaxed his strength, having no secretary and no vicar-general for several years. By his energy, by 1853 he had increased the churches in Massachusetts from twenty-seven to fifty; but he saw the necessity of bishops for the more northern States, and in 1853 was rejoiced to relinquish Maine and New Hampshire to the Bishop of Portland and Vermont to the Bishop of Burlington. Bishop Fitzpatrick encouraged the erection of a reformatory for boys, and labored to restore the college of the Holy Cross, which had been partially destroyed by fire.

The anti-Catholic excitement soon after saddened his heart by other outrages like that of Charlestown. A church at Dorchester was blown up, another burned at Bath, that at Manchester was attacked, and the houses of Catholics wrecked. The very legislature of the State stooped to infamy and appointed a committee to investigate the convents, and the Sisters of Notre Dame were grossly insulted by men appointed by the General Court of Massachusetts; yet in a few days the papers rang with exposure of the notorious character of some of these very men. In 1859 a Catholic pupil in the Eliot School was flogged for declining to repeat the spurious form of the Lord's Prayer used by Protestants. A court acquitted the teacher, but Bishop Fitzpatrick addressed the School Board in a most masterly document, in which he showed the injustice of the enforced use of the Protestant version of the Bible, the enforced learning of the Ten Commandments in the Protestant form, and the enforced repeating of the spurious form of the Lord's Prayer. The bishop at once set to work to make Catholics independent of the State schools, which were conducted in such disregard of the rights of conscience. The Jesuit Fathers opened Boston College; the Sisters of Mercy an academy and hospital at Worcester; parish schools were established in Boston, South and East Boston, Salem, and Lawrence.

As business had grown around the old cathedral, Bishop Fitzpatrick, to his sorrow, saw that it must soon be removed. He purchased a fine site, and plans were prepared for a noble edifice; but he deferred the work, so many necessary churches and institutions demanded the resources of the faithful. His health was never robust, and on the 14th of December, 1864, he was seized with violent pains, and, though his condition became critical, he would not disturb the priests in the house. When one came at last the bishop was senseless on the floor, bathed in his own blood. Extreme Unction was administered. He never regained health or strength, and expired on the 13th of February, 1866.

Reduced as his diocese was in extent, he left it with 115 churches, 110 priests, an asylum, an hospital, a reformatory, colleges, and schools.

MOST REV. JOHN JOSEPH WILLIAMS,

Fourth Bishop and First Archbishop of Boston.

JOHN JOSEPH WILLIAMS was born in Boston on the 27th of April, 1822, his parents having emigrated from Ireland to that city. His first rudiments were acquired in the public primary school, but when a Catholic school was opened at the cathedral in 1827, under the Rev. Messrs. Fitton, Tyler, and Wiley, then young seminarians, the future archbishop was one of the first scholars at the opening of this humble seat of learning. In 1833 he entered the College of Montreal, directed by the priests of St. Sulpice, and there was duly graduated after a course of eight years. Feeling called to serve God in his sanctuary, he went to the great seminary of the Sulpitians in Paris, where he made his theological course, and was ordained by Monseigneur Affre, Archbishop of Paris, in 1845.

On his return to Boston he was stationed at the cathedral, and for ten years, from November 1, 1845, directed the Sunday-school. In 1855 he was appointed rector of the cathedral, and, after discharging the duties of that position for two years, became pastor of St. James' Church, Boston, and vicar-general of the diocese. His administration as parish priest had shown his ability and discretion, as well as the possession of the highest sacerdotal qualifications.

As the health of Bishop Fitzpatrick became precarious, the Very Rev. Mr. Williams was elected titular Bishop of Tripoli and coadjutor, January 9, 1866, but before his consecration Bishop Fitzpatrick breathed his last. He was consecrated Bishop of Boston to which he had succeeded on the 11th of March, 1866, Archbishop McCloskey officiating.

Under his impulse the development of churches and institutions went on. The Sisters of Charity of Madame d'Youville's foundation, commonly called Gray Nuns, came from Montreal in 1866 to labor in the diocese, as did the Sisters of the Third Order of St. Francis. Lowell had a convent with hospital and schools : Chicopee had its convent; Boston saw a House of the Good Shepherd begun. Then came a convent of Sisters of Mercy at Worcester. The secular clergy, already aided in their labors by the Jesuits, Franciscans, Oblates, and Augustinians, were soon joined by the Redemptorists. Schools marked the real progress.

In 1870 the diocese contained 148 churches with 183 priests, and a division was deemed seasonable. A see was erected in June at Springfield, with a diocese embracing five counties; and in 1872 the diocese of Providence took from Boston Bristol, Barnstable, and part of Plymouth counties. On the 12th of February, 1875, Boston was made an archiepiscopal see, and a new ecclesiastical province was instituted, Boston being metropolitan, and Portland, Burlington, Springfield, Hartford, and Providence being the suffragans. Archbishop Williams received the pallium from the hands of Archbishop McCloskey.

One of the great desires of Archbishop Williams was gratified in 1884—the opening of a theological seminary, under the direction of the Sulpitians, in a fine building which had been for some years in progress. At this time his diocese contained about 320,000 Catholics, attended by 300 priests, and having 167 churches.

MOST REV. PATRICK J. RYAN, D.D.
Born at Cloneyharp, Ireland, in 1831.
Ordained in 1854; Consecrated Bishop of Tricomia, April 14, 1872; Promoted to Philadelphia, 1884.

MOST REV. PATRICK A. FEEHAN.
Born in County Tipperary, Ireland, Aug. 28, 1829.
Consecrated Bishop of Nashville, Nov. 1, 1865; Archbishop of Chicago, Sept. 10, 1880.

MOST REV. JOHN J. WILLIAMS, D.D.
Born in Boston, Mass., April 27, 1822.
Ordained in May, 1845; consecrated Bishop and Coadjutor of Boston, January, 1860; Bishop of Boston, March 11, 1866; Archbishop, Feb. 12, 1875.

MOST REV. WILLIAM HENRY ELDER, D.D.
Born in Baltimore, March 22, 1819.
Ordained in 1846; Bishop of Natchez, May 3, 1857; Bishop of Avara, Jan. 30, 1880, and Coadjutor of Cincinnati; Archbishop of Cincinnati, July 4, 1883.

DIOCESE OF CHICAGO.

RIGHT REV. WILLIAM QUARTER,

First Bishop of Chicago.

WILLIAM QUARTER was born in Killurine, Kings County, Ireland, January 24, 1806. The piety of his parents can be judged from the fact that three of their sons became priests. After preliminary studies at Tullamore he was preparing to enter Maynooth when the wants of the mission in the United States, as described by a priest from this country, induced him to come to America in 1822. He entered Mount St. Mary's College, where, under the direction of Rev. Messrs. Du Bois and Bruté, he was formed for his priestly career. Following Bishop Du Bois to New York, he was ordained September 4, 1829. As assistant at St. Peter's he was instrumental in introducing the Sisters of Charity into that parish, and showed such devotedness in the cholera season of 1832 that his example led to conversions. Appointed the next year to St. Mary's Church, he completed it, introduced Sisters of Charity, established a free school and academy. For eleven years he was the devoted, wise, and careful pastor of his flock, keeping up the faith in their hearts, and receiving many converts—among others a Lutheran minister, Rev. Maximilian Oertel—into the Church. Having been appointed to the see of Chicago, he was consecrated on the 10th of March, 1844. He at once set to work to organize the new diocese, beginning a cathedral, college, and seminary, and introduced the Sisters of Mercy. He made strenuous efforts to obtain priests for all congregations able to maintain them, and when he convoked his diocesan synod he could number forty-one. Bishop Quarter established conferences and sought to maintain a true spirit in his clergy, while he himself was untiring in preaching and mission work.

His health, however, failed rapidly, and he died rather suddenly April 10, 1848, in full possession of his faculties, after receiving all the sacraments.

RIGHT REV. JAMES OLIVER VAN DE VELDE,

Second Bishop of Chicago and Second of Natchez.

JAMES OLIVER VAN DE VELDE was born near Termonde, Belgium, April 3, 1795, and was educated piously by a priest who escaped from the Reign of Terror in France. He entered the seminary at Mechlin, and was teaching there when the apostolic Mr. Nerinckx visited Belgium to invite young aspirants to the priesthood to give their services to the American mission. Young Mr. Van de Velde at once volunteered, but he received an injury on the voyage, so that he had to be carried to St. Mary's College. On recovering he entered the novitiate of the Society of Jesus, and was ordained September 25, 1827. After some missionary labors in the rural districts of Maryland, he was made professor of rhetoric and mathematics in the University of St. Louis. He became successively vice-president and president of that institution, and represented the vice-province at Rome and at the Sixth Council of Baltimore. As vice-provincial he erected several churches and extended the Indian missions. Appointed to the see of Chicago in 1848, he yielded only when it was decided that the bulls were imperative. He was consecrated in the church of the university, February 11, 1849, and proceeded to Illinois. He made a visitation of his diocese, and founded two asylums to care for the orphans whose parents had been carried off by the cholera. The climate of Chicago proved very severe to Bishop Van de Velde, and a factious opposition in the diocese caused him great pain. He wished to resign, but a new see was erected at Quincy, and after a visit to Rome he resumed his visitations and other episcopal duties till he was transferred to Natchez, July 29, 1853. He left

Chicago on the 3d of November and proceeded to Mississippi, where he was hospitably and warmly welcomed. Here he labored zealously for two years. On the 23d of October, 1855, he fell, causing a compound fracture of the leg. Fever set in, which took the character of the deadly yellow fever, and, after receiving the last rites with great devotion, Bishop Van de Velde expired on the 13th of November, 1855.

RIGHT REV. ANTHONY O'REGAN,

Third Bishop of Chicago.

RIGHT REV. ANTHONY O'REGAN was born in the parish of Kiltulla, Ireland, and, becoming connected with the diocese of St. Louis, soon attained eminent positions. He was vicar-general of that diocese, president of the seminary at Carondelet, filling also the chairs of theology and Sacred Scripture.

After the transfer of Bishop Van de Velde the affairs of the diocese of Chicago fell into great disorder, and the position of bishop was declined by the clergyman first selected. The Rev. Mr. O'Regan was nominated, but declined till what was almost a peremptory order in 1854 induced him to accept the burden, and he was consecrated July 25, 1854. Possessing great administrative ability, he set to work in earnest, restored discipline and order. He introduced system into the affairs of the diocese, to which he gave much anxious thought. His methods and administration, however, excited some complaint, and, after spenping two years and a half in the diocese, Bishop O'Regan proceeded to Rome, anxious to lay down a dignity which he had never sought. His earnest petition for leave to resign was granted, and he was transferred to the see of Dora, June 25, 1858. He never returned to America, but took up his residence in London, where he died November 13, 1866, leaving bequests for the education of clergymen for the diocese over which he had presided and for erecting an hospital in Chicago.

RIGHT REV. JAMES DUGGAN,

Coadjutor-Bishop of St. Louis and Fourth Bishop of Chicago.

JAMES DUGGAN was born in the diocese of Dublin, Ireland, in the year 1825, and came early in life to this country. Having attached himself to the diocese of St. Louis, he was ordained by dispensation, under the canonical age, when only twenty-two, May 29, 1847, by Archbishop Kenrick. Notwithstanding his youth, he was made superior of the St. Louis Theological Seminary at Carondelet, and subsequently acted as one of the professors. In 1850 he was attached to the cathedral, and in 1854 was made one of the vicars-general of the diocese and pastor of the church of the Immaculate Conception. He was regarded as one of the ablest and most eloquent priests in the diocese, and his selection to aid Archbishop Kenrick in his arduous duties was cordially approved. He was appointed Bishop of Gabala and coadjutor of St. Louis January 9, 1857, and was consecrated Bishop of Antigone May 3, 1857. He rendered efficient aid to Archbishop Kenrick in the administration of the diocese; on the retirement of Bishop O'Regan he was made administrator of Chicago and finally bishop of that see. His health, never strong, soon gave way, and, leaving his diocese, he proceeded to Europe. While there complaints were made against his administration, on learning of which he returned to his diocese and removed some of the remonstrants. The matter was referred to the Archbishop of St. Louis, but, as Bishop Duggan's accusers neglected to appear and prove their charges, they fell to the ground. It was soon evident, however, that his mind had given away, and that he was not accountable for many of his acts. His mental malady increased in 1869 to such an extent that recovery was deemed doubtful. He was accordingly removed to an asylum in Missouri and arrangements were made for the administration of the unhappy diocese. Bishop Duggan never recovered.

RIGHT REV. THOMAS FOLEY,

Bishop of Pergamus and Administrator of Chicago.

THOMAS FOLEY was born in Baltimore, March 6, 1823, and, trained in piety from his youth, early evinced a vocation for the priesthood. He entered St. Mary's Seminary, where he soon became one of the prefects. The rites and ceremonial of the Church were a favorite study, and this led to his selection as master of ceremonies at the Fifth Provincial Council. He was ordained by Archbishop Eccleston August 17, 1846, and was appointed pastor of Rockville. After being assistant at St. Patrick's, Washington, he was from 1848 connected with the cathedral, Baltimore, and for some years was chancellor of the diocese. He acted as secretary at the first and second Plenary Councils, and from 1867 was vicar-general of the diocese. His merit and ability were widely known, and important duties were evidently in store for him. He was selected for the difficult task of restoring discipline and order in the diocese of Chicago, which Bishop Duggan's acts, while his malady was unsuspected, had involved in great difficulties. Rev. Mr. Foley was appointed Bishop of Pergamus and coadjutor of Chicago on the 19th of November, 1869, and was consecrated in the cathedral, Baltimore, February 27, 1870, by Bishop McCloskey, of Louisville. His experience in diocesan management enabled him to meet the wants of the diocese of Chicago. New parishes with churches were required, and in some parts there were old wooden churches no longer serviceable. Bishop Foley inspired his clergy with zeal and activity, and his financial ability kept the outlay for new churches within reasonable bounds and established a credit which made necessary loans easy. While Catholic Chicago was thus full of hope it was visited by the terrible conflagration which swept away seven churches with their pastoral residences and parochial schools, the hospital of the Alexian Brothers, an orphan asylum, the House of Providence, St. Xavier's Academy and Convent, and the select school conducted by the Christian Brothers. St. Mary's, the cradle of

Catholicity in the city, was one of the buildings devoured by the flames. The bishop and his clergy set to work with energy to repair this terrible loss, although the parishioners had been scattered far and wide by the conflagration; but as the city was rebuilt and spread Catholic churches and institutions kept pace with its progress. The cathedral of the Holy Name rose from its ashes by his energy. Eight years' labor had given the diocese a new life and spirit. Under his administration the priests in the diocese had increased from one hundred and forty-two to two hundred and six, and his churches from about two hundred to fully three hundred. Five new convents and seven academies had been begun, and he had erected a new cathedral.

Everything promised a season of needed rest for Bishop Foley amid a clergy and people who had learned to admire him, but while returning from a filial visit to his mother in Baltimore he contracted a heavy cold and was stricken down by pneumonia in February, 1879. His strength, exhausted by his years of labor, could not resist the disease, and he expired on the 19th.

During his administration the diocese of Chicago was again divided, and a new see established at Peoria, its diocese being increased, after Bishop Foley's death, by the addition of some counties taken from that of Chicago.

MOST REV. PATRICK A. FEEHAN,

Third Bishop of Nashville, First Archbishop of Chicago.

PATRICK A. FEEHAN was born in the County Tipperary, Ireland, and was educated at the celebrated Seminary of Maynooth. Having resolved to devote himself to the American mission, he came to St. Louis in 1852, and was appointed superior of the seminary at Carondelet. As pastor of the church of the Immaculate Conception in St. Louis, which position he filled for several years, he acquired reputation as a devoted priest, able in the pulpit and in the direction of the manifold affairs which devolve on the head of a parish in this country. When Bishop Whelan resigned the see of Nashville the Rev. Mr. Feehan was elected to fill the vacancy on the 7th of July, 1865. The progress of Catholicity in Tennessee has never been rapid, but under the energetic impulse given by Bishop Feehan progress was very marked. He was consecrated on the 1st of November, 1865, and proceeded to the State of Tennessee, which had been one of the battle-grounds of the war, many of the inhabitants being arrayed on each side. Amid the din of arms religion had suffered greatly, and Bishop Feehan found not more than twelve priests or churches in his diocese. By the year 1879 the diocese of Nashville reported twenty-seven priests, twenty-nine churches, a college under the Christian Brothers, academies and parochial schools under Dominican Sisters, Sisters of Mercy, of St. Joseph, Sisters of Charity, and Sisters of the Most Precious Blood. There was, too, a convent of the Sisters of the Good Shepherd with its usual Refuge, and two orphan asylums. Yet the diocese had been visited by the terrible yellow fever at Memphis the year before; nine priests and thirteen Sisters died there attending the sick, among them the vicar-general of the diocese, the Very Rev. Martin O'Riordan.

The death of Bishop Foley left Chicago unprovided; and as the lapse of years had shown Bishop Duggan's malady to be incurable, the Holy See created Chicago a metropolitan see, making Peoria and Alton its suffragans, and promoted Bishop Feehan to the newly-erected archiepiscopal throne September 10, 1880. The archbishop has more than maintained the Catholic interests in Chicago; indeed, the growth is said to exceed that at any former period. In three years nine new parishes were established in Chicago alone. He has placed on a solid basis St. Mary's Training School for Boys, an excellent institution in charge of the Christian Brothers.

On the 25th of May, 1883, the archbishop and his flock celebrated the Catholic semi-centennial, the fiftieth anniversary of the founding of St. Mary's Church, the oldest Catholic church in the city. Fifty years before Catholicity in what is now the diocese of Chicago could boast one church, one priest, and about

300 adherents. Eleven years later, in 1844, it could boast only five priests and very few churches. In 1884 the diocese, including only a portion of the State, contained 236 priests, 184 churches, two colleges, eighteen academies, four hospitals, eight asylums, a Catholic population of more than a quarter of a million, more than one-tenth being pupils in Catholic schools.

In November, 1884, Archbishop Feehan attended the grand convention of the episcopate in the Third Plenary Council of Baltimore.

DIOCESE OF CINCINNATI.

RIGHT REV. EDWARD FENWICK,

First Bishop of Cincinnati.

EDWARD D. FENWICK was born in St. Mary's County, Maryland, in 1768, of a pious Catholic family which had adhered to the faith from the colonization of the colony, and which in his person gave a second of its descendants to the young episcopate of the United States. Having been sent at the age of sixteen to the Dominican college at Bornheim, in Flanders, he went through his studies with distinction, and, feeling called to the religious life, entered the order of St. Dominic as a novice. He spent several years in the quiet seclusion, discharging the duties of professor and procurator, till the armies of revolutionary France overran the Low Countries. The convent was seized and Father Fenwick and his brethren were thrown into prison as Englishmen. Procuring his release as an American citizen, he joined the Dominicans of his province in England; but, as he was desirous of laboring in his native land, he obtained from the general of the order permission to conduct a colony of Friars Preachers to the United States. He was chosen superior of the new mission and sailed for this country with three fathers. Bishop Carroll welcomed them earnestly and assigned them to duty in Kentucky. There Father Fenwick purchased a farm in Washington County in 1805, and founded St. Rose's convent in the following year. Their missions soon extended to Ohio, where many scattered Catholics were found. Resigning the office of provincial to another, Father Fenwick devoted himself entirely to the Ohio mission, and was constantly rewarded by discovering little communities of Catholics, who hailed his advent with joy. Missions were established at Somerset, Dayton, and Cincinnati. Mr. Peter Dittoe presented him a farm in Perry County, on condition that he established a convent of his order upon it, and Father Fenwick took up his residence there with another religious, their numbers being soon increased. From this centre the missions in Ohio were regularly attended, and churches were gradually erected at different points. Bishop Flaget, whose diocese embraced that State, urged the erection of a new diocese north of the Ohio River. In 1789 there had been an attempt to colonize the Scioto country with emigrants from France, and it was proposed to give them a separate superior, subject, however, to Bishop Carroll; but the settlers were not earnestly devoted to their faith and never even had a priest. On the 19th of June, 1821, Pope Pius VII. created the diocese of Cincinnati and appointed Edward Fenwick the first bishop. Receiving consecration at the hands of Bishop Flaget, January 13, 1822, Bishop Fenwick proceeded to Cincinnati, where he hired a little house and sent out to purchase a meal. The city possessed a little frame church about a mile from the limits. Removing this into the city, Dr. Fenwick made it his cathedral, but in the course of two years it was too small for his congregation. The wants of his diocese, which he estimated as containing then eight thousand Catholics, appalled him; he borrowed a hundred dollars and set out for Rome to ask the Pope to relieve him of his episcopate. Pope Leo XII. consoled and encouraged the pious bishop, and many charitable persons contributed to aid the cause of religion in Ohio. The Association for the Propagation of the Faith, recently established at Lyons, joined in the good work. Bishop Fenwick returned to his diocese with fresh hopes; he erected a cathedral and began a series of missions, establishing churches and, where possible, schools, confiding them to the Poor Clares, Sisters of Charity, and Dominican nuns. In his laborious visitations, which extended over Michigan and Wisconsin—then called Northwest Territory--he visited the Catholic Indians, whose faith he revived. After attending the first council of Baltimore he resumed his apostolical journeys in search of souls. While thus devotedly performing the duty of a good shepherd he was struck down by the cholera at Saut Ste. Marie, but rallied sufficiently to visit Arbre Croche and Detroit. At Canton he was again seized with the cholera, but heroically kept on, only to die the next day, September 26, 1832, at Wooster, Ohio. This apostolic bishop, thus prematurely cut off, left twenty churches and thirty priests attending the large Catholic population whom his untiring labors had united in zealous congregations, in a State where he had been the pioneer priest.

MOST REV. JOHN BAPTIST PURCELL,

Second Bishop and First Archbishop of Cincinnati.

THE successor of Bishop Fenwick was for many years one of the most notable and influential members of the American hierarchy. John Baptist Purcell was born at Mallow, Ireland, on the 26th of February, 1800. After making a successful course of study he came to the United States at the age of eighteen, and soon became engaged in teaching. But his wish was to enter the priesthood, and, having secured admission into Mount St. Mary's College, he evinced such talent that he was sent to St. Sulpice, in Paris, to complete his course. On his return he became president of Mount St. Mary's College, acting also as professor. The institution flourished under his direction. He was appointed to the see of Cincinnati and consecrated October 13, 1833, his diocese comprising the State of Ohio, with Covington, in Kentucky; Michigan and the other portions of the diocese having been placed under a bishop at Detroit. The State of Ohio contained about six thousand Catholics, who had sixteen churches, attended by fourteen priests. He entered on his work with zeal, and to an advanced age performed all the duties of a missionary priest. The institutions were the Dominican convent and seminary at Somerset, and an orphan asylum and school in Cincinnati conducted by the Sisters of Charity, with the Athenæum, the nucleus of a college, at Cincinnati. By the impulse of his zeal new churches and institutions arose, exciting fanatical alarm, which was fanned by men like Beecher and Morse. Challenged to a controversy by the Rev. Mr. Campbell, Bishop Purcell refuted him and established a name as a theologian and polemic. He drew religious orders in to aid his work: the Jesuits took charge of the Athenæum, the Sisters of Notre Dame from Namur and the Brothers of Mary opened academies and schools, the Priests of the Precious Blood began mission labors among the Germans, while the Ursulines founded their prosperous convent in Brown County. In 1846 Ohio boasted seventy thousand Catholics, with seventy churches and seventy-three priests. Bishop Purcell obtained the erection of a new bishop's see at Cleveland, the diocese being that part of the State north of 40° 41'. In 1850 Cincinnati was made an archiepiscopal see by Pope Pius IX., and the bishops of Cleveland, Detroit, Louisville, and Vincennes became suffragans of Archbishop Purcell. His next great step was the establishment of a theological seminary, Mount St. Mary's of the West. The suffragan bishops and their metropolitan held the first Provincial Council of Cincinnati in May, 1855, and a second council was held three years later, after Covington had in 1853 been placed under the care of a resident bishop. It was attended by the bishops of Detroit, Cleveland, Louisville, Covington, Saut Ste. Marie, and Fort Wayne. The decrees of these councils show eminently how fully Archbishop Purcell understood the wants of the Catholic community. The necessity of giving a thorough religious education to the young was paramount in his mind. He prepared the first series of Catholic school-books; he urged the erection of Catholic schools, and introduced religious to guide them. To create churches and schools rapidly enough to meet the wants of the thousands pouring into his diocese was a problem. The new congregations, composed of people who had all to acquire, were unable to meet the cost. Borrowing became necessary. In an evil hour, as it proved, Archbishop Purcell permitted his brother, the vicar-general, to accept deposits of money. Unacquainted with business, with no financial capacity, keeping no records or accounts, that official brought ruin in time to the archbishop and the diocese.

In 1862 he obtained a coadjutor in the person of Rev.

Sylvester H. Rosecrans, an able and energetic clergyman, who was consecrated Bishop of Pompeiopolis and Auxiliary Bishop of Cincinnati on March 25, 1862. But though religion received new progress from this aid, the archbishop felt that more could be effected by again dividing the diocese, and in 1868 the diocese of Columbus was established, of which his auxiliar, Bishop Rosecrans, was made the first ordinary. After this division the once extensive diocese of Cincinnati comprised only that part of the State lying south of 40° 41', being the counties south of the northern line of Mercer, Allen, and Hardin counties, and all west of the eastern line of Marion, Union, and Madison counties, and all west of the Scioto River to the Ohio. Even thus restricted the diocese contained 139,000 Catholics, 115 churches, with 7 in course of erection, 13 chapels, and 42 stations, attended by 135 priests. There were 76 parochial schools, with 9 academies and 3 colleges.

In 1869 Archbishop Purcell attended the Œcumenical Council of the Vatican, and was prominent in its debates on the question of defining the infallibility of the Sovereign Pontiff when deciding questions of faith and morals *ex cathedra*—that is, when formally and distinctly brought before him as the supreme judicial authority in the Church. Archbishop Purcell, like some others, was averse to a distinct declaration on the question.

On the 23d of May, 1876, the golden jubilee of his ordination was celebrated by his flock with solemn services in the cathedral, attended by societies in processions, and crowds of priests and laymen, Catholic and Protestant, who came to offer their congratulations. It was the bright and brilliant prelude of a sad and terrible affliction.

Early in 1879 financial affairs which had been managed by the Very Rev. Edward Purcell ended in bankruptcy. How it all came about must ever remain a mystery. The venerable archbishop, as ignorant as a child of the system and its extent, at once came forward and assumed the whole responsibility of his brother's operations. This only complicated matters and raised a host of legal questions as to his ability, in character of trustee for the Catholic Church in his diocese, to assume an individual indebtedness contracted by another; and if he could, it became necessary to decide what property became liable for it, that owned by the diocese or the property of every Catholic church and institution in the diocese. If the debt became a just charge on the whole diocese and all its churches and institutions, it was a debt on every Catholic, which he was bound in conscience to pay. This extreme view no theologian or canonist was found to take.

The debts were at first supposed not to exceed a quarter of a million of dollars, and attempts were made to meet or reduce it materially by subscriptions; but when it was found that the indebtedness reached nearly four millions of dollars the attempt was abandoned as hopeless. The Very Rev. Edward Purcell died broken-hearted. The archbishop made an assignment of all property in his name, and long litigations began. The courts ultimately decided that the individual congregations were not liable except for moneys actually advanced to them.

The venerable archbishop asked to be permitted to resign the see which he had so long occupied, but when this was refused he obtained the appointment of a coadjutor. The choice fell upon the Right Rev. William H. Elder, then Bishop of Natchez, who in May, 1880, assumed the administration of the diocese.

Archbishop Purcell then retired to a house near the Ursuline Convent in Brown County. Here early in 1881 he was struck with paralysis and lingered till July 4, 1883, when he expired calmly and full of hope. His career had been humble, zealous, and active. In the great trial of his life all acknowledged that no money had been spent for his own purposes or extravagantly. He had been a prelate of great influence, forming many of the best bishops and clergy in the country, consecrating in his long administration eighteen bishops and ordaining hundreds of priests.

MOST REV. WILLIAM HENRY ELDER,

Third Bishop of Natchez, Second Archbishop of Cincinnati.

WILLIAM HENRY ELDER was born in Baltimore in the year 1819, and, corresponding to the pious wish of his parents, early in life looked forward to the priesthood as the work of his life. He began his studies in Mount St. Mary's College, but pursued a theological course for three years in the College of the Propaganda at Rome. He was ordained in 1846, and, returning to the United States, was for several years president and professor of theology at Mount St. Mary's. In this quiet field of labor he had impressed many bishops with his singular abilities. On the 9th of January, 1857, he was selected for the see of Natchez, and received episcopal consecration on the 3d day of May in the cathedral of Baltimore, the consecrator being the Most Rev. Francis P. Kenrick, assisted by the Right Rev. John McGill, of Richmond, and Rt. Rev. James F. Wood, coadjutor of Philadelphia. He was the twelfth bishop that Mount St. Mary's had given to the Church in the United States. Bishop Elder was actively laboring for his flock in Mississippi when the civil war began. In time the State became the scene of battle, and the bishop, with his few priests and the communities of sisters, did all in their power to alleviate suffering and to prepare men for a Christian death. One of his priests died amid his charitable labors. In 1864 the post commandant at Natchez, one of those fanatics who confound their Protestantism and their citizenship, issued an order requiring all clergymen to insert in their public worship a prayer for the President of the United States. Bishop Elder remonstrated, showing how nobly he and his clergy had acted, but taking the broad ground that Congress itself could not make alterations in the form of the Mass as offered by Catholics throughout the world, and that no Catholic priest could obey such an order. The brutal Colonel Farrar arrested Bishop Elder and sent him out of his diocese to Vidalia, Louisiana. It was one of the most daring and outrageous infringements of liberty of conscience ever perpetrated in the

United States, and was committed by an officer of the general government. General Brayman soon revoked the order, but manifested his own bigotry by the use of terms of grossest insult to the noble Catholic bishop.

When peace was at last restored Catholicity in Mississippi was in a wretched condition; flocks had been scattered, priests were gone, institutions suspended, churches in ruins. Bishop Elder went zealously to work to restore all; but when prosperity was beginning to dawn the yellow fever of 1878 visited the diocese. Bishop Elder showed his wonted zeal and was stricken down; the report even spread that he was dead, as three of his priests and many sisters were. But he lived to resume his labors and to decline in the following year the position of coadjutor to the Archbishop of San Francisco. He yielded, indeed, on the 30th of January 1880, to the command that he should proceed to Cincinnati to assume, as Bishop of Avara, a duty before which many had quailed—the administration of the diocese amid its financial wreck. The diocese of Natchez was endeared to him by his missionary labors and his patient care; he left it with a population of 12,500, attended by twenty priests, who offered the Holy Sacrifice in 41 churches scattered through the State. The Catholic body was gaining by natural increase and by conversion, nearly one-fourth the baptisms being of adults, and there were several religious orders laboring by good example and sound instruction to diffuse the gospel of truth. Still retaining the administration of Natchez, Bishop Elder took up his residence in Cincinnati. Difficulties beset him, but his wise, temperate, and prudent course soon restored order and rallied around him the best elements in the diocese. In February, 1882, he presided in the Fourth Provincial Council of Cincinnati, where decrees were adopted based on the necessities of the time. By the death of Archbishop Purcell, July 4, he became Archbishop of Cincinnati, and soon received the pallium. Archbishop Elder took a prominent part in the work of the Third Plenary Council of Baltimore, the sessions of which were continued through nearly the whole month of November, 1884.

DIOCESE OF MILWAUKEE.

MOST REV. JOHN MARTIN HENNI,

First Bishop and Archbishop of Milwaukee.

JOHN MARTIN HENNI was born of a family in comfortable circumstances at Obersaxen, in the Swiss canton of the Grisons, in the year 1805. After studying at St. Gall and Luzerne he proceeded to Rome to complete his course; there he and another young Swiss, Martin Kundig, moved by the appeal of Bishop Fenwick, of Cincinnati, for priests to aid him, volunteered to join his diocese. They arrived in Baltimore in 1829, and, completing their theology in the seminary at Bardstown, were ordained by Bishop Fenwick February 2, 1829. The Rev. Mr. Henni took charge of the Germans in Cincinnati, who then attended St. Peter's Church, giving them instructions in their own language. He also taught philosophy in the Athenæum. His next field of labor was in Northern Ohio, extending from Canton to Lake Erie. Bishop Purcell recalled him to Cincinnati in 1834, making him vicar-general and pastor of the German church of the Holy Trinity. The next year he visited Europe and published there an interesting account of the state of religion in the Valley of the Ohio, in order to stimulate interest in the missions. Returning to Cincinnati, he established in 1837 the *Wahrheits Freund*, the first German Catholic paper in the United States. He also organized the St. Aloysius' Orphans' Aid Society. Among his projects was a seminary for the education of priests to labor among the Germans in this country. His plan was laid before the Provincial Council in Baltimore, but that body, soliciting the erection of a see at Milwaukee, recommended him as admirably fitted by learning, piety, sacerdotal zeal, and experience for the new mitre. On the feast of St. Joseph, March 19, 1844, he was consecrated in St. Xavier's Church, Cincinnati, by Archbishop Purcell, assisted by Bishops Miles and O'Connor. The diocese of Milwaukee was just the field for his zeal. The only church in his episcopal city was a wooden one, thirty feet by forty in size. Indeed, Mass had been said for the first time in Milwaukee only seven years before in the house of Solomon Juneau. A stone church had been begun at Prairie du Chien, but the few other churches in the dioceses were log structures, and the Catholics, estimated at from eight to ten thousand, had only five priests to attend them. Bishop Henni found his old friend, Rev. Mr. Kundig, at Milwaukee, and had brought with him a learned young priest, Rev. Michael Heiss. He began a visitation of his diocese, borrowing money to pay his expenses, and soon found that his flock was nearly double what had been supposed. To supply them with priests and churches was his urgent task. By the end of the first year he had nine priests, eighteen churches, and six more going up. The activity of the Catholic body under the impulse of their bishop excited the hostility of fanatics, who began their usual misrepresentations. A Rev. Mr. Miter was especially active in endeavoring to excite violence against Catholics, but Bishop Henni, in a pamphlet entitled "Facts against Assertion, by Philalethes," placed them so clearly in the wrong that a better feeling soon prevailed.

In 1847 he began the erection of a new cathedral and introduced the Sisters of Charity, who took charge of a hospital. The next year he visited Rome to report the condition of his diocese and obtain aid of various kinds. On his return he suspended work on his cathedral in order to build an orphan asylum; he introduced the School Sisters of Notre Dame, and, by giving them a thorough system of training, made the order one of the most successful bodies of teachers in the country. Meanwhile churches and institutions were increasing, the Dominicans opened a college at Sinsinawa, Brothers of St. Francis and Sisters of the same order at Nojoshing, Dominican nuns at Benton. Some zealous priests organized a Capuchin convent, reviving that order in this country. At the end of his first ten years his flock was one hundred thousand and his clergy numbered seventy-three.

The very year after his arrival he opened a little theological seminary under the direction of the Rev. Mr. Heiss, and maintained it, gradually preparing to place it on a solid basis. After the consecration of his cathedral by Archbishop Bedini in 1853 he was able to lay, in 1855, the corner-stone of the Salesianum, or Seminary of St. Francis de Sales, and opened it for the reception of students on the feast of that saint. This seminary, under the able management of Rev. Messrs. Heiss and Salzmann, became one of the best in the country. By the year 1868 the State contained three hundred thousand Catholics, and at the request of Bishop Henni it was divided into three dioceses. His Holiness Pope Pius IX. established the sees of Green Bay and La Crosse, yet the portion of the State left in the diocese of Milwaukee contained two hundred and forty-three churches and one hundred and forty-three priests. Bishop Henni had won the esteem and attachment of all men, and his silver jubilee in 1869 was a spontaneous ovation. The eloquent sermon preached on that occasion by the Rev. Father Garesché, S.J., was long remembered.

In 1875 the Holy See created him an archbishop, giving him as suffragans the bishops of Green Bay, La Crosse, Marquette, and St. Paul. The golden jubilee of his priesthood in 1879, when the sermon was preached by Archbishop Purcell, who had consecrated him, evoked the most enthusiastic expressions of respect. But the aged archbishop was ready to lay down his burdens. The death of his old friend, Very Rev. Mr. Kundig, was a severe blow to him, and a visitation during the summer, in which he gave confirmation in several places, completely prostrated his enfeebled frame.

On the 14th of March, 1880, the Right Rev. Dr. Heiss was made coadjutor and relieved Archbishop Henni of much of the care of the administration. The aged archbishop soon became too weak to perform any official act, though he retained all his faculties. He died on the 7th of September, 1881, at half-past eleven, having received the sacraments in full possession of his senses.

MOST REV. MICHAEL HEISS,

First Bishop of La Crosse and Second Archbishop of Milwaukee.

The successor of Archbishop Henni, the Most Rev. Michael Heiss, was born in Pfahldorf, Bavaria, April 12, 1818, and, entering the Latin school at the age of nine, was graduated with distinction from the gymnasium of Newburg in 1835. He first studied law, but, feeling called to the service of God, went through a theological course in the University of Munich, where Goerres, Moehler, and Döllinger were his professors. He then entered the ecclesiastical seminary at Eichstadt, and was ordained by Cardinal Reisach October 18, 1840. He received a curacy, but came to the United States in 1843, and was appointed to the church of the Mother of God in Covington, Ky. On the appointment of Dr. Henni to Milwaukee Rev. Mr. Heiss accompanied him, acting as secretary, and doing mission work for fifty miles north of the city. He founded St. Mary's Church in 1846; but his health failed, and he spent two years in Europe. On his return he became president of the Salesianum, and by learned theological works showed his ability and erudition. On the division of the diocese he was selected for the see of La Crosse and consecrated September 6, 1868. The diocese, which embraces the portion of the State north and west of the Wisconsin River, had an early French settlement at Prairie du Chien about 1689. In the present century it was first visited by a priest in 1817, and the corner-stone of a church was laid in 1839. Under the administration of Bishop Henni religion had made such progress in this part of the State that the new diocese of La Crosse contained forty churches, attended by fifteen priests. Bishop Heiss proceeded to develop the good work; he established Franciscan Sisters at La Crosse, and their mother-house soon supplied teachers for twenty-five parochial schools and two asylums. The Christian Brothers opened St. John's College at Prairie du Chien, and the School Sisters of Notre Dame had excellent schools under their care. At the end of ten years the diocese of La Crosse

MOST REV. MICHAEL HEISS, D.D.
Born in Pfahldorf, Bavaria, April 12, 1818.
Ordained Oct. 18, 1840; Consecrated Bishop of La Crosse, Sept. 6, 1868; Bishop of Adrianople and Coadjutor of Milwaukee, March 14, 1880; Archbishop of Milwaukee, Sept. 7, 1881.

MOST REV. MICHAEL A. CORRIGAN.
Born in Newark, N. J., Aug. 13, 1839.
Ordained Sept. 19, 1863; Consecrated Bishop of Newark, May 4, 1873; Archbishop of Petra and Coadjutor of New York, Oct. 1, 1880; succeeded to the See of New York, Oct. 10, 1885.

MOST REV. FRANCIS X. LERAY, D.D.
Born near Rennes, France, April 20, 1825.
Ordained March 19, 1852; Consecrated Bishop of Natchitoches, April 22, 1877; Bishop of Janopolis and Coadjutor of New Orleans, Oct 23, 1879; Archbishop of New Orleans, Dec. 27, 1883.

MOST REV. C. J. SEGHERS, D.D.
Born at Ghent, Belgium, Dec. 26, 1839.
Ordained June, 1863. Consecrated June 29, 1873, Bishop of Vancouver's Island; Coadjutor of Archbishop Blanchet, Dec. 10, 1878; succeeded as Archbishop of Oregon City, Dec. 12, 1880; resigned 1884; appointed Archbishop of Vancouver's Island, 1885.

had thirty-six churches with resident pastors, fifty others regularly visited, forty priests, and forty-five thousand Catholics.

When the failing health of Archbishop Henni required the aid of a more vigorous prelate, Bishop Heiss was promoted to the see of Adrianople, March 14, 1880, and appointed coadjutor. The whole administration of Milwaukee diocese soon devolved upon him, and on the death of Archbishop Henni he became second archbishop of that see.

As theologian Dr. Heiss took an active part in the councils of St. Louis and the Second Plenary Council of Baltimore. He attended the Vatican Council in 1869-70, and was appointed by Pope Pius IX. a member of one of the four great commissions, each being composed of twelve bishops representing all parts of the world.

The pallium was conferred on Archbishop Heiss, in his cathedral, on the 23d of April, 1882. On the 3d of June in the following year he laid the corner-stone of a new cathedral, a building to be worthy of the great and flourishing diocese. He attended the Third Plenary Council of Baltimore in November, 1884.

DIOCESE OF NEW ORLEANS.

MOST REV. LOUIS IGNATIUS PEÑALVER Y CARDENAS,

First Bishop of Louisiana and the Floridas, Archbishop of Guatemala.

Don Louis Ignatius Peñalver y Cardenas was born in Havana, on the island of Cuba, on the 3d of April, 1749, and at an early age was placed in the college which the Fathers of the Society of Jesus maintained for nearly half a century in that city. His higher studies were pursued in the University of St. Jerome, and, feeling that God called him to the ecclesiastical state, he in time received the order of priesthood. His learning, ability, and charity made him a remarkable man, and in 1773 he was appointed provisor and vicar-general of the diocese of Santiago de Cuba. His functions as ecclesiastical judge made him familiar with the whole diocese, and especially with that portion situated on the mainland, Louisiana and Florida, to which the ancient jurisdiction was extended once more between 1776 and 1784. He was thus aware of the state of religion, and especially of the difficulties which had embarrassed Bishop Cyril. His exemplary and austere life, and the immense liberalities in which he expended the wealth he had inherited, made Dr. Peñalver beloved and respected in his native city. He was the first director of the Patriotic Society, and the founder of the Casa de Benificencia, purchasing the ground and expending nearly twenty-six thousand dollars on the buildings. When the Holy See erected the diocese of Louisiana and the Floridas Dr. Peñalver was chosen as the first bishop, and was consecrated in 1793. He reached New Orleans the following year, and proceeded to organize a chapter for the diocese, appointing two canons. The cathedral had just been completed by Don Andres Almonaster. He found religion at a very low ebb and many of the clergy unfit for their positions. Immorality prevailed; not one-fourth of those able attended Mass on Sundays, and there were not more than three or four hundred Easter communions in New Orleans out of a population of 11,000; days of fast and abstinence were utterly neglected. The infidel doctrines of France were finding in such a soil a rapid and dangerous growth. Even the officers of the colony, who ought to have set an example of virtue and morality, sanctioned by their own lives what they should have prevented. The good bishop set to work, however, to repair the evils and recall the people, as far as possible, to a life of Christian duty. He found this no easy task, and parishes that had maintained some sense of religion were gradually yielding to the torrent of evil caused by the influx of adventurers of all kinds. The bishop's charity and zeal to relieve the poor and afflicted were exerted in vain; they failed to win the attachment of the flock confided to his care. He became discouraged, but on the 20th of July, 1801, he was promoted to the see of Guatemala, and he left the colony. On his voyage from New Orleans to Havana his vessel was pursued by an English man-of-war, and he narrowly escaped being made a prisoner. In Guatemala he founded a hospital and established several schools; but, finding the burden of the episcopate too great, he obtained leave to resign the mitre, and did so March 1, 1806. Returning to his native city, he devoted the remainder of his life to charity, and died July 17, 1810. His property he bequeathed to pious institutions and to the poor.

On the retirement of Bishop Peñalver the Rev. Francis Porro, of the convent of the Holy Apostles in Rome, is said to have been nominated to the diocese of Louisiana, but, according to the accurate Benedictine Gams, he was never consecrated, the probability of the speedy termination of Spanish authority in the province having doubtless prevented the bishop-elect from attempting to assume direction of the diocese, where there would be no provision for his maintenance, and where little could be expected from the people.

MOST REV. WILLIAM LOUIS DUBOURG,

Second Bishop of Louisiana, First Bishop of New Orleans, Bishop of Montauban, and Archbishop of Besançon.

LIKE his predecessor, William Louis Du Bourg was a native of the West Indies, having been born at Cap François, Saint Domingo, February 14, 1766. He was sent to France for his education. There he embraced the ecclesiastical state, and after his ordination joined the Society of St. Sulpice. He was superior of the seminary at Issy when the French Revolution declared war on religion. He retired at first to his family at Bordeaux, but when he saw that there was no hope of change he resolved to come to America. He arrived at Baltimore in December, 1794, and joined Rev. Mr. Nagot in the new Sulpitian house. He was president of Georgetown College for three years; he then with some other Sulpitians visited Havana to found a house in that city; and, though the project failed, he obtained pupils for St. Mary's College, Baltimore, of which he became president. His labors as missionary priest were never abated, and in the French refugees from the West Indies he and his associates found a new field for their charity and zeal. He was the first to persuade Mrs. Seton to found a religious community in this country rather than go to Europe, and he not only aided her in the great work, but was appointed by Archbishop Carroll the first ecclesiastical superior of the Sisters of Charity. He showed ability as a controversialist in his able replies to attacks on the Church.

The diocese of Louisiana and the Floridas had, after Bishop Peñalver's departure, fallen into complete anarchy. It had been in time placed under the administration of Dr. Carroll, but the vicars-general appointed by the Archbishop of Baltimore found their authority defied. In 1812 the Rev. Mr. Dubourg was elected apostolical administrator. It was during our war with England, and soon after reaching New Orleans he found it menaced by a powerful English army. He aroused the patriotism and piety of his flock, and offered prayers for the success of the

American arms. On General Jackson's signal victory Rev. Mr. Dubourg went out and congratulated him in an eloquent address.

Having ascertained the condition of affairs in the vast diocese, which then comprised all the territory of the United States west of the Mississippi, with Florida and the strip on the Gulf of Mexico, he proceeded to Rome, where he was consecrated September 24, 1815. Returning to France, his appeals for aid led to the foundation of the great Association for the Propagation of the Faith. He returned in 1817 with several Lazarists and other priests, and, proceeding towards St. Louis, took possession of his diocese near St. Genevieve on the 28th of December. He made St. Louis his episcopal residence, deterred by the experience of his predecessor and the administrators, during the vacancy of the see, from attempting to settle in New Orleans. He founded a theological seminary and college at the Barrens, which he confided to the Lazarists; the Sisters of Loretto came from Kentucky to open schools, and the Ladies of the Sacred Heart founded their first American convent at St. Louis, soon followed by a second at Florissant. Religion in what was known as Upper Louisiana received a great impulse from these institutions, and the bishop, aided by the Association for the Propagation of the Faith, was rapidly increasing churches, priests, and schools. New Orleans and the lower part of the diocese he visited annually, gradually overcoming all opposition to his jurisdiction and authority. In 1823 he obtained as coadjutor the Right Rev. Joseph Rosati, and a plan was formed for dividing the diocese. He then took up his residence in New Orleans, the old Ursuline convent becoming at once the episcopal residence and a college. After laboring zealously and judiciously he proceeded to Europe in 1826 for affairs of the diocese, but there resolved to resign the see, convinced that another bishop would effect more good. By the division of the diocese Bishop Rosati became Bishop of St. Louis, and the Right Rev. Dr. Portier Vicar-Apostolic of Alabama and the Floridas. Dr. Dubourg was too well known and esteemed to be left in retirement; he was transferred to the see of Montauban, and in 1833 was promoted to the archiepiscopal throne of Besançon. In both dioceses he elicited the warmest and most devoted affection. He died calmly and piously December 12, 1833.

RIGHT REV. LEO RAYMOND DE NECKERE,

Second Bishop of New Orleans.

LEO DE NECKERE was born in Wevelghem, Belgium, June 6, 1800, of a pious family. He pursued his classical course at the College of Roulers, and was in the Lazarist Seminary when he was selected as one of those who were to go with Bishop Dubourg to America. He spent some time at the seminary at Bardstown and in that at the Barrens, and was ordained October 13, 1822. He was soon made a professor, and in time superior, at the Barrens, combining mission labors with his other duties. The excessive labor began to tell on a frame never vigorous, and he was placed for a time at New Orleans. In 1827 he visited Europe, hoping to gain relief, but while resting at Amiens was summoned to Rome, where, notwithstanding his remonstrance, he was elected Bishop of New Orleans August 4, 1829. He returned to his native Belgium, but for a time his health was such that his recovery seemed miraculous. As soon as his increased strength permitted a sea-voyage Bishop Neckere returned to America, and a day was fixed for his consecration at New Orleans; a new attack of disease, however, deferred it till June 24, 1830, when he was consecrated by Bishop Rosati, assisted by Bishop England and Bishop Portier. He took up the duties of the episcopate with all the zeal his feeble strength permitted, aided greatly by the Very Rev. Anthony Blanc, whom he made his vicar-general, and who was appointed coadjutor, but refused the dignity. In the summer of 1833 Bishop Neckere was at St. Michel when the yellow fever appeared at New Orleans. He at once set out for that city, although all his friends endeavored to dissuade him. It was, he felt, his post of duty, and he labored assiduously among his afflicted people for their spiritual and corporal relief until he was himself seized with the disease. "He died," says Archbishop Spalding, "the death of a saint," September 4, 1833.

MOST REV. ANTHONY BLANC,

Third Bishop and First Archbishop of New Orleans.

THIS prelate was born at Sury, in France, October 11, 1792, and was ordained at the age of twenty-four, coming the next year to the United States as one of the young priests who volunteered to accompany Bishop Dubourg. Having been stationed at Vincennes, he extended his labors to a considerable distance, building log chapels where Catholics were numerous. He then joined Bishop Dubourg and was employed in New Orleans, Natchez, Pointe Coupée, and Baton Rouge. In 1831 he was made vicar-general of the diocese, and the next year sent back to Rome the bulls which arrived appointing him coadjutor to Bishop de Neckere. On the death of that prelate he became administrator, and, yielding at last to the decree appointing him to the vacant see, he was consecrated Bishop of New Orleans November 22, 1835, by Dr. Rosati, assisted by Bishop Purcell and Bishop Portier. The labors of Bishop Dubourg and his successor, and the zealous priests whom they called around them, had greatly changed the diocese. Communions, instead of being numbered by tens, could be counted by thousands. In 1838 Bishop Blanc established a diocesan seminary, under the direction of the Lazarist Fathers, in the parish of the Assumption. It was subsequently at Jeffersonville and then removed to New Orleans. The Society of Jesus also came to his aid, founding colleges at Grand Coteau and New Orleans. At a later period the Redemptorists began their work among the Germans. On the death of the rector of the cathedral of New Orleans the trustees refused to recognize the priest whom Bishop Blanc appointed, and it was not till after long litigation that his rights were recognized. In the rest of his diocese he saw a better spirit, and churches and institutions increased.

The State of Mississippi had, from the time of Bishop Dubourg, been merged in the diocese of New Orleans; but in 1837 a see was established at Natchez, and the State formed its diocese.

Bishop Blanc had attended the first Provincial Council of Baltimore as theologian; he sat in all from the first to the seventh as bishop. At the request of the last of these New Orleans was, on the 19th of July, 1850, made an archiepiscopal see, Mobile, Natchez, Little Rock, and Galveston being the suffragans.

In 1855 Archbishop Blanc was one of the hierarchy who attended the definition of the dogma of the Immaculate Conception in Rome. The following year he held the first Provincial Council of New Orleans, which was attended by the four suffragan bishops and their theologians, with the superiors of several bodies of regulars. In 1858, while hastening to the relief of sufferers by yellow fever, he stepped into a hole in the wharf and broke both bones of his leg. This did not prevent his activity in the subsequent discharge of his duties, but it caused a shock from which he never fully recovered. In June, 1860, he made visitations, giving confirmation at a distance from New Orleans. He returned from Thibodeauxville on Monday, and on Wednesday offered the Holy Sacrifice and began his usual duties of the day, seeing several persons. While alone for a moment he was seized with fatal illness and had just time to ring his bell before throwing himself on his bed. The servant who came called Vicar-General Rousselon. He arrived just in time to administer Extreme Unction and the last absolution. Archbishop Blanc died June 20, 1860. During his active career the churches in Louisiana increased from twenty-six to seventy-three, and his clergy from twenty-seven to ninety-two. He left his diocese with a seminary, two colleges, eight academies, thirteen orphan asylums, Brothers of the Christian Schools, Sisters of Charity, of Notre Dame, of the Good Shepherd, and of the Holy Cross, as well as Carmelite nuns, all introduced by his zeal.

MOST REV. JOHN MARY ODIN,

First Bishop of Galveston and Second Archbishop of New Orleans.

JOHN MARY ODIN was born at Ambierle, France, February 25, 1801, and in early life was received into the Congregation of the Mission. At the age of twenty-two he was sent to the Barrens, Missouri, where he continued his studies, while acting as teacher of logic and theology. Having received sacerdotal orders about a year after his arrival, he made a visit to Texas with the Rev. Mr. Timon, performing missionary duties throughout the journey. After Dr. Rosati's elevation to the episcopate he became president of the college at the Barrens. He attended the Second Provincial Council of Baltimore as theologian, and subsequently made a voyage to Europe for the benefit of his health, but he devoted the time to obtaining aid for the Lazarist establishments in the United States, which were at this time constituted into a province. In 1836 he became for a time pastor at Cape Girardeau, but he was soon recalled to the seminary.

In 1840 the Very Rev. Dr. Timon, who had been appointed Prefect-Apostolic of Texas, selected Father Odin as vice-prefect, and despatched him to that field. Rev. Mr. Odin acted with energy; he freed the Prefecture from scandals, and on the arrival of the prefect co-operated with him in his missionary labors. Among other important services which the two Lazarists rendered to religion at this time was their forecast in securing from the legislature of the Republic a confirmation of the right of the Catholic Church to the old ecclesiastical property in Texas. Summoned to Missouri, Father Odin reached New Orleans fairly in rags, and there received bulls appointing him coadjutor of Detroit; but by the advice of his superior he declined the nomination. Pope Gregory XVI. erected Texas into a vicariate-apostolic in 1841, and Rev. Mr. Odin was appointed Bishop of Claudiopolis and invested with its direction. Submitting to a dignity which required hard missionary labor, he was consecrated at New Orleans, March 6, 1842, and entered on the discharge of his new duties. He soon erected churches at Galveston, Houston, St. Augustine, Nacogdoches, Lavaca, and Fort Bent, and restored those which dated from Spanish times and were not utterly ruined. He visited Europe in 1845 to obtain priests and means, and returned with several missionaries. Two years after the Ursuline nuns at his request began a convent of their order in Galveston, which was that year made a bishop's see. Bishop Odin soon introduced the Sisters of the Incarnate Word and the Brothers of Mary to conduct schools, and received in the Oblate Fathers a community of zealous missionaries. His visitations of his diocese, accomplished at great personal fatigue and danger—for he was nearly drowned in 1857—were apostolic missions, as he performed all the duties of a priest in many parts where none had been seen.

On the death of Archbishop Blanc the general voice of the bishops of the province nominated Dr. Odin for the vacancy, and he was promoted to the see of New Orleans on the 15th of February, 1861. The Church in Texas was in a manner his own work, and he left it with regret. He had found it without a priest, or aught but ruined churches; he left it with fifty churches attended by forty priests, with a thriving college and four academies. He assumed his new duties with his usual zeal, although advanced in life and broken by mission work. The civil war called forth his zeal and prudence, and the services of his clergy in the field and the hospital were most consoling. Though a constant sufferer from neuralgia from the period of his arrival in New Orleans, Archbishop Odin gave himself no relaxation; in his nine years' occupancy of that see he nearly doubled the number of priests and churches, and notably increased the religious institutions. In 1869 he set out to attend the General Council of the Vatican, and at Rome obtained the appointment of the Rev. Napoleon J. Perché as coadjutor. He was soon after compelled to leave Rome by the state of his health, and reached his native place only to die there, after having endured most intense pain with all the serenity and piety of a martyr, on the feast of the Ascension, May 25, 1870.

MOST REV. NAPOLEON J. PERCHÉ,

Third Archbishop of New Orleans.

NAPOLEON JOSEPH PERCHÉ was born at Angers, in France, January 10, 1805, and was so precocious that he could read and write at the age of five, and began his philosophy at thirteen, actually teaching it as professor five years later. Completing his studies at the Seminary of Beaupreau, he was ordained September 19, 1829. His first charge was Murr, near Angers, a difficult parish, where he conquered the good-will of all. As parish priest of Turquand he effected great good among the convicts, and did much to reorganize the Dames du Bon Pasteur. He came to the United States with Bishop Flaget in 1837, and took charge of Portland and its missions, laboring with his wonted zeal. Having visited New Orleans to appeal for aid in building a church, he received every encouragement from Archbishop Blanc, but was urged by that prelate to come to Louisiana permanently, as a field where he could accomplish more than he was likely to effect in Kentucky. To the change Bishop Flaget reluctantly consented. In Louisiana the eloquence of the young priest soon acquired for him both fame and influence. In the schism of the trustees he supported the bishop with pen and voice; but, feeling the want of a truly Catholic organ in the diocese, he founded *Le Propagateur Catholique*, which still exists, and of which he was for many years editor. He also founded a Catholic society to give those who loved religion a mutual support. For twenty-eight years he remained chaplain of the Ursuline convent, seeking no advancement, ever ready to preach when summoned. When Archbishop Odin, in Europe, felt that he might never return to his diocese, or could do so only an invalid, he requested the appointment of Rev. Mr. Perché as his coadjutor. Having accepted his bulls, the Abbé Perché sailed to Europe, and was consecrated Bishop of Abdera May 1, 1870, succeeding to New Orleans before the close of the month.

He returned to America as archbishop and assumed the direction of a diocese the difficulties of which he knew full well. The cathedral had hitherto been in the hands of a body of trustees, who had on several occasions shown, probably from ignorance of real Catholic principles, an open hostility to the discipline and life of the Church. Repeated litigation resulted from their resistance to episcopal authority and their attempts to manage the church and cemetery according to their own fancy. Archbishop Perché, who had already taken part in the controversy, not only with ability but with the gentleness of a St. Francis de Sales, had gained much, and had at the same time retained the good-will of the party in opposition. By his influence the wardens of the cathedral at last transferred that edifice and other ecclesiastical property standing in their name to him and his coadjutor. He endowed his diocese with a contemplative community—Carmelite nuns of the reform of St. Teresa, a filiation of the convent in St. Louis; and one of his latest acts was an appeal in their behalf on the occasion of the centenary of the great Spanish Carmelite nun.

Under his zealous direction Thibodeaux College and St. Mary's Commercial College were opened; the Ladies of the Sacred Heart established a third academy; three other academies and thirteen parish schools were opened in his time; the Little Sisters of the Poor founded an Asylum for aged colored women. Ten new churches and as many chapels marked the growth of the diocese, and the number of priests increased one-fifth. His energy, sound judgment, and an eloquence which caused Pope Leo XIII. to compare him to Bossuet, as well as his unbounded charity, endeared Archbishop Perché to the people of Louisiana. Towards the course of the year 1883 his vital powers began to fail, and, though a removal to the country seemed to invigorate his frame, he grew weaker on his return to the city. In December he saw that the end was at hand; fortified by the sacraments, he died of old age on Thursday, December 27, 1883.

MOST REV. FRANCIS XAVIER LERAY,

Second Bishop of Natchitoches and Fourth Archbishop of New Orleans.

FRANCIS XAVIER LERAY is a native of Brittany, born in a small town near Rennes on the 20th of April, 1825, of a respectable family, being one of thirteen children. He was sent to school at Rennes at an early age, and pursued a classical course, partly under the Eudist Fathers, and partly at the university but still under their guidance. When the Eudist Fathers began a mission of their order in the United States, Mr. Leray came to Vincennes with them in 1843, and during his two years' stay in Indiana knew some of the pioneer priests of the West, like the venerable Badin. In 1845 he was sent for a short time to Spring Hill College, near Mobile, and subsequently made a journey on horseback from Vincennes to St. Louis. Recalled thence, he was sent to St. Mary's Seminary, Baltimore, where, after his many wanderings and changes, he was allowed to complete his theology, and was ordained priest at Natchez, Mississippi, by the Right Rev. J. J. Chanche, on March 19, 1852, fully prepared by his intercourse with the hard-working missionaries for the labors before him. After the death of Bishop Chanche he was sent to Jackson, the capital of the State. Here he labored with Rev. J. B. Babonneau, a priest of great talent and zeal, till his brother-priest was struck down by yellow fever in the autumn of 1853. The young Breton priest deemed that his associate was ripe for heaven, but that he was not. Left in charge of a district more extended than the diocese to which he was ultimately appointed, he labored to the best of his power and ability, travelling on horseback wherever the wants of scattered Catholics required it. When the yellow fever returned in 1854 he attended Jackson, Vicksburg, and Brandon. The next year the State was agitated by the Know-Nothing movement, and the Rev. Mr. Leray, on whom devolved the task of defending the faith in public, was compelled to take a prominent part. Actions speak more powerfully than words. During the fall of that very year the yellow fever came to wash away the stains of Know-Nothingism and to put to the test the necessity and truthfulness of the Catholic priest. The result was that many were converted to the faith, and others, filled with respect for a Church which could produce such results, apologized amply for their ignorant assaults. The illustrious archbishop says, indeed, that "the times of epidemics have been for me the times of the most abundant harvests." In 1857 Bishop Elder sent the Rev. Mr. Leray to Vicksburg, where he found a large Catholic population sadly in need of a priest to organize and instruct them. Obedience alone induced him to undertake the difficult duty. To meet the wants of his parish he obtained from Baltimore, in 1860, a few Sisters of Mercy to begin an establishment of their order, and everything betokened a prosperous result, when the war broke on them. The Sisters, with their superior, went to share with the clergy the misfortunes of the war. Meanwhile Vicksburg endured all the horrors of a long siege, and when in 1865 the Rev. Mr. Leray returned to his sorely-tried parish he had to seek his scattered flock and restore the house of God. The next two years the city was visited by the cholera, and no epidemic in the long missionary career left a deeper impression on his mind than the scenes of this time, which exceeded anything that he had witnessed. "I have read," he says, "of many pestilences and plagues in Europe in past ages, but I think, without exaggeration, I have seen worse in Jackson, Vicksburg, Yazoo City, Canton, and Greenville."

While laboring in this toilsome and dangerous mission he was summoned by the voice of the successor of St. Peter to assume what he regarded as a much more onerous burden—that of the episcopate. Having been selected to succeed the Right Rev. Dr. Martin, he desired to receive the episcopal character in his own native province, and on the 23d of April, 1877, he was consecrated Bishop of Natchitoches in the cathedral of Rennes by His Eminence Godefroy Cardinal Broussais Saint-Marc, Archbishop of Rennes, assisted by the Right Rev. Celestine de la Hailandière, formerly Bishop of Vincennes, and Mgr. Nouvel, Bishop of Quimper.

The diocese to which Bishop Leray was called comprised the

northern part of the State of Louisiana, with thirty thousand Catholics scattered over it, but with only seventeen priests to attend the sixty-eight churches and chapels. Two religious communities, the Daughters of the Cross and the Sisters of the Order of Mercy, conducted a number of schools. The new bishop began to build on this foundation, in order to afford his flock all possible religious aid, but in little more than two years he was summoned to a new toil. The temporal affairs of the diocese of New Orleans were in a difficult position. The losses during the war, and perhaps even greater losses during the period of reconstruction, had entailed debts which were increasing and required a skilful and energetic hand to control. Bishop Leray was accordingly transferred to the see of Janopolis October 23, 1879, and made coadjutor of New Orleans. He was to retain the care of the diocese of Natchitoches as administrator-apostolic. In the extraordinary burdens thus imposed he evinced all his energy, and on the death of the Most Rev. Archbishop Perché in December, 1883, became apostolic administrator of the diocese of New Orleans, and was thus charged with the care of the whole State of Louisiana. He was soon after appointed Archbishop of New Orleans, and was one of the most honored of the fathers who assembled at Baltimore in the Third Plenary Council in the month of November, 1884.

DIOCESE OF NEW YORK.

• RIGHT REV. RICHARD LUKE CONCANEN, O.S.D.,
First Bishop of New York.

RICHARD LUKE CONCANEN was a native of Ireland, and at an early age entered the Order of St. Dominic in the Irish convent of the Holy Cross in Lorraine, and was soon after sent to Santa Maria sopra Minerva at Rome. He became distinguished for his learning and virtue, and after his ordination was prior of the Irish Dominicans in Lisbon and at Rome, and in the latter city was professor at St. Clement's and director of the famous Casanate Library. His merit led to his nomination to an episcopal see in Ireland, but the humble religious steadily refused to accept the honor.

As agent for the Irish bishops in Rome during those troubled times he had rendered essential service to the Church, and his merit was so well known that when, at the request of Bishop Carroll, the diocese of Baltimore was divided and new sees erected, Father Concanen was selected for the newly-created see of New York. He was consecrated in Rome, April 24, 1808, by Cardinal Antonelli, Prefect of the Congregation *de Propaganda Fide*. The Catholics of New York looked forward to his speedy arrival, and he obtained from friends donations of every kind for his diocese, and prepared to reach it at once.

The French, however, were then in full sway in Italy, and all British subjects were liable to arrest. Bishop Concanen spent time and money at Leghorn in ineffectual efforts to obtain passage to America. The anxiety and difficulty brought on a dangerous fit of illness, and on his recovery he returned to Rome and wished to resign a dignity which it seemed the will of Providence he should never assume. His courage was, however, revived, and from information given him there was a hope that he might secure a passage to America by visiting Naples. Once more he made the attempt to reach his diocese; but the officials of King Murat at Naples were even more exacting than those at Leghorn, and the Bishop of New York was held virtually as a prisoner. Again was time lost in appealing to higher authorities. His constitution, enfeebled by age and recent illness, gave way, and Bishop Concanen closed his edifying life in the great convent of St. Dominic in Naples, on the 19th of June, 1810, in the seventieth year of his age. When the sad tidings arrived of his death a solemn requiem was offered for New York's first bishop at St. Peter's Church on the 7th of October, 1810.

RIGHT REV. JOHN CONNOLLY, O.S.D.,

Second Bishop of New York.

JOHN CONNOLLY was a native of Drogheda, Ireland, born in 1750, and, like his predecessor, entered the Order of Friars Preachers at an early age. After holding other positions he became prior of St. Clement's at Rome and agent of the Irish bishops. In this latter capacity he showed great ability and courage in saving the property of the English and Irish institutions from the hands of the French. After the decease of Bishop Concanen the trials which befell the Holy See prevented the Sovereign Pontiff from appointing a bishop for the vacant see, and it was not till 1814 that Father Connolly received bulls making him Bishop of New York. He was consecrated in Rome, November 6, 1814, but did not arrive at his episcopal city till the same month of the following year. He brought with him some priests, and found in his diocese only four clergymen to receive him. The institutions which had been begun had all been abandoned. His flock, scattered over the State, numbered seventeen thousand, but was in great spiritual want. Bishop Connolly bravely began the difficult task of building up religion. Many difficulties beset him, but he visited his diocese and began churches at Utica and Rochester. Priests were sent to remote points in New York and New Jersey to collect the Catholics. In New York City he founded an Orphan Asylum, for which he obtained from Mother Seton some members of the Sisters of Charity. He assisted in the consecration of Archbishop Marechal, and was highly esteemed for his learning and virtue. His zeal during the yellow fever excited unusual admiration. In 1824 he solicited the appointment of a coadjutor, but during the winter ensuing the diocese was deprived by death of two priests. While officiating at the funeral of one of them Bishop Connolly caught a severe cold, which, at his age, proved fatal. He died at his residence on the Bowery, February 6, 1825, and was laid under his cathedral.

RIGHT REV. JOHN DU BOIS,

Third Bishop of New York.

JOHN DU BOIS was born in Paris, August 24, 1764, of a family blessed with a spirit of piety and a competency which they used in a Christian spirit. The training of a pious mother led the youth to seek to serve God in his sanctuary. He studied at the college of Louis le Grand, where Robespierre and Camille Desmoulins were also pupils. Formed for the ecclesiastical life in the seminary of St. Magloire, he was ordained priest September 22, 1787. The young priest at once received the appointment of assistant at the great church of St. Sulpice, Paris, and was also made chaplain to a large asylum. The Revolution had already begun its war on the clergy, and the Abbé Du Bois ere long resolved to leave France. He arrived at Norfolk, Va., in 1791, and, having been received into the diocese of Baltimore by Bishop Carroll, exercised the ministry at Norfolk and Richmond, then at Frederick, Maryland, making this last a centre whence his pastoral visits extended to Emmittsburg and Winchester, visiting the remote points at imminent danger in all seasons and weathers. He built churches where all deemed it impossible to do so, and in 1805 began a brick church at Mount St. Mary's. Here, too, he opened a school, which soon developed into Mount St. Mary's College, of which he was long president. His log college was succeeded by a stone building, which was burned to the ground just as it was ready for use. When Mother Seton planted the first house of her community of Sisters of Charity near the college, the untiring priest added to his duties the direction of that community. His college was also a theological seminary, where some of the greatest bishops and priests of the country were formed.

From this scene of labor so productive of good he was summoned by the voice of the Vicar of Christ to assume the direction of the diocese of New York. He was consecrated October 29, 1826, in Baltimore. He found but few churches in his diocese; yet, with all the energy of youth, the sexagenarian bishop set to work. Six other churches soon rose on New York island alone, and others in various parts of the State.

A college on the plan of Mount St. Mary's was one of the great projects of Bishop Du Bois, and he began such an institution at Nyack; but in this, and in the establishment of parochial schools, he failed to elicit a hearty co-operation among the people. A faction arrayed itself against him, the centre of the opposition being in the board of trustees of his own cathedral. He visited Europe in 1829 for the benefit of his diocese, and at the Second Council of Baltimore aided by his experience and advice in framing regulations for the benefit of religion. Cramped and hampered as he was, Bishop Du Bois obtained many zealous clergymen for the congregations that were beginning to form in all parts of his diocese, and, by the alms from the Association for the Propagation of the Faith and other sources, aided the congregations in erecting churches. When, in 1836, his failing health required the aid of a coadjutor, Bishop Du Bois had forty-three priests in the diocese, where he found only a few; there were twenty-six churches, a college, two academies, five asylums, and several parish schools. The next year the Rev. John Hughes, of Philadelphia, was appointed his coadjutor, and a few months later the venerable Bishop of New York was struck with paralysis while walking in the street. He never recovered his health or vigor, and, by the counsel of the Sovereign Pontiff, resigned the administration of the diocese into the hands of Bishop Hughes. His life of active usefulness for God and his people was thus brought to a close. He lingered a few years in retirement, devoting himself to devotion and good works, till his death on the 20th of December, 1842. His body was laid in one of the vaults under the cathedral, but after the completion of the new cathedral was transferred to it, together with the remains of his predecessor.

MOST REV. JOHN HUGHES,

Fourth Bishop and First Archbishop of New York.

JOHN HUGHES, born at Annalogan, County Tyrone, Ireland, June 24, 1797, was one of the greatest bishops of the Church in the United States. Emigrating with his family to America in 1817, he applied for entrance to Mount St. Mary's in order to receive the theological instruction to fit him for the priesthood. There was no vacancy, but he took charge of the garden to be able to remain and study. He was soon guiding and directing others as teacher and prefect, employing his pen even then in defending his faith against newspaper assailants. After having been ordained priest October 15, 1826, he was stationed at Bedford, but was soon removed to Philadelphia, where his abilities were displayed at St. Joseph's and St. Mary's. A popular preacher, an able writer, the Rev. John Hughes was ere long a notable man. He founded St. John's Orphan Asylum, attended the First Provincial Council as theologian, erected St. John's Church, and by his singular skill and learning in an oral controversy with a Presbyterian minister, Rev. John Breckenridge, acquired a national reputation.

THE MOST REV. JOHN HUGHES,
FIRST ARCHBISHOP OF NEW YORK.

In 1837 he was selected as coadjutor to Dr. Du Bois, by whom he was consecrated to the see of Basileopolis on the 26th of November, Bishops Fenwick of Boston, and Kenrick of Philadelphia, being assistants. The churches, under the unwise management of trustees, had generally become loaded with debt, and the very men who so abused their trust were active in arraying the weak and ignorant against their pastors and bishop. Nyack College was destroyed by fire. Everywhere a firm and energetic hand was needed. When Bishop Hughes was appointed to the sole direction of the diocese as administrator he broke the power of the trustees, restored the credit of the Catholic congregations, gave a new impulse to the erection of churches, and founded St. John's College at Fordham. For higher education of young ladies he introduced into the diocese the Ladies of the Sacred Heart, who opened an academy at Astoria, subsequently transferred to Manhattanville.

After a visit to Europe for the good of his diocese Bishop Hughes took an active part in a movement of Catholics to recover State aid for their parochial schools, such as had been given till a fraud practised by a Baptist church brought denominational schools into disfavor. Bishop Hughes defended the rights of Catholics before the New York common council against an array of eminent lawyers and clergymen whom the Protestant sects sent to prove that a system under which they themselves had received thousands of dollars was a very improper one, simply because Catholics advocated it. The common council rejected the claim, and both political parties took ground against it. The Catholics thereupon ran a ticket of their own, and developed such strength that the bigoted Public-School Society gave up its schools, and the State organized a series of schools from which all offensive religious matter was to be excluded.

In 1842 Bishop Hughes held the first diocesan synod of New York. It was attended by sixty-four priests. At the close of the year he became, by the death of Dr. Du Bois, Bishop of New York. The diocese comprised the whole State of New York and half of New Jersey—a territory in which there were seven bishoprics in 1884. The increase of churches and institutions made this vast field too much to govern unaided, and in 1844 Dr.

Hughes obtained as coadjutor the Right Rev. John McCloskey. That same year Bishop Hughes, by his firmness and decision, saved New York from scenes of arson and murder such as had been beheld in Philadelphia, where Catholics were shot down, their houses and churches given to the flames. Finding that the public mind, debauched by fanatics, would never allow the public schools to be anything but a weapon in their hands against the faith of his flock, Bishop Hughes declared that the time had come when Catholics must build the school first and the church afterwards. Under his impulse schools started up in all parts, erected and sustained by sacrifices such as no other body has ever made. To give the educational institutions of the diocese every efficiency he invited the Jesuit Fathers to assume the direction of St. John's College and of St. Joseph's Theological Seminary, which he had founded near it. He reorganized the Sisters of Charity as a body distinct from those of Emmittsburg, who had abandoned the rule of Mother Seton, though the Sisters in New York adhere to it.

In time he obtained Brothers of the Christian Schools, and other teaching orders for both sexes—Sisters of Mercy, Sisters of the Good Shepherd, and for the increasing German Catholic body the Redemptorist Fathers. Bishop Hughes took a prominent part in the deliberations of several of the Provincial Councils, and in the sixth obtained the recommendation of a division of his diocese. A see was accordingly erected at Albany, of which Bishop McCloskey took possession, and another at Buffalo. He was a keen observer of the public mind, and when religion was assailed or misrepresented his keen, clear, vigorous words came forth like clarion notes, and were echoed through the press over the whole land. He was recognized as the leader of Catholic thought. When war broke out with Mexico our government tendered him a diplomatic appointment with a view of restoring peace. On the 3d of October, 1850, Pope Pius IX., on the recommendation of the Council of Baltimore, promoted him to the rank of archbishop and erected new sees at Brooklyn and Newark. Soon after he held the first Provincial Council of New York, which was attended by his seven suffragans, the bishops of New England, New York, and New Jersey.

In 1854 he visited Rome on the occasion of the definition of the Dogma of the Immaculate Conception by the great Pope, Pius IX. Soon after he saw the legislature propose an act to wrest the Catholic Church property from the hands of the bishops. In a controversy with Hon. Erastus Brooks he refuted the falsehoods on which the proposed legislation was based, and placed on record evidence of the iniquity and unconstitutional character of the law; the legislature yielded to public clamor fanned by fanatics, but soon cancelled its own weak work. The care of the diocese and the burden of responsibility began to weigh heavily on the archbishop; he even begged the Holy Father for permission to resign his see. Yielding, however, to the encouraging words of the Sovereign Pontiff, he set to work to begin for his diocese a grand cathedral worthy of the Catholic Church and of the great city. St. Patrick's Cathedral had for nearly half a century owned land on Fifth Avenue, which had now become the most fashionable street in New York. On this site the archbishop in 1858, with great pomp, laid the corner-stone of a noble cathedral, for which Mr. Renwick had prepared the plans. Work was immediately commenced, and continued till the civil war made it impossible to proceed.

When that great struggle came on—which Archbishop Hughes had prophetically foretold, reminding the people that the Catholic clergy and people had had no share in producing the angry feelings which had engendered and precipitated it—he gave his earnest support to the national government, and went to Europe on a diplomatic mission with a view to counteract the feeling unfavorable to the United States which envoys of the seceding States had excited in more than one European cabinet. While in Europe he visited Rome and took part in the canonization of the Japanese Martyrs. He held a second Provincial Council after his return, and continued his plans for the increase of religion in his flock; his pastorals, addresses, and writings, as well as his oral discourses, being stamped with vigor, manliness, a sense of the greatness and dignity of the Catholic Church, that infused itself into his people, making them proud to be American Catholics and eager to live so as to maintain that high character with credit among their fellow-citizens. During the terrible Draft Riots, Archbishop Hughes, then in feeble health, addressed the people from his balcony and did all in his power to allay the excited feelings. It was his last public appearance; disease was sapping his vital powers, and at last he was even unable to offer the Holy Sacrifice. He felt that the end was approaching and calmly prepared for his last moment. He died on the 3d of January, 1864.

No man ever exercised greater influence in the Catholic Church in the United States than Archbishop Hughes; on all important occasions his words were awaited by the faithful throughout the country and the public at large as the exposition of the Catholic view. The archbishop had attained this influence without an effort, held it without envy, and used it only for the highest ends.

HIS EMINENCE JOHN CARDINAL McCLOSKEY,

First Bishop of Albany, Second Archbishop of New York.

JOHN McCLOSKEY was born in Brooklyn, N. Y., March 10, 1810, and was baptized in St. Peter's Church, New York, then the only Catholic church in or near the city. At the age of twelve he was sent to Mount St. Mary's, where he was honorably graduated in 1829. Deciding to become a priest, he returned to Emmittsburg, and, after completing his divinity course, was ordained by Bishop Du Bois, January 12, 1834. After spending a few years in Rome for more thorough study, he became pastor of St. Joseph's Church, N. Y., in 1838, and in 1842 assumed also the office of director of St. Joseph's Theological Seminary, Fordham. When Bishop Hughes sought a coadjutor the Rev. Mr. McCloskey, the choice of the bishop and clergy alike, was consecrated Bishop of Axiern, March 10, 1844. Residing at St. Joseph's, Bishop McCloskey assumed much of the labor, visiting remote parts of the State to confirm, examine, and adjudicate. When the diocese was divided he was, in May, 1847, transferred to the see of Albany. Already familiar with the clergy of the new

diocese and its wants, he set to work energetically and infused into his flock a spirit of faith and sacrifice. Schools, academies, asylums, and churches sprang up in all parts. Every year beheld new progress. In 1864 the diocese of Albany had one hundred and thirteen churches, eight chapels, and fifty stations, attended by eighty-five secular and regular priests, the latter embracing members of the Augustinian Order, Minor Conventuals of St. Francis, and Oblates of Mary Immaculate. The Ladies of the Sacred Heart directed a fine academy at Kenwood; Sisters of Mercy devoted themselves to works of charity; Brothers of the Christian Schools, Sisters of Charity and of St. Joseph, Gray Nuns from Montreal, and Sisters of the Third Order of St. Francis controlled schools and asylums. From this flourishing diocese, which owed so much to his zeal, he was, on the death of Archbishop Hughes, summoned to fill the archiepiscopal throne of New York.

As Bishop of Albany his great theological learning, as well as his experience and prudence, had been manifested in the Seventh Council of Baltimore in 1849 and in the Plenary Council of Baltimore in 1852, as well as in the Provincial Councils held in New York in 1854 and 1861. In his own diocese he convoked synods in 1868 and 1882, and adopted wise regulations for its better administration.

On his return to New York the Catholic Protectory felt his fostering care and grew to be an institution of immense benefit to the State. He felt the want of church accommodation in New York City, and after creating new parishes, in which he placed active priests to build up church and school, he resumed the work on the cathedral, which had been suspended during the war. After the Second Plenary Council, which he attended, in 1866, he promulgated its decrees in the synod which he held at New York in September, 1868.

The next year he attended the General Council of the Vatican, where his piety and learning won general esteem. In 1873 he dedicated his diocese to the Sacred Heart of Jesus. The young Church of the United States had never been represen in the Sacred College, and there was universal joy when Pope Pius IX., in the Consistory held March 15, 1875, created Archbishop McCloskey Cardinal Priest of the Holy Roman Church. The insignia of the high dignity were despatched to him, and the beretta was formally presented to him in St. Patrick's Cathedral. The cardinal soon after proceeded to Rome, where, with the usual ceremonies, he took possession of the church of Santa Maria supra Minervam, of which he bears the title.

On the death of the great Pontiff, Pius IX., Cardinal McCloskey was summoned to attend the Conclave. He set out for Europe in obedience to the call, but before he reached the Eternal City the voice of the Sacred College, guided by the Holy Ghost, had elected Cardinal Pecci, who assumed the name of Leo XIII.

Religion was progressing in his diocese. The Dominican Fathers came at last to open the church of St. Vincent Ferrer; the Capuchin Fathers took charge of German churches; the Reformed Franciscans founded an Italian church, while Brothers of Mary, Franciscan Brothers, Presentation Nuns, Sisters of Christian Charity, and Sisters of the Immaculate Heart of Mary came to aid the communities devoted to education and works of mercy. The Sisters of Charity met a want that New York had long felt, by opening a Foundling Asylum. The Little Sisters of the Poor opened houses for the aged poor; the Rev. Mr. Drumgoole founded a great institution for homeless boys, the Mission of the Immaculate Virgin, for which in time an imposing building was erected in the city and a farm acquired in the country. The Bon Secours Sisters came from France to nurse the sick in their homes, and soon found that the calls for their services demanded numbers of Sisters. Meanwhile the Catholic Union and its vigorous branch, the Xavier Union, united and strengthened the Catholic laity.

The magnificent cathedral of St. Patrick was at last completed, the finest ecclesiastical structure in America; it was dedicated on the 25th of May, 1879, by His Eminence Cardinal McCloskey, assisted by forty-two archbishops and bishops, with a pomp such as never had been witnessed in the United States.

The advanced age and increasing infirmities of the venerable cardinal called for the services of a coadjutor, and on the 1st of October, 1880, the Right Rev. Michael A. Corrigan, Bishop of

Newark, was promoted to the archiepiscopal see of Petra and made coadjutor to the Archbishop of New York. In November, 1882, Cardinal McCloskey held a synod of his diocese, and soon after presided in a Provincial Council. When the Third Plenary Council assembled in Baltimore in November, 1884, His Eminence, owing to his advanced age and infirmities, was not summoned, and all regretted the absence of one whose long experience would have been so useful to the hierarchy gathered in the cathedral church of a Carroll, a Marechal, and a Spalding.

Cardinal McCloskey offered the sacrifice of the Mass for the last time on the feast of the Ascension, 1884, the exertion even for that solemn rite having become gradually too much for his waning strength. After that he was unable to read or write or take a single step without assistance. Sinking slowly, he bore with serenity the utter helplessness, looking patiently to the end, never murmuring or complaining. With the Hail Mary on his lips he expired October 10, 1885.

The funeral obsequies drew crowds which filled the vast cathedral, and no more impressive sight was ever witnessed in New York City.

In person Cardinal McCloskey was nearly six feet high, straight and thin; his features were regular, his brow lofty, his eye keen; his countenance calm and serious, inclining to sternness, but relieved by a pleasant expression which it almost always wore. The sensitiveness of his eyes gave portraits taken by the strong light of the camera a frown-like contraction between the eyes that was not habitual to him. He avoided all notoriety and parade, and sought to accomplish his high duties simply and thoroughly.

MOST REV. MICHAEL A. CORRIGAN,

Second Bishop of Newark and Third Archbishop of New York.

MICHAEL AUGUSTINE CORRIGAN was born in Newark, New Jersey, of Irish parents, August 13, 1839. While prospering in life, the family retained such piety and love for religion that three of the sons became priests, and a daughter a nun at Meaux, in France. Michael was sent in 1855 to St. Mary's College, Wilmington, but four years later entered Mount St. Mary's at Emmittsburg, where his ability and studious character won a high rank. When the American College at Rome, which had been founded by Pope Pius IX., was opened for students, Michael A. Corrigan was the first seminarian chosen and the first to enter. He was ordained in the Lateran Basilica, September 19, 1863, by Cardinal Patrizi, but prolonged his residence in Rome in order to pursue special studies and win his doctor's cap. On his return to Newark in July, 1864, Bishop Bayley, who had the highest esteem for his learning and piety, appointed him professor of dogmatic theology and Sacred Scripture in the seminary at Seton Hall. He soon became director of that institution and vice-president of Seton Hall College, and its president after the elevation of Dr. McQuaid to the see of Rochester. In his devotion to the cause of education Dr. Corrigan bent all his energies to render Seton Hall a college of the highest rank.

During the absence of Bishop Bayley at the Vatican Council in 1870 Dr. Corrigan was vicar-general and administrator of the diocese, discharging the onerous additional duties with singular prudence. When Bishop Bayley was promoted to the see of Baltimore Dr. Corrigan was elected Bishop of Newark on the 14th of February, 1873, and on the feast of Patronage of Saint Joseph (May 4) was consecrated in his own cathedral by His Grace Archbishop McCloskey, of New York, seventeen bishops being present, and was at once enthroned. He was the youngest member of the American hierarchy, but showed the maturity and experience of years. Retaining the presidency of the college to which he was so greatly attached, he devoted his mind to the increase of religion. His diocese was already a flourishing one, with 121 churches and mission stations, 116 priests, 57 parochial schools. He introduced the Jesuits, Dominicans, and Conventual Franciscans; established a Catholic Protectory for Boys at Denville, under the care of the Franciscan Brothers, a House of the Good Shepherd at Newark, and an hospital in charge of the Little Sisters of the Poor of St. Francis. Besides these orders engaged in active works of mercy, he wished to endow the diocese with a contemplative order, convinced that it would draw down blessings on all. The Dominican Nuns of the Perpetual Adoration from Lyons, France, came to fulfil his wish.

A diocesan synod held in 1878 renewed and extended the statutes previously promulgated by Bishop Bayley for the Church under his care. Meanwhile the Catholic schools received an impulse, so that towards the close of 1880 there were in New Jersey one hundred and fifty-three, with more than twenty-six thousand pupils. The churches had increased to one hundred and fifty, with forty stations, and the priests to one hundred and ninety-two.

The advanced age of Cardinal McCloskey made the appointment of a coadjutor a necessity, and, to the regret of the Catholics of New Jersey, Bishop Corrigan was, on the 1st of October, 1880, promoted to the see of Petra and made coadjutor to the Archbishop of New York with the right of succession.

In his new position the active part of the episcopal work soon devolved upon him—the visitation of the diocese, ordinations, confirmations, dedications. The Fourth Provincial Council and Fourth Synod of New York, were mainly directed by him, and for the use of such assemblies he prepared a useful manual. He was summoned to Rome as one of the archbishops whom the Holy See wished to consult in regard to the work of the proposed Plenary Council, and when that body met in November, 1884, he represented the diocese of New York.

On the death of his Eminence Cardinal McCloskey, Archbishop Corrigan became, on the 10th of October, 1885, third Metropolitan of the province of New York.

DIOCESE OF OREGON.

MOST REV. FRANCIS NORBERT BLANCHET,

First Bishop and First Archbishop of Oregon.

FRANCIS NORBERT BLANCHET was born in Canada, in the parish of St. Pierre, Rivière du Sud, on the 3d of September, 1795, and was educated at the Petit Seminaire, Quebec. After passing through the course of the Theological Seminary he was ordained priest by Archbishop Plessis, July 18, 1819. He spent some years on the mission at Richibouctou, and in 1828 was appointed curé, or parish priest, of Soulanges. He was parish priest of Les Cédres, in 1838, when Archbishop Signay, of Quebec, asked for priests in his diocese to undertake a mission in Oregon. Canadians, led to the shores of the Pacific by the great fur companies, had settled in Oregon, and after applying to Bishop Provancher, of Red River, for a priest, had, at his advice, as he was unable to help them, appealed to the successor of Laval. Rev. Mr. Blanchet responded to the call, and, having been appointed vicar-general for Oregon, set out with one priest, Rev. Modest Demers. They reached Fort Vancouver on the 24th of November, and Rev. Mr. Blanchet began the labors which were to occupy the rest of his life. He found Canadians to be attended, Indians ready for instruction to embrace the faith—a field not for one priest but for many. Other priests soon arrived, many Indians were converted, a college opened, and Father De Smet arrived from Europe with Jesuit Fathers for the Indian mission, and Sisters of Notre Dame from Namur to establish a school. By this time Oregon was a vicariate-apostolic, erected December 1, 1843, and Rev. Mr. Blanchet, who at this time received his bulls, returned to Canada and was consecrated Bishop of Drasa, July 25, 1845, by Right Rev. Dr. Bourget, assisted by Bishops Gaulin and Turgeon. He then proceeded to Rome, where he ex plained the position of the Territory; in view of the rapid settlement of Oregon, which seemed certain, Pope Pius IX. resolved to erect an archiepiscopal see with suffragans. Oregon City was made the see of the archbishop, and Wallawalla and Vancouver's Island, with six other places, established as bishoprics or districts. Thus Dr. Blanchet became in July, 1846, Archbishop of Oregon. He returned to his diocese in August, 1847, bringing eight secular and regular priests and seven Sisters of Notre Dame, besides several ecclesiastics. After the consecration of Bishops Blanchet and Demers the First Provincial Council of Oregon was held in February, 1848. The diocese of Oregon had then ten secular priests, two Jesuits, and a community of Sisters. The discovery of gold in California diverted emigrants from Oregon, and even drew away much of the population of that Territory. Indian wars also tended to check emigration, a Protestant missionary having been killed, and another saved only by the heroic interference of a Catholic priest, whose only reward has been the most unblushing calumny from sectarian writers. Under these circumstances Oregon languished, religious communities left the diocese, and in 1855 Archbishop Blanchet visited South America, and subsequently Canada, to solicit aid. He attended the First and Second Plenary Councils of Baltimore, but most of his life was spent in his diocese as a zealous missionary, building up slowly the Church confided to him. In 1865, as Oregon City had made no progress, he removed to Portland. Infirmities began to weaken him in 1878, and the Right Rev. Charles J. Seghers, of Vancouver's Island, was made coadjutor. The diocese of Oregon had by this time grown. It had twenty-three priests, twenty-two churches, a college, nine academies, a hospital, an orphanage, and schools for a population of 20,000. The venerable archbishop soon after resigned the see and announced his retirement in a touching pastoral on the 27th of February, 1881. The patriarch of the Northwest remained at the scene of his lifelong labors, preparing for his last end. His strength gradually failed him, and he passed away painlessly on the 18th of June, 1883, closing a holy life with a most edifying death. As he had desired, he was interred in the cemetery of St. Paul amid the oldest Canadian settlement in Oregon.

MOST REV. CHARLES JOHN SEGHERS,

Second Bishop of Vancouver's Island, Second Archbishop of Oregon.

CHARLES JOHN SEGHERS was born at Ghent, Dec. 26, 1839. Like many devoted men of that truly Catholic country, he resolved to devote himself to the American mission. The poorest and most laborious diocese on the northern continent was his choice. Bishop Demers, of Vancouver's Island, placed him in his cathedral as one of the assistant priests, and till the death of that zealous pioneer prelate, Rev. Mr. Seghers labored with the utmost devotedness among the white and Indian population. He was finally made vicar-general, and became, on the death of Bishop Demers, administrator of the diocese. To fill the vacancy the choice of the Holy See was soon fixed on the humble and laborious priest. He was elected Bishop of Vancouver's Island, and was consecrated June 29, 1873. He assumed charge of the diocese, extending his missionary labors to the bleak Territory of Alaska.

When the veteran of the Pacific, the Most Rev. Dr. Blanchet, found that his advanced age and infirmities announced the close of his long labors, he selected Bishop Seghers as his coadjutor, and in 1878 that prelate was transferred to the archbishopric of Emesa and made coadjutor. He reached Portland on the 1st of July, 1879, and was received by the venerable founder of the diocese. He aided him so acceptably that in February, 1881, the aged archbishop resigned the see, and the whole burden devolved on Mgr. Seghers. He was soon called to officiate on the funeral of his predecessor, whose zeal and virtues he imitates. He went to Rome in 1873 and remained in Europe for the interests of his diocese. When Bishop Brondel was transferred to Montana, and none of the clergymen selected for the vacant see seemed willing to accept that laborious and straitened position, Archbishop Seghers applied to the Holy Father to be restored to the diocese of Vancouver's Island, as another could be more readily found for the see of Oregon.

He attended the Third Plenary Council of Baltimore in November, 1884, after having taken part in the assembly in Rome during the preceding year. Then, his resignation having been accepted, he was made Archbishop Bishop of Vancouver's Island.

MOST REV. WILLIAM H. GROSS,

Fifth Bishop of Savannah and Third Archbishop of Oregon.

WILLIAM H. GROSS was born in the city of Baltimore on the 12th of June, 1837, his parents being also natives of that city. On his father's side he was descended from an Alsatian family who came to this country while Maryland was still a British colony; on his mother's side his family was Irish. Their son was for many years a student in St. Charles' College, the preparatory seminary of the diocese of Baltimore. Feeling a vocation for the religious state, he entered the novitiate of the Redemptorist order at Annapolis on the Feast of the Annunciation, 1857. After his novitiate and theological course he was ordained priest by Archbishop Kenrick, March 21, 1863, in the Redemptorist church, Annapolis. The young priest was immediately employed by his superiors in attending the numerous wounded soldiers in the military hospitals around Annapolis, and he also preached to the soldiers in the camp of paroled prisoners near that city. He was also directed to do all in his power to infuse some clear religious ideas into the minds of the neglected negroes. From the year 1864 he was assigned by his superiors to a band of the Redemptorist Fathers engaged in giving missions in all parts of the country, reviving faith in the tepid by clear and forcible sermons, and by assiduous and careful guidance in the confessional. In these missions Father Gross was recognized as a talented and able religious. He was attached to St. Alphonsus' Church, in New York City, for five years, and then became superior at the church of his order in Boston. In 1873 he was elected to the see of Savannah, and, having received consecration on the 27th of April, was installed by his predecessor.

Bishop Gross has done much to spread the Gospel among the colored population, the Benedictines and Priests of St. Joseph having come to labor in a field which has not yet gladdened the patient missionaries with remarkable results. Deeming schools almost the only successful means of saving the poor colored people, he bent every effort to establish them wherever possible.

When Archbishop Seghers resigned the see of Oregon in 1884 Bishop Gross was promoted to the vacant metropolitan throne.

DIOCESE OF PHILADELPHIA.

RIGHT REV. MICHAEL EGAN,

First Bishop of Philadelphia.

MICHAEL EGAN was born in Ireland, and at an early age entered the Franciscan Order. He came to the United States in 1802, and was received into the diocese of Baltimore by Bishop Carroll, who stationed him at Lancaster, Pennsylvania, as assistant to the Very Rev. Mr. de Barth. He soon became pastor of St. Mary's Church in Philadelphia. Dr. Carroll had recognized in him a learned, modest, and humble priest, who maintained, though alone and far from a convent of his order, the true spirit of St. Francis. One great desire that animated him was to establish the Order of Friars Minor in the United States, and on the 29th of September, 1804, he obtained an apostolic rescript authorizing him to erect here a Franciscan province. On the division of the diocese of Baltimore and the creation of the see of Philadelphia Father Egan was recommended for its first bishop, and was appointed April 8, 1809. The bulls did not arrive till late in the following year, and it was not till October 28, 1810, that he was consecrated in the cathedral of Baltimore. Archbishop Carroll had as a preliminary step required that a suitable income should be secured to the bishop, but Dr. Egan, soon after arriving and selecting St. Mary's Church as his cathedral, found himself at the mercy of trustees, who made his life a martyrdom. His diocese contained fourteen priests, eleven being Jesuits and Augustinians. He labored to increase the churches and clergy, but his infirm health and the constant opposition of factious men paralyzed his efforts and hastened his end. He died on the 22d of July, 1814.

RIGHT REV. HENRY CONWELL,

Second Bishop of Philadelphia.

HENRY CONWELL was born in the diocese of Armagh, Ireland, about the year 1748, and, full of the spirit of faith, studied for the priesthood amid all the dangers of the penal laws. He was ordained in 1776, and as curate and parish priest labored in his native diocese with all zeal. His merit raised him to the position of vicar-general, and on the vacancy of the see his name was one of those sent on to Rome. When experienced priests declined the appointment to the see of Philadelphia Dr. Conwell was nominated, and, accepting the bulls, received consecration in London in 1820. He came immediately to Philadelphia, and, notwithstanding his advanced age, began a visitation of his diocese. At St. Mary's Church, Philadelphia, he found a priest who had been received during the vacancy of the see. This clergyman's credentials were not satisfactory to Bishop Conwell, but his attempt to remove him was resisted by the trustees of the church, who opposed the bishop even after the unfortunate priest had apostatized. Philadelphia became rent with a schism that was fatal to religion and caused many to lose the faith. After years of strife Dr. Conwell relinquished the control of the diocese to the Very Rev. William Matthews, who had been appointed administrator, and proceeded to Rome, to which city he had been summoned in 1827. He was urged, for his own peace and that of the diocese, to resign the see, but declined and returned to Philadelphia. When the First Provincial Council of Baltimore met in 1829 Bishop Conwell attended, but took no active part. By the judgment of that body a coadjutor was recommended, and the Holy See appointed Right Rev. Francis Patrick Kenrick, who assumed the administration. Bishop Conwell gradually lost his sight, and was thus prevented from performing any episcopal duty. His life was prolonged, however, for many years, and he died at St. Joseph's Church, April 22, 1842, at the age of ninety-four.

RIGHT REV. JOHN NEPOMUCENE NEUMANN,

Third Bishop of Philadelphia.

JOHN NEPOMUCENE NEUMANN was born in Prachatitz, Bohemia, March 28, 1811, his father, Philip, a native of Obernburg, in Bavaria, having married and settled there. Trained by a pious mother in devotion to Mary, John lost none of his fervor in his studies there and at Budweis. A solid rather than a brilliant scholar, he entered the seminary at Budweis and completed his course at Prague. Resolved to devote himself to the American mission, he left his home in February, 1836, to offer his services to the Bishop of Philadelphia, little dreaming that he was himself to die in that office: Circumstances, however, led him to New York. Having been received by Bishop Du Bois, he was ordained in New York and sent to Williamsville, in the western part of the State. A parish of fifty miles here devolved on him, but he discharged his duties with scrupulous fidelity. He had long yearned to enter the religious state, and at last, with the consent of Bishop Hughes, joined the Redemptorists in 1840. In Baltimore, New York, Philadelphia, and Rochester his labors bore fruit. He became superior at Pittsburgh, and in 1846 provincial of his order. On the promotion of Bishop Kenrick to the see of Baltimore Father Neumann was appointed Bishop of Philadelphia, peremptory orders requiring him to accept the bulls. He was consecrated on Passion Sunday, 1852, by Archbishop Kenrick. The diocese of Philadelphia had, under the able rule of his predecessor, attained great prosperity. Although the western part had been assigned to the new see of Pittsburgh, the diocese of Philadelphia contained more than a hundred churches and priests. Bishop Neumann made visitations, encouraged the erection of churches, stimulated the establishment of parochial schools. He held synods to give his clergy strength, renewing the constitutions already in force. In the councils of Baltimore in 1852 and 1855 Dr. Neumann edified his brethren in the episcopate by his learning and sound, practical experience. After . visiting Rome at the time of the definition of the dogma of the

Immaculate Conception he asked to resign his see and return to the religious life, which was his choice. The Rev. James F. Wood was appointed coadjutor, and Bishop Neumann, submitting to the will of the Pope, retained his see. He set out to attend some business on the 5th of January, 1860, but was struck down in the street; he sat down on the nearest steps and expired. His native city erected a statue of him, the inscription styling him a "Servant of Mary." His virtues were of so extraordinary character that he was invoked by many after his death, and in 1884 steps were taken to introduce the process of his canonization.

MOST REV. JAMES FREDERIC WOOD,

Fourth Bishop and first Archbishop of Philadelphia.

JAMES FREDERIC WOOD was born in Philadelphia, April 27, 1813, of a family which had adopted the belief of the Unitarians. His parents came from England in 1809, and, after he had acquired the rudiments in Philadelphia, sent him, at the age of twelve, to the school of St. Mary de Crypt in Gloucester, where he remained five years, completing his education in Philadelphia. In November, 1827, he became clerk in the United States Branch Bank in Cincinnati, and rose to important positions. In 1833 he entered the Franklin Bank in that city, of which, three years subsequently, he became cashier. During this period his mind turned to more serious things than finance. The truth of the Catholic doctrines became clear to him, and he was baptized by Archbishop Purcell, April 7, 1836. In September of the ensuing year he resigned his position and entered the College of the Propaganda at Rome as a student. After seven years of serious study he was ordained, March 25, 1844, by Cardinal Fransoni, Prefect of the Propaganda. On his return to Cincinnati in October he was appointed assistant at the cathedral, and for nearly ten years was a laborious priest in that capacity. He was then pastor of St. Patrick's till he was selected as coadjutor to Bishop Neumann, of Philadelphia. On the 26th of April, 1857, he was consecrated by Archbishop Purcell Bishop of Antigona. The financial affairs of the Philadelphia diocese were soon reduced to order by him, and the great works of the diocese placed on a safe footing for their speedy completion. By the death of Bishop Neumann in January, 1860, Bishop Wood succeeded to the see and to the whole burden of the episcopate. He completed the cathedral of St. Peter and St. Paul, which was dedicated, November 20, 1864, with great solemnity, a medal struck to commemorate the event being the only fine numismatic work of art the Church has given in this country. To meet the wants of educational and charitable institutions he introduced the Sisters of the Good Shepherd, Servants of the Immaculate Heart of Mary, Sisters of the Third Order of St. Francis, the Little Sisters of the Poor, and developed the work of the Sisters of the Holy Child Jesus. He established a Catholic Home for Destitute Orphan Girls and enlarged St. Vincent's Orphan Asylum.

In 1862 he attended the canonization of the Japanese Martyrs in Rome, and in 1867 the centenary of St. Peter. He was present at the opening of the Vatican Council, and took part in its sessions till a severe illness compelled him to return home; he left his recorded vote in favor of a distinct declaration of the infallibility of the Sovereign Pontiff when defining *ex cathedra*. In 1868 the diocese of Philadelphia was reduced by the erection of the dioceses of Harrisburg, Scranton, and Wilmington. On the 15th of February, 1875, Dr. Wood was made Archbishop of Philadelphia, and a new ecclesiastical province was formed, the Bishops of Pittsburg, Harrisburg, Scranton, and Wilmington being his suffragans; Allegheny, which received a bishop in 1876, being then added. After taking part in the Second Plenary Council of Baltimore he celebrated in 1882 the silver jubilee of his episcopal consecration. One of the great acts of his later life was the erection of the fine seminary of St. Charles Borromeo at Overbrook, formally opened September 16, 1871.

In the early part of the year 1883 the aged archbishop was attacked with that fatal malady, Bright's disease of the kidneys, and in June the case became critical. He at once appointed

Vicar-General Walsh administrator, and, making a solemn profession of faith in the presence of his physicians and members of the clergy, moving all to tears, he received the last sacraments and prepared to meet his end. He expired on the 20th of June, shortly after eleven o'clock at night.

MOST REV. PATRICK JOHN RYAN,

Second Archbishop of Philadelphia.

PATRICK JOHN RYAN was born in Cloneyharp, near Thurles, in the county of Tipperary, Ireland, in 1831, of a pious and worthy family of farmers. He lost his father, Jeremiah, at an early age, but his mother placed him at the school of the Christian Brothers in Thurles, where he studied diligently. Showing a decided vocation for the priesthood, he was sent to a classical school in Dublin, where his talents and industry soon attracted attention, and he was selected to read the address of the school to Daniel O'Connell, then in prison. Young Ryan entered Carlow College to study for the priesthood as an ecclesiastic of the diocese of St. Louis, to which he had offered himself. In his course of philosophy, theology, and canon law he showed more than ordinary abilities, and essays which he contributed to periodicals attested his talent in presenting the knowledge he had acquired in an attractive form. Having received deacon's orders, he came to St. Louis in 1853, not having yet attained the age requisite for the priesthood. After a short stay in the seminary at Carondelet he was ordained by the archbishop in 1854 and stationed at the old cathedral. He was made pastor of the church of St. John the Evangelist, and vicar-general of the diocese some years later. Accompanying the archbishop to Rome in 1868, he preached the Lenten sermons in that city, winning the highest admiration for his learning and eloquence. When the venerable archbishop sought a coadjutor the Very Rev. P. J. Ryan was elected Bishop of Tricomia, February 15, 1872, and was consecrated on the 14th of April. After discharging for twelve years much of the diocesan work at St. Louis, and earning the reputation of a most eloquent and able bishop, he was, in 1884, transferred to the see of Philadelphia. His reception in that city was an ovation unparalleled in the history of the Church in this country. He attended the Third Plenary Council of Baltimore in November, 1884, preaching with his wonted eloquence the opening sermon on "The Church in her Councils."

DIOCESE OF ST. LOUIS.

RIGHT REV. JOSEPH ROSATI,

First Bishop of St. Louis.

JOSEPH ROSATI was born at Sora, in Italy, January 30, 1789, of a respectable and pious family. After his studies he entered the novitiate of the Priests of the Mission at Rome, and made his theological course at Monte Citorio under the apostolic Father de Andreis, and after his ordination was frequently his companion. When Bishop Du Bourg visited Rome in 1815 to obtain priests for the diocese of Louisiana, Father de Andreis was selected as one of the missionaries. He at once wrote to Father Rosati, asking him to join them if he wished. Father Rosati at once resolved to go; he made the journey to Toulouse, and, accompanying Father de Andreis thence to Bordeaux, embarked June 12, 1816. They reached Baltimore after a voyage of six weeks, and proceeded to Bardstown, where they set to work to learn English. Father Rosati the next year began his labors by a mission at Vincennes, and then proceeded to St. Louis. When the first log seminary of the Lazarists was established at the Barrens, Father Rosati was made superior, manfully meeting all the poverty and hardships incident to a new institution on the frontier. In 1820 he became superior of the Lazarists in this country, and three years afterwards opened a college, never ceasing constant missionary work amid all his other responsibilities. With the increasing community under his direction, Dr. Rosati did much to give Catholicity order and life in Missouri. Bishop Du Bourg, seeking a division of his diocese, proposed Father Rosati as vicar-apostolic of Florida; but the Lazarist declined the appointment, preferring to remain at his post in Missouri. In 1823 he was appointed coadjutor to Bishop Du Bourg, and it was ordained that in 1826 a see should be established at New Orleans and another at St. Louis, Bishop Du Bourg to select which he preferred, the other to be filled by his coadjutor. Father Rosati was accordingly consecrated Bishop of Tenagra on the 25th of March, 1824, but continued to reside in Missouri. On the resignation of Bishop Du Bourg he administered the diocese till he was made first Bishop of St. Louis in 1827, and a new bishop was consecrated for New Orleans. Able at last to devote himself to the diocese of St. Louis, he aided the Jesuit Fathers in their good work and the Ladies of the Sacred Heart, introduced the Sisters of Joseph, Visitation Nuns, and Sisters of Charity, thus endowing Missouri with communities for education and works of mercy. He began a cathedral, and by his energy soon had a large and elegant edifice, which was dedicated with great pomp in October, 1834, five bishops taking part in the ceremony. Bishop Rosati held a synod of his clergy in 1839, adopting wise statutes. Though not in the province of Baltimore, he took part in the first four Provincial Councils held in that city. After the close of the fourth council, in 1840, he visited Rome, and the Sovereign Pontiff then confided to him a mission to the republic of Hayti to arrange for the re-establishment of episcopal sees in that island. Meanwhile he had obtained the appointment of the Rev. Peter Richard Kenrick as coadjutor, and, returning to the United States, consecrated him at Philadelphia. Bishop Rosati then proceeded to Hayti, where his negotiations were most successful, and the terms of a concordat were agreed upon, which was to be signed at Rome by a Haytian envoy. After confirming a great number in Hayti he set out for Rome to make his report to Pope Gregory XVI. He was seized with a serious illness in the Eternal City, but, recovering, set out for his diocese by the way of Paris. There his disease returned, and his physicians counselled a return to Rome. He reached it only to die on the 25th of September, 1843. Bishop Rosati was eminent for his holy life, his zeal as a priest, his successful administration as a bishop, his learning, his eloquence. He built up the diocese from a very slender beginning, organized the Indian missions, and extended the work of the Church beyond the Rocky Mountains.

MOST REV. PETER RICHARD KENRICK,

Second Bishop and first Archbishop of St. Louis.

THE Most Rev. Peter Richard Kenrick, a younger brother of Francis Patrick, Bishop of Philadelphia and Archbishop of Baltimore, was born in Dublin August 17, 1806. At the close of his studies the piety instilled into him from his youth led him to embrace the ecclesiastical state. He entered the seminary and was ordained priest.

Coming to the United States, to which his brother had been sent from Rome, he was in 1833 received into the diocese of Philadelphia and became assistant at the cathedral, and in 1835 pastor. His learning and abilities led to his selection as superior of the diocesan seminary, in which he filled also the chair of dogmatic theology. As vicar-general he aided greatly in reorganizing the diocese; become thus widely known, he was chosen by Bishop Bruté, of Vincennes, as his theologian at the Third Provincial Council of Baltimore. When Rev. Father Timon declined the appointment of coadjutor of St. Louis, Bishop Rosati selected the Very Rev. Mr. Kenrick, "whose apostolic zeal," he declared, "had been so conspicuous, and to whose merits all the prelates of the American Church had on several occasions given honorable testimony." An express command of the Sovereign Pontiff precluded every way of shrinking from the dignity to which he had been called. Submitting to an honor he had not sought, he was consecrated Bishop of Drasa by Dr. Rosati, assisted by Bishop Francis P. Kenrick and Bishop Lefevere, in St. Mary's Church, Philadelphia, on St. Andrew's day, November 30, 1841. Bishop Rosati proceeded to Hayti, to which he had been sent by the Holy See, and Bishop Kenrick repaired to St. Louis to assume the administration of the diocese during his absence. Bishop Rosati never returned to Missouri; his health failed, and he died at Rome September 25, 1843, when the Right Rev. Dr. Kenrick succeeded to the see of St. Louis. From his arrival in the diocese he had given an impulse to all good works. He encouraged the building of churches, and, with far-seeing wisdom,

MOST REV. WILLIAM H. GROSS, D.D.
Born in Baltimore, June 12, 1837.
Ordained March 21, 1863; Consecrated Bishop of Savannah, April, 27, 1873; promoted to Oregon City, 1884.

MOST REV. P. R. KENRICK, D.D.
Born in Dublin, August 17, 1806.
Consecrated Bishop of Drasa, and Coadjutor of St. Louis, Nov. 30, 1841; Bishop of St. Louis, Sept. 25, 1843; created Archbishop, 1847.

MOST REV. J. B. SALPOINTE, D.D.
Born in France, Feb. 22, 1825.
Consecrated Bishop of Doryla and Vicar-Apostolic of Arizona, June 20, 1869; Coadjutor of Santa Fe, June 8, 1884, succeeded 1885.

MOST REV. PATRICK W. RIORDAN, D.D.
Born August, 27, 1841.
Ordained in 1865; Consecrated Bishop of Cabasa, and Coadjutor of San Francisco, Sept. 16, 1883; Archbishop of San Francisco, 1884.

erected some where not a house was to be seen, but where thriving towns soon gathered. He gave a series of lectures on the doctrines of the Church which attracted general attention, and established *The Catholic Cabinet*, a magazine to diffuse religious knowledge among his flock. The diocese of St. Louis, when Dr. Kenrick reached it, embraced the States of Missouri, Arkansas, half of Illinois, and the Territories now constituting Kansas, Nebraska, and Indian Territory, with all east of the Rocky Mountains. The city of St. Louis had six churches and chapels, a theological seminary, a university, convent of the Sacred Heart, two asylums, four free schools, and 16,000 Catholics out of a population of 30,000. The diocese contained 65 churches and 74 priests, and had several Indian missions. The erection of the sees of Little Rock in 1843, Chicago in 1844, of the vicariates-apostolic of Indian Territory and of Nebraska in 1851, of St. Joseph in 1868, and of Kansas City in 1880, have in his time reduced his diocese greatly, so that in 1885 it comprises only the eastern portion of the State of Missouri.

Bishop Kenrick introduced the Brothers of the Christian Schools, the Sisters of St. Joseph, and other orders to aid in education or works of mercy. In 1847 Pope Pius IX. made St. Louis an archiepiscopal see, to which the bishops of Dubuque, Nashville, Chicago, and Milwaukee were assigned as suffragans. Archbishop Kenrick held a synod of his diocese in 1850, and in September, 1855, convened the First Provincial Council of St. Louis, which was attended by the bishops of the sees already named, and of those of Santa Fé and St. Paul, who had also been made suffragans, and by the vicar-apostolic of Indian Territory. A second council was held in September, 1858. Both by their wise provisions bear testimony to the zeal and prudence of Archbishop Kenrick. During the civil war the State became a battlefield; the citizens were divided in their sympathies, and bitter feelings prevailed. The archbishop, with his clergy and religious, was unremitting in attending all, especially the sick and wounded, without distinction; but Catholics suffered from the petty fanaticism of bigots in temporary power. At the close of the war a new constitution, carried by excluding thousands of citizens from the polls, forbade any bishop, priest, or religious to preach, officiate, or teach, unless a test oath of a stringent character as to men's very thoughts was first taken. Archbishop Kenrick, in a circular, directed his clergy not to take it, and several priests and Sisters were indicted under the shameful provision before the Supreme Court declared its nullity.

Archbishop Kenrick took an active part in the three Plenary Councils held at Baltimore, and at the Vatican Council was one of those who opposed the definition of the infallibility of the Pope as unnecessary and dangerous to the peace of the Church. His arguments show the full liberty of discussion given in the Œcumenical Council, and his prompt acceptance of the dogma when defined gave his character new lustre. To aid him in the administration of his diocese he obtained, in 1857, a coadjutor in the person of the Right Rev. James Duggan, who became Bishop of Chicago two years after, and at a later period in the person of Patrick John Ryan, who was consecrated Bishop of Tricomia, April 14, 1872. Dr. Ryan was the eloquent and trusted assistant of the venerable archbishop till he was transferred to the see of Philadelphia in 1884.

In 1876 the Catholics of St. Louis celebrated the centenary of the erection of the first church in their city.

The progress of the diocese under the care of Archbishop Kenrick may be seen in its condition in 1885, when it contained 254 priests, 40 ecclesiastical students, 216 churches and chapels. The religious orders are well represented: Lazarist Fathers direct the theological seminary and a college; the Jesuits have the university; the Christian Brothers a college; Redemptorists and Franciscan Fathers labor chiefly among the Germans. There are academies conducted by the Ladies of the Sacred Heart, Visitation Nuns, Sisters of Loretto, Ursulines, and Sisters of St. Joseph; Carmelite Nuns follow their contemplative life; Sisters of the Good Shepherd reclaim the fallen; Sisters of Charity and of Mercy minister to all human miseries and care for the orphan; the Servants of the Divine Heart attend the sick at their homes. There are orphan asylums; a Protectorate for Boys; 88 parochial schools, with 17,180 pupils, conducted by Christian and Franciscan Brothers, Ladies of the Sacred Heart, Sisters of Notre Dame, St. Joseph, the Precious Blood, Christian Charity, St. Francis, Oblates of Mercy, Sisters of Loretto; and the total population of the diocese is estimated at 196,000.

DIOCESE OF SAN FRANCISCO.

RIGHT REV. FRANCIS GARCIA DIEGO, O.S.F.,

Bishop of the Two Californias.

WHEN California was reached by the Jesuit missionaries who founded their reductions of converted Indians in the lower peninsula, and little Spanish settlements grew up near the crosses they planted, jurisdiction over the peninsula was claimed by different sees; but the distance and difficulty of travel prevented any bishop from visiting it. Ultimately the superior of the mission was made a prefect-apostolic by the Holy See, with power to confer the Sacrament of Confirmation. A similar power was conferred upon the venerable Franciscan Father Juniper Serra when he founded the missions in the Upper Province. At the solicitation of the Mexican government the Two Californias were erected into a diocese by Pope Gregory XVI in 1840. Father Francis Garcia Diego y Moreno, the first bishop, was born at Lagos, in the State of Jalisco, and pursued his course of Latin, rhetoric, and philosophy at Guadalajara, and entered the order of St. Francis in the Apostolical College at Zacatecas. Here he was ordained about the year 1824, and became master of novices and vicar. As a missionary he was distinguished for his strict observance of his rule, his eloquence and zeal. In 1832 he was appointed prefect of the California mission, and made Santa Clara his abode. The grand missions, that once numbered more than thirty thousand Catholics, were sinking under the Mexican misgovernment which had robbed them and turned the Indians adrift. The prefect did all in his power to save these Catholic Indians and animate them to persevere. Even the Pious Fund of California for the support of the missions was seized and its income withheld. so that Fathers died of actual starvation. Father Garcia went to Mexico to endeavor to obtain redress for all these evils, but was detained at Zacatecas by duties conferred on him in his order. Meanwhile he was appointed bishop, and accepted only on a solemn promise from the Mexican government that the income of the Pious Fund should be restored, and because the salary promised him would support several missionaries. He was consecrated bishop October 4, 1840, but the preliminaries to his taking possession of his diocese were prolonged so that he did not reach San Diego, which was named in the bull as his residence, till December, 1841. He found the desolation complete, most of the missions in ruins and abandoned, the fertile mission lands and vineyards, with the herds of cattle, seized, the Indians reduced to about four thousand and utterly destitute. Obtaining all the aid he could, the good bishop traversed the province, endeavoring to save his flock. He began a seminary at Santa Ynez, having obtained at last a grant of thirty-five thousand acres. As San Diego was in ruins, he took up his residence at Santa Barbara. He was not, however, permitted by Providence long to survive; his health failed in 1845, and on the night of April 13 in the ensuing year he died piously amid his faithful missionaries. His remains were interred in the church at Santa Barbara.

MOST REV. JOSEPH SADOC ALEMANY, O.S.D.,

First Bishop of Monterey and First Archbishop of San Francisco.

JOSEPH SADOC ALEMANY was born in 1814 in Vich, a city in the province of Catalonia which has sent many zealous missionaries to America. After making his primary studies young Alemany entered the Dominican Order at the age of fifteen. Upon completing his theological course at a very early age he was ordained at Viterbo in 1837 by Bishop, afterwards Cardinal, Pianetto. The young priest was then made sub-master of novices at Viterbo, and, having been summoned to Rome, was an assistant to the rector of the church of Santa Maria sopra Minerva till the year 1841, when he solicited the American mission. Soon after reaching St. Joseph's Convent in Ohio Father Alemany was sent to Tennessee at the request of Bishop Miles, and began his missionary career in Nashville, but was soon assistant at Memphis, aiding to erect the first Catholic church in that city. He remained in this severe mission, attending the few Catholics scattered over a large district, till 1847, when he was elected provincial and returned to Ohio. Having gone to Rome in 1850 to attend a General Chapter of the order, he was appointed Bishop of Monterey, the Rev. Mr. Montgomery having declined the nomination. He was consecrated by Cardinal Franzoni in the church of San Carlo, June 13, 1850, and set out for his diocese, taking with him Father Vilarrasa to found a convent of Friar Preachers, and Mother Mary Goemare to establish one of Dominican Nuns. A new population of American and other English-speaking people had by this time flocked into California, including many Catholics, so that Bishop Alemany had to provide priests for Spanish, English, and Indian tongues. The new population was in the more northerly districts, San Francisco growing rapidly to be a great city. Bishop Alemany had few priests, few churches, no institutions for charity or education. The abundant provision which the Spanish monarchs and pious Catholics in their day had made for the maintenance of religion was gone. The year before his consecration a little wooden shanty had been reared as the first Catholic church in San Francisco. The year of his arrival the two priests there had to cope with the cholera, and the priest at Sacramento, Father Anderson, a native of Elizabeth, N. J., and a convert, died while attending the sick. In 1852 the bishop attended the First Plenary Council, and exerted himself to procure priests and religious, and succeeded to some extent, obtaining several Sisters of Charity from Emmittsburg, two of whom died on the way. The others courageously went on, and soon opened an asylum for the many orphans.

The extent of California and the diversity of population called for a division of the diocese of Monterey. In July, 1853, San Francisco was erected into an archiepiscopal see, to which Dr. Alemany was transferred, and Bishop Amat succeeded him at Monterey. The archbishop then devoted him wholly to the wants of the increasing flock. Presentation Nuns and Sisters of Mercy came; a diocesan seminary was begun under Rev. Dr. Eugene O'Connell; the cathedral was completed and dedicated. As cities and towns grew up a new division of the diocese became necessary, and in 1860 the Holy See set off the northwestern portion of the diocese as the vicariate-apostolic of Marysville, and the northeastern as that of Colorado. By this time the Jesuit Fathers who had entered the diocese had founded their college at Santa Clara; academies and parochial schools were increasing in number and efficiency. Reduced as the diocese has been, the 15 priests and 24 churches of California in 1850 have developed, in the diocese of San Francisco alone, in 1884 to 128 churches and 175 priests, with a seminary, 6 colleges, 18 academies, and 200,000 Catholics; with Jesuits, Dominicans, Marists, Brothers of the Christian Schools, Presentation, Ursuline, and Dominican Nuns, Sisters of Charity, of Mercy, of Notre Dame, of the Holy Names.

Archbishop Alemany was one of the Fathers of the Third Plenary Council of Baltimore, and delivered a Latin sermon to the clergy on the virtues that should adorn the priesthood. Soon after its close he resigned his see and returned to his order.

MOST REV. PATRICK W. RIORDAN,

Second Archbishop of San Francisco.

PATRICK WILLIAM RIORDAN was born August 27, 1841, and was taken by his parents to Chicago in his seventh year. He made his studies at the university of St. Mary's of the Lake, and, feeling himself called to the ecclesiastical state, asked to be received as a seminarian. His talents led to his being sent to the American College at Rome, but, having suffered greatly from malaria, he left Rome and completed his course in Paris and Louvain. He was ordained in Belgium in 1865 by Cardinal Sterckx, and after his return to the United States was appointed in 1866 professor of ecclesiastical history and canon law in the theological seminary of St. Mary's of the Lake at Chicago; the next year he filled the chair of dogmatic theology. From 1868 to 1871 he was in the active discharge of missionary duties at Joliet, after which he was appointed rector of St. James' Church in the city of Chicago. Here he gave all his energy to the spiritual good of his people, upholding and extending the parochial schools under the Sisters of Mercy. His abilities and zeal marked him as one destined to render great services to the Church.

While pastor of St. James' Church in 1883 he received the notification of his appointment as titular Bishop of Cabasa, and coadjutor, with the right of succession, to the Most Rev. Archbishop Alemany, of San Francisco. He was consecrated in St. James' on Sunday, September 16, 1883, by Archbishop Feehan. Bishop Riordan reached San Francisco on the 6th of November, and was received by a delegation, who conveyed him to the residence of the archbishop.

Archbishop Riordan at once, by visitations and otherwise, relieved Archbishop Alemany of many of the heavier burdens of the episcopate, and took part with Archbishop Alemany in the great Plenary Council of 1884. By the resignation of that venerable prelate he became the second archbishop of San Francisco.

DIOCESE OF SANTA FÉ.

MOST REV. JOHN B. LAMY,

First Bishop and First Archbishop of Santa Fé.

JOHN BAPTIST LAMY was born in 1814 in Auvergne, France, and came, after his ordination, to the United States to give his services to the cause of religion. In 1839 he was stationed at Sapp's Settlement, Ohio, afterwards called Danville, where he erected a fine church dedicated to St. Luke; the next year he was attending also Mount Vernon and a German settlement at Newark, obtaining sites for churches, and in the former had already begun a large and handsome edifice, which he completed only to see it destroyed by fire; but he set to work to rebuild it, extending his missions to Millersburgh, in Licking County. In this field he labored till about 1848, when he was appointed pastor of St. Mary's Church, Covington, Ky., then in the diocese of Cincinnati. When the province of New Mexico was acquired by the United States religion had greatly declined among its inhabitants. No bishop had visited New Mexico for eighty years; the Franciscans who had ministered for centuries to the Spaniards and Indians had been removed; schools had ceased. The Holy See, to remedy the evils, formed the territory into a vicariate-apostolic, and the Rev. John Baptist Lamy was consecrated Bishop of Agathonica, November 24, 1850. The territory contained sixty thousand whites and eight thousand Indians, with twenty-five churches and forty chapels. Bishop Lamy endeavored to obtain exemplary priests to revive the faith of the neglected flock. Sisters of Loretto opened an academy with the commencement of the year 1853. On the 29th of July in that year the see of Santa Fé was erected, and Dr. Lamy was elected the first bishop. He visited Europe to obtain aid, and returned with four priests, a deacon, and two subdeacons. He soon after obtained

RT. REV. BENEDICT JOSEPH FLAGET.
Born at Contournat, in Auvergne, France, Nov. 7, 1763.
First Bishop of Bardstown and Louisville; Consecrated Nov. 4, 1810; died Feb. 11, 1850.

RT. REV. JOHN ENGLAND.
Born at Cork, Ireland, Sept. 23, 1786.
Ordained Oct. 10, 1808; first Bishop of Charleston; Consecrated Sept. 21, 1820; appointed Vicar-Apostolic of Santo Domingo, March 15, 1833; died April 11, 1842.

RT. REV. JOHN VERTIN, D.D.
Born at Rudolfswerth, Austria, July 17, 1844.
Ordained Aug. 31, 1865; Consecrated Bishop of Marquette, Sept. 14, 1879.

MOST REV. J. B. LAMY, D.D.
Born in Auvergne in 1814.
Consecrated Bishop of Agathonica and Vicar-Apostolic of New Mexico, Nov. 24, 1850; Bishop of Santa Fe, July 29, 1853; created Archbishop, 1875; resigned 1885.

Brothers of the Christian Doctrine, who in time founded a college; Sisters of Charity for hospitals and asylums; and in 1867 Jesuit Fathers, who opened a college at Las Vegas and established a Catholic journal. In 1875 the see was made archiepiscopal, with Dr. Lamy as archbishop. In 1885 the diocese contained 34 parish churches, 203 chapels regularly attended, 56 priests, with 111,000 Catholics of Spanish origin, 3,000 English-speaking Catholics, and 12,000 Pueblo Indians. One of Archbishop Lamy's great labors has been to defeat the government proselytizing schemes which aimed at converting the Catholic Pueblo Indians to Protestantism.

MOST REV. JOHN B. SALPOINTE,

Second Archbishop of Santa Fé.

JOHN B. SALPOINTE was born in France on the 22d of February, 1825, and made his classical studies in the preparatory seminary of Agen in the Department of Creuse, and of Clermont in that of Puy de Dôme. After passing through a thorough theological course at the seminary of Clermont Ferrand he was ordained priest December 21, 1851. He spent three years in the parochial exercise of the sacred ministry, and five more as teacher in the preparatory seminary of Clermont. He left his native land to devote himself to the missions of New Mexico, on the 4th of August, 1859, and was sent to Arizona as vicar-general by Right Rev. Bishop Lamy in 1866. Arizona was made a vicariate-apostolic in 1869, and Very Rev. Dr. Salpointe, having been appointed Bishop of Doryla, on the 25th of September, 1868, was consecrated at Clermont, France, June 20, 1869. The vicariate comprised Arizona, the southern part of New Mexico, known as the Mesilla valley, and the county of El Paso in Texas. There were churches at Tucson and St. Xavier del Bac, and Las Cruces, which had priests, as had the chapel of San Agustin. Churches were needed for the new population, and these soon rose at Colorado City and other points. Bishop Salpointe labored to save his Spanish and Indian flock from perversion, the United States government having assigned the Catholic Indians to Protestant sects in order to debauch their faith. The vicar-apostolic introduced Sisters of St. Joseph, who established schools and hospitals; Sisters of Mercy and of Loretto to open academies. At the commencement of 1884 he had sixteen priests, eighteen churches built and five more going up, fifteen chapels, six parochial schools, a white Catholic population of thirty thousand, and one thousand Catholic Indians. On the 8th of June, 1884, Pope Leo XIII. transferred Bishop Salpointe to Santa Fé, and made him coadjutor to Archbishop Lamy.

DIOCESE OF ALBANY.

RIGHT REV. JOHN JOSEPH CONROY,

Second Bishop of Albany.

JOHN JOSEPH CONROY was born in Clonaslee, Queen's County, Ireland, about the year 1829, and came to this country at the age of twelve. He received his earlier training in New York City, where his uncle was for many years a zealous priest. His classical studies he pursued under the Sulpitians at Montreal; his higher course and theology at Mount St. Mary's and St. Joseph's Seminary, Fordham. His ability was such that he was made a professor before his graduation. He was ordained priest June 4, 1842, and was made vice-president of St. John's College at Fordham in the following year, and subsequently president of that institution. In March, 1844, he was appointed pastor of old St. Joseph's Church, Albany, and held that position till he was raised to the episcopate. During his rectorship he rebuilt the church, introduced the Sisters of Charity, and founded St. Vincent's Orphan Asylum. His abilities and zeal made the parish prosper, and he was in time made vicar-general of the diocese about the year 1857, and during the absence of the bishop he acted as administrator. When the Right Rev. Dr. McCloskey was promoted to the see of New York, the Very Rev. Mr. Conroy administered the diocese of Albany till July 7, 1865, when he was appointed bishop, receiving episcopal consecration October 15 in the same year.

Bishop Conroy governed the diocese for several years, churches, priests, and institutions of all kinds increasing. Among these may be noted the establishment of an Industrial School, St. Peter's Hospital, St. Agnes' Rural Cemetery, and the introduction of the Little Sisters of the Poor. He attended the First Plenary Council of Baltimore as theologian, and sat in the second as bishop of Albany. He visited Rome on the occasion of the centenary of St. Peter, and took part in the sessions of the Council of the Vatican. In August, 1869, he held a diocesan synod in which salutary regulations were adopted. But in 1872 infirmities made it a matter of prudence for Bishop Conroy to secure a coadjutor. After the appointment of Bishop McNeirny, Dr. Conroy continued as far as possible to direct the diocese till January, 1874, when he relinquished the administration to his coadjutor. On the 16th of October, 1877, he resigned the see and removed to New York City. The Sovereign Pontiff subsequently appointed him to the see of Curium. He has since on several occasions rendered essential service to the Most Rev. Archbishop of New York, and attended the Plenary Council of Baltimore in 1884.

RIGHT REV. FRANCIS S. McNEIRNY,

Third Bishop of Albany.

FRANCIS S. MCNEIRNY was born in the city of New York on the 21st of April, 1828, and began his studies in the school of Mr. Sparrow, a Catholic teacher. In September, 1841, he was sent to Montreal, and entered the college in that city directed by the priests of the community of St. Sulpice. Here he remained till he terminated the course of philosophy. He then resolved to enter the ecclesiastical state, and pursued his theological studies in the Grand Seminary from 1849 to 1854, acting as procurator of the institution for one year, and for two years directing the class of belles-lettres in the college. Returning to New York, he received the tonsure, minor orders, and subdeaconship at the hands of Archbishop Hughes in St. Patrick's Cathedral. He was ordained deacon on the feast of the Assumption, 1854, and priest two days later. The young clergyman was immediately stationed at the cathedral and made chaplain to the archbishop. His perfect knowledge of the rites and offices of the Church caused Rev.

RT. REV. PETER J. BALTES, D.D.
Born at Ensheim, Bavaria, April 7, 1827.
Ordained May 21, 1853 ; Consecrated Bishop of Alton, Jan. 23, 1870.

RT. REV. FRANCIS S. McNEIRNY, D.D.
Born in New York, April 21, 1828.
Ordained Aug. 17, 1854 ; Consecrated Bishop of Rhesina and Coadjutor of Albany, April 21, 1872; Bishop of Albany, Oct. 16, 1877.

RT. REV. WM. G. McCLOSKEY, D.D.
Born in Brooklyn, N. Y., Nov. 10, 1833.
Ordained Oct. 6, 1852; Consecrated Bishop of Louisville, May 24, 1868.

RT. REV. DENIS M. BRADLEY, D.D.
Born in Ireland, Feb. 25, 1846.
Ordained June 3, 1871; Consecrated Bishop of Manchester, June 11, 1884.

Mr. McNeirny to be selected on all solemn occasions as master of ceremonies, and he did much to give dignity to the services of the Church. In 1857 he was made chancellor of the diocese of New York, and from 1859 he was, as secretary to Archbishop Hughes or secretary of the diocese or the council, constantly and intimately connected with the management of affairs. When the health of Bishop Conroy, of Albany, required relief from duty, the Rev. Mr. McNeirny was appointed; he was consecrated Bishop of Rhesina and coadjutor of Albany April 21, 1872. On the 18th of January, 1874, the administration of the diocese was confided to him, and on the resignation of Bishop Conroy, October 16, 1877, he became third Bishop of Albany. Under his careful and prudent administration the diocese has prospered and acquired order and solidity. Although the diocese of Ogdensburg was set off in 1872, the churches and chapels have increased from 170 to 210; the priests from 120 to 197; the parochial schools number twelve thousand pupils, while the religious orders have been increased by the accession of Brothers of the Good Works, Little Sisters of the Poor, Sisters of Christian Charity, Sisters of St. Dominic, and Presentation Nuns. The Jesuit Fathers, Augustinians, and Franciscan Conventuals have houses in the diocese of Albany, and in it is situated the Provincial Seminary at Troy, a large theological institution with an able corps of professors.

DIOCESE OF ALTON.

RIGHT REV. HENRY DAMIAN JUNCKER,

First Bishop of Alton.

HENRY DAMIAN JUNCKER was born at Fénétrange, in the province of Lorraine, while it was still part of the French territory. During his studies he felt called to devote himself to the American mission, and, coming to this country, entered the seminary of the diocese of Cincinnati, showing ability as a student and as a teacher. He was ordained priest March 16, 1834, being the first one who received holy orders from the hands of Bishop Purcell. He was appointed to Holy Trinity, the first German church in Cincinnati, and in 1836 became pastor of St. Mary's, Canton, attending it, with its numerous missions, for ten years, when he was removed to Urbana, also a position of no little labor. In 1854 the Holy See divided the diocese of Chicago and established a see at Quincy. The clergymen nominated to the new bishopric declined the mitre, and the diocese was temporarily administered by Bishop O'Regan. On the 9th of January, 1857, the see was transferred to Alton, and the new diocese embraced that of Quincy with several additional counties. Rev. Mr. Juncker was appointed first Bishop of Alton, and, having received consecration from Archbishop Purcell on the 26th of April, 1857, he proceeded to organize the Alton diocese, in which he found only eighteen priests; in the first year he obtained twenty-four others, and eight new churches were erected. After laying the cornerstone of the cathedral of St. Peter and St. Paul he visited Europe to obtain aid, and on the 19th of April, 1859, gathered his flock to witness the dedication of the cathedral by Archbishop Kenrick. Bishop Juncker's visitations were constant; in many places he was the pioneer missionary priest, gathering Catholics and organizing congregations, administering the sacraments, and preparing the way for the pastor, whom it was his next care to send them. By the year 1868 he had brought the diocese to a flourishing condition, with colleges, academies, hospitals, and asylums; fifty-six parochial schools, one hundred priests, and 123 churches; the Franciscan Fathers, Ursuline Nuns, Sisters of St. Joseph, School Sisters of Notre Dame, Sisters of Charity and of the Holy Names, as well as the Sisters of the Poor of St. Francis, joining in the good work.

After a long and severe illness Bishop Juncker was **removed** from the scene of his energetic labors October 2, 1868.

RIGHT REV. PETER JOSEPH BALTES,

Second Bishop of Alton.

PETER JOSEPH BALTES was born in the village of Ensheim, in the diocese of Spire, Bavaria, April 7, 1827, and came to this country with his parents when only six years old. The family settled in the State of New York, and their son made his classical course in New York and at the College of the Holy Cross, Worcester, completing his theology in the University of St. Mary's of the Lake, Chicago. Desiring to devote his life to the service of God, he was accepted for the diocese of Chicago, and, after a theological course at the Sulpitian Seminary in Montreal, was ordained May 21, 1853. His first mission labors were at Waterloo, Monroe County, from which he was transferred to Belleville, both in the new diocese of Quincy. He remained at Belleville, devoting himself to his missionary duties and acquiring a reputation for ability and zeal, till the death of Bishop Juncker, when he was made administrator of the diocese. The appointment foreshadowed his election to the bishopric by Pope Pius IX., September 24, 1869. He was consecrated on the 23d of January, 1870, in St. Peter's Church, Belleville, where he had so long ministered, and was the first bishop consecrated in the State of Illinois, though Catholicity had flourished there for nearly two centuries. Bishop Baltes has been a watchful and energetic bishop, laboring earnestly to guard his flock. Under his care the religious orders already in the diocese developed, and Brothers of the Holy Cross, Sisters of the Holy Cross, of Mercy, of the Precious Blood, of Loretto, and of St. Dominic, with the Poor Handmaids of Christ, came to labor in his bishopric. In 1884 the diocese had two colleges under the Franciscan Fathers, nine academies, 100 parochial schools with 11,000 pupils, three asylums, eleven hospitals, 169 priests, and 190 churches. The diocese sustained a terrible loss in 1884 by the conflagration of St. Joseph's Convent and Academy of Notre Dame in the bishop's former parish of Belleville, where 27 lives were lost. Bishop Baltes has held a synod, and by wise regulations provided for the maintenance of discipline in the diocese confided to him.

His health began to decline, but early in 1886 he was supposed to be recovering from a disease of the liver, when he suddenly grew worse, and died between eight and nine o'clock on the morning of February 15, 1886. At his solemn obsequies Archbishops Kenrick, Feehan, and Heiss, with Bishop Hogan, attended.

DIOCESE OF BROOKLYN.

RIGHT REV. JOHN LOUGHLIN,

First Bishop of Brooklyn.

JOHN LOUGHLIN was born in the County Down, Ireland, in the year 1816, and came at an early age to this country. His boyhood was spent in Albany. To secure him a thorough Catholic education he was sent to Mount St. Mary's, Emmittsburg, where as a student and teacher he attracted attention by his ability. On completing his divinity course he was ordained priest by Bishop Hughes, at his first ordination, October 18, 1840. Rev. Mr. Loughlin was appointed assistant pastor at St. Patrick's Cathedral, and in 1844 became rector. Five years later he was chosen by Bishop Hughes vicar-general of the diocese, and discharged the important duties to the satisfaction of that great prelate. When Long Island was formed into a diocese with Brooklyn as the episcopal see, the Very Rev. John Loughlin was chosen the first bishop. He was consecrated by Archbishop Cajetan Bedini, in St. Patrick's Cathedral, on the 30th of October, 1853. He was installed in St. James' Church, which he had taken as his pro-cathedral, on the 9th of November, and began the labors which, extending over more than thirty years, have raised so many monuments of his zeal.

On taking possession of his diocese Bishop Loughlin had ten churches in Brooklyn and Williamsburg, and eleven others in the rest of Long Island, attended by twenty-three priests. There were two orphan asylums and a few schools under the Brothers of the Christian Schools and Sisters of Charity. In 1855 he introduced the Sisters of St. Joseph and Sisters of Mercy, and the Visitation Nuns founded a monastery of their order in Brooklyn. Under the impulse of his zeal churches were established in all parts of Long Island, and especial efforts made to give children a really Catholic training. On the 20th of June, 1868, the corner-stone of a cathedral church under the invocation of the Immaculate Conception was solemnly laid by Archbishop McCloskey. The site is on Lafayette Avenue, between Clermont and Vanderbilt Avenues, and the edifice has gone slowly on ever since.

In July, 1869, the corner-stone of the college of St. John the Baptist on Willoughby Avenue was laid. The edifice was soon completed, and the institution opened under the direction of the Lazarists, or Priests of the Mission. About the same time the Sisters of the Good Shepherd began an asylum for penitent women. The Franciscan Sisters of the Poor opened St. Francis' Hospital, and the Little Sisters of the Poor an Asylum for the Aged, which was unfortunately destroyed by fire in March, 1876, with the loss of several lives in spite of the heroic efforts of the Sisters. The diocese has also been endowed with a Home for Boys.

Bishop Loughlin took part in several councils of Baltimore, two of them Plenary, as well as in the Provincial Councils of New York, and held a Diocesan Synod for the purpose of establishing in his diocese the decrees of the councils.

In 1884 the city of Brooklyn had 45 churches, Kings County 9, Queens County 25, and Suffolk County 12; the priests of the diocese of Brooklyn numbered 156; there were 76 parish schools with 21,500 pupils; seven orphan asylums under Sisters of St. Joseph, of St. Dominic, of Mercy, and of Charity; hospitals under Sisters of Charity, St. Dominic, and the Franciscan Sisters of the Poor; an Institute for Deaf Mutes, two Homes for Destitute Children, a Nursery, an Invalids' Home, and a House of the Good Shepherd.

DIOCESE OF BUFFALO.

RIGHT REV. JOHN TIMON, C.M.,

First Bishop of Buffalo.

JOHN TIMON was born in Conewago, Pennsylvania, of Irish parentage, on the 12th of February, 1797. When a young man he went to St. Louis with his family and engaged in mercantile life, but in April, 1823, he entered the Lazarist Seminary of St. Mary's of the Barrens with the intention of becoming a priest. Having been received into the order, he was ordained in 1825. He had already made an essay of mission life, accompanying Rev. Mr. Odin on an excursion through Arkansas and Texas. Rev. Father Timon's first missions were in the vicinity of the Barrens, extending to Cape Girardeau, Jackson, and New Madrid. In his labors he encountered opposition, and was occasionally compelled to enter the lists with Protestant ministers. In 1835 he was appointed visitor of the Lazarists in the United States. This office entailed new and difficult labors on him, requiring a visit to the East and to Europe, from which he returned in 1837 with several missionaries. The due organization of the order at this time was mainly his work. The next year he established a theological seminary in Louisiana, and, at the request of Archbishop Blanc, visited Texas to ascertain the condition of the Church there. His visit was a laborious mission for the benefit of the Catholics in that territory. Returning to Missouri, Father Timon began a series of missions in that State and Illinois, amid which he received bulls appointing him coadjutor of St. Louis, but he refused the dignity. In April, 1840, he received letters naming him Prefect-Apostolic of Texas, with power to administer confirmation. He accepted the position and sent Rev. Mr. Odin to Texas, and soon after wrote to Rome to request the appointment of that clergyman as prefect. He went to Texas himself at the close of the year, and gained the good-will of the members of the government of the Republic of Texas, from whom he solicited a confirmation of the right of the Church to the property held by it under Spain. Having visited the chief towns in Texas, he left Rev. Mr. Odin in charge of the missions and returned to Missouri, from which business of the order soon required him to set out for France.

Father Timon maintained this life of incessant activity as superior of the Lazarists till he received, on the 5th of September, 1847, bulls appointing him Bishop of Buffalo. His humility prompted him to decline the honor; but prudent priests urged him to accept, and he yielded because his duty as visitor had become extremely onerous. He was consecrated on the 17th of October in the cathedral of New York, and at once proceeded to his diocese, taking up his residence at the church of St. Louis till the trustees requested his departure. The first year he spent in the visitation of his diocese, giving missions and confirming. In the course of this constant travel he was thrown from a sleigh and severely injured. When fully acquainted with his diocese and its wants he attempted to establish a college, but his first efforts failed; he founded a hospital, introduced the Ladies of the Sacred Heart, who opened an academy, and also the Sisters of Our Lady of Charity and Sisters of St. Joseph. The charitable Nicholas Devereux, of Utica, was instrumental in obtaining from Rome a colony of Recollects, or Reformed Franciscans, who in time established a prosperous seminary and college at Allegany. The trustees of St. Louis' Church renewed the insubordinate conduct which had already caused scandal, and they refused to submit even to the delegate of the Sovereign Pontiff. Their rebellion led to the closing of the church, and for years was a source of pain to Bishop Timon. In 1857 the Lazarists, to the bishop's joy, opened the seminary of Our Lady of the Angels, near Niagara City—an institution which has prospered. Besides his labors in the diocese, in which Bishop Timon held several synods, he went to Rome at the time of the definition of the Immaculate Conception, on the anniversary of St. Peter, and at the time of the canonization of the Japanese martyrs; he also attended the Provincial Councils of New York.

RT. REV. JOHN LOUGHLIN, D.D.
Born in County Down, Ireland, 1810.
Ordained Oct. 18, 1840; Consecrated Bishop of
Brooklyn, Oct. 30, 1853.

RT. REV. LOUIS DE GOESBRIAND, D.D.
Born at St. Urbain, France, Aug. 4, 1816.
Ordained July 13, 1840; Consecrated Bishop of
Burlington, Oct. 30, 1853.

RT. REV. STEPHEN VINCENT RYAN, D.D.
Born at Almonte, Canada, Jan. 1, 1825.
Ordained June 24, 1849; Consecrated Bishop of
Buffalo, Nov. 8, 1868.

RT. REV. HENRY P. NORTHROP, D.D.
Born in Charleston in 1841.
Consecrated Bishop of Rosaha and Vicar Apostolic of
North Carolina Jan. 8, 1882; Bishop of
Charleston, Jan. 27, 1883.

In 1852 he laid the corner-stone of St. Joseph's Cathedral, which was dedicated in 1855. Bishop Timon continued his labors till he was attacked in 1866 with erysipelas—a disease that in his enfeebled state was highly dangerous. He took medical advice, but continued to discharge his duties till Monday in Holy Week, when at the close of the devotions he asked prayers for a happy death. With great difficulty he reached his bed, and died piously the next day, April 16, 1867.

RIGHT REV. STEPHEN VINCENT RYAN, C.M.,

Second Bishop of Buffalo.

STEPHEN VINCENT RYAN was born near the village of Almonte, Upper Canada, January 1, 1825, his parents having emigrated some time before from the County of Clare, in Ireland. While he was still a child the family removed to Pottsville, in Schuylkill County, Pennsylvania. In 1840, when Stephen was about fifteen years of age, he was sent to St. Charles' Seminary, Philadelphia. On the 5th of May, 1844, he entered the order of the Lazarist Fathers at Cape Girardeau, Missouri, and completed his studies for the ministry at St. Mary's of the Barrens. He was ordained priest in St. Louis, June 24, 1849, by the Most Rev. Archbishop Kenrick. The young priest remained for a time in Perry County, Missouri, as professor and prefect in St. Mary's of the Barrens, and was subsequently professor at Cape Girardeau. He then became president of St. Vincent's College, and filled that important position until the year 1857, when he was made visitor of the Congregation of the Mission in the United States. While holding this position he resided at St. Louis till it was decided to remove the mother-house and novitiate of the community to Germantown, Philadelphia. The Very Rev. Dr. Ryan took an important part in creating the new establishment, and made it his residence till he was elected to the see of Buffalo. He was consecrated in his episcopal city, by Archbishop, now Cardinal, McCloskey, on the 8th of November, 1868. The original diocese of Buffalo had been diminished by the erection of a see at Rochester, and, when Bishop Ryan assumed the administration, comprised only the counties of Erie, Niagara, Genesee, Orleans, Chautauqua, Wyoming, Cattaraugus, Steuben, Chemung, Tioga, Allegany, and Schuyler. It contained a Catholic population of probably 90,000 souls, who had a hundred churches, attended by more than a hundred priests. Besides the seminary established at the bishop's house, the Fathers of the Congregation of the Mission had a fine seminary, dedicated to Our Lady of the Angels, at the Suspension Bridge, and the Reformed Franciscans had a college and seminary at Allegany; Redemptorists, Passionists, and Oblates had establishments; the Christian Brothers and several orders of Sisters were engaged in training the young or employing the resources of Catholic charity for the relief of human miseries. In a few years the Fathers of the Society of Jesus from Germany came to open Canisius College, in Buffalo.

The Catholic population has not of late years increased much by immigration, and the natural progress by births has been reduced by the removal of many westward.

DIOCESE OF BURLINGTON.

RIGHT REV. LOUIS DE GOESBRIAND,

First Bishop of Burlington.

LOUIS DE GOESBRIAND was born at St. Urbain, in the diocese of Quimper, in the Catholic province of Brittany, France, on the 4th of August, 1816. After pursuing a classical course at Quimper and Pont Croix-Finisterre he entered the seminary at Quimper, and there and at St. Sulpice, Paris, went through a thorough theological course. He was ordained priest in Paris on the 13th of July, 1840, by the Right Rev. Dr. Rosati, Bishop of St. Louis, and, devoting himself to the American mission, came to the diocese of Cincinnati, where he exercised the ministry from September, 1840, to October, 1847, chiefly as pastor of St. Louis' Church, near Canton, and St. Genevieve's, in Holmes County, and at Toledo, whence he attended Manhattan, Providence, Napoleon, and Decatur. On the erection of the diocese of Cleveland Bishop Rappe made Rev. Mr. de Goesbriand his vicar-general and rector of his cathedral, which positions he discharged zealously till he was appointed bishop of the newly-erected see of Burlington, Vermont. Catholicity had made slow progress in that State, although a French fort and chapel were built on Isle La Motte as early as 1666. Rev. Mr. Matignon visited the Vermont Catholics in 1815, followed by Rev. Messrs. Mignault, Paul McQuade, James Fitton, and Bishop Fenwick. About 1830, for the first time, the Catholics in Vermont had a resident pastor, Rev. Jeremiah O'Callaghan. Their numbers increased in spite of opposition, and converts began to come into the Church. When Bishop de Goesbriand took possession of his see on the 6th of November, 1853, there were in the whole State only eight churches and five priests, but not a school or institution of any kind. With his missionary experience in the West, Bishop de

Goesbriand began the work of building up a diocese with all the zeal of a chivalric French priest of ancestral renown.

He appealed to France for priests, and from that country and elsewhere gradually gathered a set of devoted clergymen. Very soon after he assumed the administration he introduced Sisters of Providence, who opened a day-school, took charge of the orphans, and visited the sick. Bishop de Goesbriand was already making progress to meet the wants of the twenty-five thousand Catholics. By 1860, though the number of the faithful had not increased rapidly, there were twenty-nine churches and thirteen priests. The next decade showed an increase of Catholic population to 34,000, with 38 churches and 28 priests. The Sisters of Providence extended their houses to Winooski, and there were Catholic schools in Burlington, Winooski, Rutland, and Burlington. The episcopal city had a fine Gothic cathedral, built of stone quarried on Isle La Motte, the cradle of Catholicity in Vermont. In the next fifteen years the population had increased steadily, the Catholic baptisms in 1883 being 2,037 out of 7,350 infants born in the State in the year. The churches had nearly doubled, numbering 71 in 1884, with 37 priests, 15 parochial schools with 2,846 pupils. The Sisters of Providence are aided by Sisters of Mercy, Sisters of St. Joseph, and Sisters of the Congregation of Our Lady.

DIOCESE OF CHARLESTON.

RIGHT REV. JOHN ENGLAND,

First Bishop of Charleston.

JOHN ENGLAND, destined to be one of the greatest of American bishops, was born in Cork, Ireland, September 23, 1786, of a family that had suffered severely under the unchristian penal laws. Inheriting their piety, he grew up deeply attached to his faith. After spending two years at the study of law John England renounced the world and entered Carlow College to prepare for the priesthood. While a seminarian he showed his missionary spirit by undertaking the spiritual instruction of the militia quartered near the college, and by founding an asylum for unprotected women and a free school. Before his ordination he preached in Carlow cathedral, and was appointed president of the Theological Seminary at Cork. After his ordination, October 10, 1808, he delivered a series of lectures in the cathedral, and became chaplain of the prison. Soon after he was placed at the head of St. Mary's Theological Seminary by Bishop Moylan, and appointed by his successor, Bishop Murphy, parish priest of Bandon, a most bigoted place, where Catholics and their clergy were subjected to every form of insult.

When the diocese of Charleston was established, embracing the Carolinas and Georgia, Dr. England was selected for the mitre, and was consecrated on the 21st of September, 1820, by Bishop Murphy in Cork. On reaching his diocese Bishop England found only two churches and two priests. He made a visitation of his diocese, gathering Catholic families together, encouraging them to persevere in the faith till he could obtain priests for them. To recruit his clergy he established a classical school in Charleston, the teachers being candidates for holy orders, who pursued their theology under the bishop. He revived classical studies in the South and took part in scientific and literary associations. As a preacher he was universally admired, Protestants flocking to hear his discourses. So deeply did the Catholic bishop impress them that, at the instance of the Southern members, he was invited to preach before the members of the House of Representatives at Washington.

The diocese committed to Dr. England's charge involved great exertion and labor, from which he never shrunk, but he was alive to the wants of the Church in the whole republic. He identified himself with the country from his consecration, and became thoroughly American in feeling. He endeavored to organize the Church in each of the States under his care by giving it an annual convention of the clergy with lay delegates from the various congregations. In these conventions affairs of general interest were discussed. He was the first, too, to establish a Catholic paper, so as to give the Church a medium for spreading information, exciting faith and perseverance, and refuting error by the clear assertion of dogmatic truth. The *United States Catholic Miscellany*, founded and conducted by Bishop England, met and repelled attacks on the Church with wonderful ability, forcing men who wished a fair fame to be guarded in repeating the oft-refuted and stale calumnies against Catholics. Bishop England's articles were read and copied in all parts of the country, producing incalculable good. But while his mind was given to the greatest topics, he never neglected his duties as bishop or as what he had always to be—a hard-working missionary priest. He was devoted in his attention to his flock, and when the yellow fever and other epidemics visited Charleston he was untiring in his attention to the sick, hastening in the hottest days to the bedside of the dying, from whom all others shrunk in horror. The condition of the colored people excited all his sympathy, but his efforts to educate and improve them were at that time too little in unison with the public spirit to be maintained. He made sacrifices to save some from the evils of slavery. In one case a Catholic had bought a beautiful quadroon, and, finding her possessed of a refined and pure mind, married her. Their two daughters were educated in the best schools of the North, and possessed all the accomplishments and manners of cultivated ladies. On their father's death they supposed themselves heiresses of his property, but, to their indescribable horror, found that their father had neglected to make out the legal papers freeing their mother. They were slaves and part of their father's property, which all devolved on a distant relative. The hard-hearted man not only took the property, but sent the two girls to be sold, that he might add the price to his wealth. Bishop England gave all his own means and what he could procure to rescue the girls from the terrible fate before them.

Bishop England, in 1834, obtained a colony of Ursuline nuns from Ireland, and organized the community of Sisters of Our Lady of Mercy, founded in 1829 by Misses Mary and Honora O'Gorman and Teresa Barry. This order still maintains its good work.

Bishop England was one of the most earnest promoters of the project of a Provincial Council, and sat in the first four held at Baltimore, where his learning and sound judgment contributed greatly to the good accomplished. He thus exercised an influence on the whole Church in the United States; and the Holy Father employed him even beyond the limits of our territory, appointing him, March 15, 1833, Visitor-Apostolic of Santo Domingo. He twice visited that island to negotiate such arrangements as would enable the Pope to appoint bishops for that long-bereaved Church. In fulfilment of the duties thus imposed upon him Dr. England twice visited the island where the first bishopric in America had been established, and did much to prepare for a revival of discipline.

Besides all these labors Bishop England found time to write important works on religious subjects. His incessant labors at last told on a frame naturally vigorous. Returning from Europe in 1841, he was no fewer than fifty-two days at sea, and when dysentery broke out on the vessel he was constantly beside the sick till he himself was prostrated. Landing at Philadelphia in an extremely enfeebled condition, he refused all rest, but preached and lectured with all his wonted brilliancy in Philadelphia and Baltimore. After reaching Charleston he rallied, but the recovery was only transient. He prepared for the last moment with calmness. After addressing his clergy he received the last sacraments, and expired April 11, 1842, mourned by all the inhabitants of the city.

His successor, Bishop Reynolds, collected the writings of Bishop England in six volumes, which form one of the most prized works in the libraries of the clergy. A selection of the most remarkable writings of Bishop England, edited by Hugh P. McElrone, was published at Baltimore in 1884.

RIGHT REV. WILLIAM CLANCY,

Bishop of Oriense, Coadjutor of Charleston, and Vicar-Apostolic of British Guiana.

WILLIAM CLANCY, a native of Cork, Ireland, a graduate of Carlow College, after acting as curate at that institution and filling a chair of theology, was selected, October 30, 1834, as coadjutor to Bishop England, and was consecrated Bishop of Oriense in Carlow cathedral, February 1, 1835, by the Right Rev. Dr. Nolan. Owing to a serious illness he did not reach Charleston till November 21. He remained only a short time in the diocese, but aided Bishop England materially, and sat in the Third Provincial Council of Baltimore in April, 1837. On the 12th of that month, however, he had been appointed Vicar-Apostolic of British Guiana, and proceeded to that province. His administration proved so unsatisfactory that he incurred censure, and the management of the vicariate was in 1838 committed to another. Bishop Clancy returned to Ireland, and died there in 1847.

RIGHT REV. IGNATIUS ALOYSIUS REYNOLDS,

Second Bishop of Charleston.

IGNATIUS ALOYSIUS REYNOLDS was born near Bardstown, Kentucky, August 22, 1798, of one of the Catholic families that emigrated from Maryland to that State. Trained under Bishop Flaget and Dr. David, he early showed a real vocation, and was one of the first students in the Theological Seminary at Bardstown. Completing his course at St. Mary's, Baltimore, the young Kentuckian was ordained there October 24, 1823. Returning to his native State, he became professor and subsequently president of St. Joseph's College and professor in the seminary. He bore his share in the missionary duties, especially during the visitations of the cholera. He succeeded Bishop David as ecclesiastical superior of the Sisters of Charity, and was for many years vicar-general of the diocese, before and after the removal of the see to Louisville.

The Fathers of the Fifth Council of Baltimore nominated Rev. Mr. Reynolds as successor to Dr. England, and he was consecrated, by Archbishop Purcell, Bishop of Charleston March 19, 1844, in the cathedral of Cincinnati. He made frequent visitations of his diocese, gathered the scattered Catholics, besides winning many converts to the faith. His flock numbered about twelve thousand in a population of two millions, but the diocese of Charleston was heavily in debt; the frame cathedral and bishop's house were fast falling into ruins. Bishop Reynolds visited Europe to obtain aid, and on his return assembled his clergy for a retreat. He began to collect means for a suitable cathedral, and secured a site, but the work was not begun till May, 1850. Bishop Reynolds had the consolation of seeing it dedicated in April, 1854. His labor in his diocese was active and unremitting, although his health was never rugged. He attended the Sixth and Seventh Councils of Baltimore and the First Plenary Council; but his strength failed and he died of congestion of the lungs, March 9, 1855, having, as his fellow-bishops declared, "worn himself out in the service of his

Church." The whole diocese of Charleston deplored the loss of the kind, generous, and laborious bishop.

RIGHT REV. PATRICK NIESEN LYNCH,

Third Bishop of Charleston.

PATRICK NIESEN LYNCH was born at Clones, Ireland, March 10, 1817, but when only two years old was brought to this country by his parents, who settled at Cheraw, South Carolina. He was one of the first to enter the seminary of St. John the Baptist when it was opened by Bishop England in Charleston, and after his preparatory training there was sent to the College of the Propaganda at Rome. There he took rank as one of the remarkable scholars, winning his doctor's cap with honor, and storing his mind with theological and scientific learning. After his ordination in 1840 he returned to Charleston and was stationed at the cathedral. In 1844 he was appointed to St. Mary's Church, of which he was pastor for eleven years, securing the love, respect, and admiration of his flock, especially during the yellow fever of 1848. Besides his parochial duties he was principal of the Collegiate Institute, and for many years vicar-general of the diocese. On the death of Bishop Reynolds the Very Rev. Dr. Lynch became administrator of the diocese, and on the 11th of December, 1857, was elected to the see. He was consecrated on the 14th of the ensuing March. Catholicity had not grown in the Southern States, as it had at the North, by immigration, and difficulties of many kinds embarrassed the bishops. Dr. Lynch took up his burden zealously, but the Civil War, which began near his episcopal city, proved almost fatal to his diocese. In the first year of the war his cathedral, his residence, with the fine library and the diocesan archives, were swept away by a conflagration, and the bombardment and siege of Charleston ruined and scattered his flock. In the burning of Columbia by Sherman the church, college, and convent in that city perished.

During the war Bishop Lynch visited Europe in the interests of the Confederacy, and bore to the Pope a letter from President Davis. He returned to his diocese to find all in ruins, priests and people scattered, a debt of more than a hundred thousand dollars, and a debt of even larger amount to be incurred to restore what was absolutely necessary; for the governments created after the peace were more ruinous even than the desolating armies. Resources in his own diocese there were none. Bishop Lynch was forced into a kind of exile to raise means to pay off the load of debt, and by his exertions he reduced it to a comparatively small amount. His mission duty in his diocese, especially in the yellow fever of 1871, was unremitting. In 1877 he underwent a surgical operation in Boston which gave him temporary relief from a distressing malady, but in a year or two the difficulty returned, and it was evident that it would ultimately prove fatal. Physicians urged quiet, but the necessities of the diocese required on the part of the bishop almost constant travel in visitations through the diocese or collecting tours without. Bishop Lynch returned from a visitation in the northern part of the State of South Carolina in December, 1881, so prostrated that he was brought to the brink of the grave. He rallied, and there was hope that a change of air might restore him; but his strength waned, and he prepared for death. He made his profession of faith, asked forgiveness for all his shortcomings, and, having received the last sacraments, he gave his last benediction to his clergy, and expired Feb. 26, 1882. He had previously forbidden all display, and especially any sermon, at his funeral. Bishop Lynch was a learned and forcible writer, and for years contributed to Catholic publications. His articles on the Vatican Council, the liquefaction of the Blood of St. Januarius, and on Galileo are among the most notable.

RIGHT REV. HENRY P. NORTHROP,

Second Vicar-Apostolic of North Carolina and Fourth Bishop of Charleston.

HENRY PINCKNEY NORTHROP was born in Charleston, S. C., in 1841, and, after preliminary studies in his native city, entered Georgetown College, and concluded his university course at Mount St. Mary's, where he was graduated. Feeling himself called to the priesthood, young Northrop entered the seminary at Emmittsburg, but soon proceeded to Rome, where he was one of the early students of the American College. After his ordination in Rome he remained some time in that city pursuing special studies till his father's death recalled him to his native land. Entering on his life as a missionary, the Rev. Mr. Northrop was stationed at Wilmington and then at New Berne, N. C. In 1871 he was called to Charleston and made assistant at the cathedral. There he remained till 1877, when he was made pastor of St. Patrick's. His piety, zeal in the discharge of his priestly duties, and his skill in management of affairs led to his election as Bishop of Rosalia and Vicar-Apostolic of North Carolina in 1881. He was consecrated in the cathedral of Baltimore by Archbishop Gibbons on the 8th of January, 1882. He carried on the good work so successfully begun in that State by Archbishop Gibbons, but on the death of Bishop Lynch he was, by a brief of Pope Leo XIII., translated, on the 27th of January, 1883, to the see of Charleston, still remaining Vicar-Apostolic of North Carolina. He has 17 priests with 26 churches and chapels in South Carolina; and 9 priests attending 20 churches and chapels in the North State. The Catholic population of South Carolina is about 10,000, that of North Carolina 2,200.

DIOCESE OF CLEVELAND.

RIGHT REV. AMADEUS RAPPE,

First Bishop of Cleveland.

AMADEUS RAPPE was born in the diocese of Arras, France, in the year 1797, and enjoyed so few educational advantages that he began life as a shepherd boy. He possessed talent and ambition, and acquired an education. After his ordination he came to America and joined the diocese of Cincinnati about 1840. He was assigned to laborious missions—Delaware, Pikestown, and Portsmouth—but soon had charge of St. Joseph's, Maumee, with Manhattan, Providence, Napoleon, and Defiance as stations. By 1845 he had churches at Providence and Defiance. Soon after he obtained as assistant the Rev. Louis de Goesbriand, now Bishop of Burlington, the two priests living at Toledo and attending all the Catholics in the valley of the Maumee. When the portion of Ohio lying north of latitude 40° 41' was erected into a separate diocese in 1847, with a see at Cleveland, the energy and zeal of Rev. Mr. Rappe induced his selection to wear the mitre. He was consecrated bishop of Cleveland at Cincinnati on the 10th of October, 1847. His diocese, when he took possession of it, contained about twenty-five thousand Catholics, having thirty-four churches attended by twenty-eight priests, including some Fathers of the Precious Blood. Some Sisters of the same rule maintained an academy. Trained as a hard-working missionary, he labored to give his flock more priests and churches, establishing a theological seminary at an early date. In 1850 he founded an orphan asylum and introduced Sisters of the rule of St. Augustine to direct an hospital at Cleveland. The next year the Ursulines opened an academy in the same city, and in a few years others at Toledo and Tiffin. St. John's College, succeeded by a Preparatory Seminary, was founded in

1854. Brothers of Mary and of the Holy Cross, Sisters of the Sacred Heart of Mary, the Sisters of Charity of Madame d'Youville's foundation in 1864, the Sisters of the Humility of Mary in 1868, and in the following year the Franciscans at Cleveland, the Jesuit Fathers at Toledo, all came to labor among the Catholics of his diocese, who had by 1870 increased to the number of one hundred thousand. The 34 churches and 28 priests were represented by 107 priests and 160 churches. The schools in the diocese of Cleveland numbered ninety, and charitable institutions abounded; Sisters of the Good Shepherd, Little Sisters of the Poor, Franciscan Sisters of the Poor directing institutions for the care of the sick and erring. Bishop Rappe had built up the diocese, and might have expected in his declining years to enjoy a happy old age amid the clergy and people whom he had guided as a faithful pastor for twenty years; but this was not to be. An ungrateful opposition sprang up, calumny assailed even the venerable bishop, who with a broken heart resigned his see on the 22d of August, 1870, and retired to the diocese of his good friend Bishop de Goesbriand, of Burlington. There he resumed his old missionary life, laboring assiduously among the people, giving missions and retreats, and earnestly advocating the cause of temperance. He died piously at St. Alban's, Vermont, on the 9th of September, 1877. Cleveland claimed the remains of her first bishop, which were conveyed to that city and interred with all the honor due to his life and services.

RIGHT REV. RICHARD GILMOUR,

Second Bishop of Cleveland.

RICHARD GILMOUR was born in Glasgow, Scotland, on the 28th of September, 1824, of a family of stanch Covenanters. When he was only four years of age his parents emigrated to Canada, and finally settled in Pennsylvania. When young Gilmour was about nineteen he one Sunday entered a Catholic church some five miles from his home, and was so struck by the sermon he heard and by the devotion of the people that he began to read, and, corresponding to the grace of God, became a Catholic. Resolving to devote himself to the service of the altar, Mr. Gilmour entered Mount St. Mary's Seminary, and at the close of his studies was ordained priest by Archbishop Purcell, August 30, 1852. He was first appointed to missions in southern Ohio—Portsmouth, Ironton, Gallipolis, Wilkesville—laboring for five years to give every mission a church and a school. When he was made pastor of St. Patrick's Church, Cincinnati, in 1857, he set to work to erect a school-house, and in time had the finest building of the kind in the State. No one took a more active part towards advancing Catholic education than Rev. Mr. Gilmour. Besides his labors in building schools, he compiled "School Recreations," a collection of songs and hymns, a Bible History, and a series of readers. After being assigned to a professor's chair in the seminary of Mount St. Mary's of the West, Rev. Mr. Gilmour was made pastor of St. Joseph's Church, Dayton, and there at once prepared the plans for a school-house. On the resignation of Dr. Rappe the bishops of the province of Cincinnati nominated this zealous priest for the see of Cleveland, and he was elected to it on the 15th of February, 1872, and was consecrated on the 14th of April in the cathedral of Cincinnati by Archbishop Purcell. From his entrance into his diocese Bishop Gilmour advanced Catholic interests with all the activity and energy of his nature. Catholic education was made paramount, and, to defend the interests and principles of the Church against the bigots who swarmed in that part of the State, he founded the *Catholic Universe*, which, under the editorship of Manly Tello, Esq., is one of the ablest papers of the country. The increase of Catholic churches and schools excited the bitterest feelings, and the advocates of the Protestant system of public schools attempted to hamper, if not crush, them by heavy taxation. Bishop Gilmour met them in the courts and won a complete victory. The Catholics of the diocese, roused to the importance of preserving the faith in their families, are active and alert. At the close of the year 1884 the population of the diocese of Cleveland was estimated at nearly 170,000; the annual baptisms at 7,965; the average number of children attending the 123 parochial schools is 23,500. One hundred and eighty-four priests attend 217 churches, 21 chapels, and 71 stations; and a theological seminary, with forty-four seminarians, promises priests to fill vacancies and continue the work of the ministry.

DIOCESE OF COLUMBUS.

RIGHT REV. SYLVESTER H. ROSECRANS,

First Bishop of Columbus.

SYLVESTER HORTON ROSECRANS was born in Homer, Licking County, Ohio, February 5, 1827, his parents, Crandall and Johanna Rosecrans, of Wilkesbarre, Pennsylvania, being both Protestants. Stephen Hopkins, one of the signers of the Declaration of Independence, was one of his maternal ancestors. While a student at Kenyon College, Ohio, young Rosecrans received a letter from his brother, then an officer in the United States Army and professor at West Point, announcing his conversion to the Catholic faith, and giving his reasons for the grave step. Sylvester too examined, prayed, and was convinced. He was received into the Church, and completed his university course at St. John's College, Fordham. Bishop Purcell, of Cincinnati, received him as a seminarian, and sent him to Rome to study at the Propaganda. After his ordination in 1852 he was appointed to St. Thomas' Church, Cincinnati, but was soon made assistant at the cathedral. There for seven years he discharged his duties as a missionary priest, besides giving his daily attendance as a professor in the theological seminary. One night, returning from the seminary, he was attacked by two ruffians and received a pistol-ball in his body. Without informing any one on reaching the house, he attempted to extract the ball, but was discovered and a surgeon summoned. From 1859 to 1861 he was president of a college connected with the seminary, and edited the *Catholic Telegraph*. In 1862 he was appointed Bishop of Pompeiopolis and Auxiliary of Cincinnati, and was consecrated by Archbishop Purcell on the feast of the Annunciation. For six years Bishop Rosecrans continued to aid the venerable archbishop in the affairs of the diocese in which he was so well known. On the election of the Rev. Mr. Fitzgerald to the see of Little Rock, Dr. Rosecrans assumed the pastorship of St. Patrick's Church, Columbus, and a few months afterwards the diocese of Columbus was created. It embraced the part of the State south of 40° 41', and lying between the Ohio and Scioto rivers, as well as the counties of Franklin, Delaware, and Morrow. The Right Rev. Dr. Rosecrans became Bishop of Columbus March 3, 1868. The portion of the State thus assigned to his exclusive care contained about forty churches and as many priests, with forty thousand Catholics. St. Joseph's, with its Dominican convent, the cradle of Catholicity in Ohio, was in his diocese. At Columbus there were three Catholic churches, Sisters of the Good Shepherd, of Notre Dame, and Franciscan Sisters of the Poor, the first organization of the faithful dating back to 1833. Soon after the erection of the see the Dominican Sisters, aided by two charitable gentleman, erected their academy of St. Mary's of the Springs near Columbus. Bishop Rosecrans soon began the erection of St. Joseph's Cathedral near the State House, and made it the most substantial and imposing edifice in the capital of the State. In 1871 St Aloysius' Seminary for young men, erected by his efforts, was opened for scholars. Bishop Rosecrans fixed on the 20th of October, 1878, for the consecration of his cathedral, and the solemnity was attended by eight bishops and some fifty priests. In the afternoon, about the time of Vespers, he was seized with a hemorrhage, and, though medical aid was summoned, it was soon evident that the case was hopeless. After receiving the last sacraments Bishop Rosecrans expired on Monday, the 21st, the next solemn function in the cathedral being his own funeral rites.

Bishop Rosecrans was a man of solid learning and an active administrator. In life he was simple, averse to all ostentation, living at the orphan asylum, and making the fatherless his companions.

The diocese during his episcopate did not increase greatly in the number of Catholics, but he left 52 priests, 77 churches, and 28 parochial schools, with hospitals and asylums for the fifty thousand Catholics under his care.

RT. REV. RICHARD GILMOUR, D.D.
Born at Glasgow, Sept. 28, 1824.
Ordained August 30, 1852; Consecrated Bishop of Cleveland, April 14, 1872.

RT. REV. CAMILLUS PAUL MAES, D.D.
Born at Courtrai, Belgium, May 13, 1846.
Ordained Dec. 18, 1868; Consecrated Bishop of Covington, Jan. 25, 1885.

RT. REV. JOHN AMBROSE WATTERSON, D.D.
Born at Blairsville, Penn., May 27, 1844.
Ordained Aug. 8, 1868; Consecrated Bishop of Columbus, Aug. 8, 1880.

RT. REV. HENRY COSGROVE.
Born at Williamsport, Pa., Dec. 19, 1834.
Ordained Aug. 1857; Consecrated Bishop of Davenport, Sept. 14, 1884.

RIGHT REV. JOHN AMBROSE WATTERSON,

Second Bishop of Columbus.

JOHN AMBROSE WATTERSON was born at Blairsville, Indiana County, Pennsylvania, May 27, 1844. At an early age he was sent to Mount St. Mary's, Emmittsburg, in which time-honored institution he was graduated in 1865. After pursuing theological studies there he was ordained priest at St. Vincent's Abbey by Bishop Domenec, August 8, 1868. By permission of his bishop he returned to Emmittsburg and became a member of the faculty of his Alma Mater. In October, 1877, he was chosen to succeed the Rev. John McCloskey, D.D., as president of the college, and on the 24th of June following the degree of Doctor of Divinity was conferred upon him by the faculty of Georgetown College. He was selected in 1880 to succeed Bishop Rosecrans in the see of Columbus, and, even before his consecration, was called upon to grapple with the financial difficulties of the diocese to which he had been called. He was consecrated on Sunday, August 8, 1880, in St. Joseph's Cathedral, Columbus, by the Right Rev. William H. Elder, administrator of Cincinnati. As he passed out of the sanctuary he stepped aside to raise his consecrated hands in benediction over the head of the mother who had taught him his first prayer to God.

The diocese of Columbus is a compact one, increasing by natural growth rather than by immigration. Feeling that the future of his flock depends on the education of the young, Bishop Watterson, who had so long been engaged in training youth, had by the close of 1884 established a Catholic college at Columbus, and has besides three academies, thirty-two parochial schools attended by 6,482 children—a very large proportion out of a population which the parish reports fixed at 50,500, the annual baptisms being 2,291.

DIOCESE OF COVINGTON.

RIGHT REV. GEORGE A. CARRELL,

First Bishop of Covington.

GEORGE ALOYSIUS CARRELL was born in the Penn mansion, Philadelphia, June 13, 1803, of a family that had settled in that city before the Revolutionary War. At the age of ten he was sent to Mount St. Mary's, but was graduated at Georgetown. He then entered the Society of Jesus, but completed his theological course at Mount St. Mary's, and was ordained in Philadelphia in 1829. After being assistant at St. Augustine's, in that city, attending missions in New Jersey, and afterwards pastor of Holy Trinity, he was stationed at Wilmington, Delaware. There for several years he effected great good, establishing an academy and a school on a solid basis. Having been admitted to the Society of Jesus, he was appointed professor in the University of St. Louis, and subsequently president of that institution, and at a later date of one near Cinciunati. When the eastern part of Kentucky was formed into a diocese, with a see at Covington, Father Carrell was elected to it, July 29, 1853, and received consecration on All Saints' Day. The district was large, but contained only ten churches and seven priests. His first care was to meet the wants of his flock, especially by giving them schools; for this purpose he introduced the Ursuline, Benedictine, and Visitation Nuns, the Sisters of Charity, and Sisters of the Poor of St. Francis. Self-denying and laborious, Bishop Carrell lived to gather thirty-three priests in his diocese, to see forty-two churches and many stations attended by them. The Benedictine Fathers came to minister to the Germans, Rev. Dom Louis M. Fink being prior. Though Kentucky was the scene of many military operations during the Civil War, the diocese of Covington was spared much of the horrors, and religion steadily advanced. Bishop Carrell lived to repair to some extent the evil caused by the war. He died on the 25th of September, 1868, after having long endured with cheerful patience the sufferings caused by a complication of diseases.

RIGHT REV. AUGUSTUS MARY TOEBBE,

Second Bishop of Covington.

AUGUSTUS MARY TOEBBE was born on the 17th of January, 1829, at Meppen, in the kingdom of Hanover. After passing through the Gymnasium in that place he began to prepare for commercial life, but his pious inclinations led him to seek to serve God in the ecclesiastical state. To this end he came to America in 1852, and entered St. Mary's Seminary, Cincinnati. He was ordained by Archbishop Purcell, September 14, 1854, and assigned to a laborious district extending from Columbia to Ripley. Here he labored night and day with the utmost zeal till January, 1857, when he was made pastor of St. Boniface's Church, Cumminsville; after about a year's duty here Rev. Mr. Toebbe became rector of St. Philomena's Church in Cincinnati. Esteemed as a learned no less than a zealous priest, he was one of the theologians at the First Plenary Council. On the 27th of September, 1869, bulls issued naming Rev. Mr. Toebbe to the see of Covington, and he was consecrated on the 9th of January, 1870, in St. Philomena's Church, by Bishop Rosecrans. On taking possession of his see Bishop Toebbe gave his attention to those Catholics who, isolated from churches, neglected their duties and were overlooked. By this good work he rescued many, and, inspiring parents with a zeal for the salvation of their children, saved another generation. Under his prudent and careful direction churches increased, and the clergy emulated his zeal. He visited Rome in 1878, returning by way of Germany, France, and Ireland. On the 14th of September, 1879, he celebrated the silver jubilee of his priesthood, and two days after opened his Diocesan Synod. He introduced the Sisters of the Good Shepherd and the Sisters of Notre Dame. His life was one of labor, privation, and prayer. He lived to see fifty-two churches in his diocese for his forty thousand Catholic souls, attended by fifty-six priests, with orphan and foundling asylums, a hospital, and, best of all, thirty-five parochial schools. He died, universally regretted, May 2, 1884.

RIGHT REV. CAMILLUS PAUL MAES,

Third Bishop of Covington.

THE third Bishop of Covington, Right Rev. Camillus Paul Maes, is a native of Belgium, born at Courtrai, in West Flanders, March 13, 1846. He made his classical studies in the college of his native city, and entered the seminary at Bruges to prepare for the priesthood. Desirous, however, of devoting himself to the missions in this country, he proceeded to the American College at Louvain, where he completed his theological course and was ordained for the diocese of Detroit, December 18, 1868. On his arrival in Michigan he was made pastor of St. Peter's, Mount Clemens; and, after two years' service there, was assigned to Monroe, one of the oldest seats of Catholicity. Here he became pastor of St. Mary's Church in 1871, and two years later of St. John's. In this city he was soon known as a learned and studious priest, full of zeal in the discharge of his ministry, and devoted to everything that bore on education and charity. His leisure was given to study, and he became greatly interested in the early history of the Church in this country. He obtained a mass of papers relating to the Rev. Charles Nerinckx, a Belgian priest who labored as a saint on the Kentucky mission and founded the Sisters of Loretto; but they were given to him on condition that he should write the life of that pioneer priest. His work is one of the most thorough and interesting in the Catholic libraries. In 1880 Rev. Mr. Maes became secretary to Bishop

Borgess, and in that capacity he organized the collections for the support of the diocesan seminary and rendered essential services in every department of administration.

In September, 1884, he was elected to the see of Covington, and attended the Plenary Council of Baltimore. After its close he was consecrated in the cathedral at Covington by Archbishop Elder, of Cincinnati, assisted by Bishop Borgess of Detroit and Bishop McCloskey of Louisville, on the 25th of January, 1885.

DIOCESE OF DAVENPORT.

RIGHT REV. JOHN McMULLEN,

First Bishop of Davenport.

JOHN MCMULLEN was born on the 8th of March, 1833, at Ballinahinch, County Down, Ireland. When he was in his fourth year his family emigrated to Canada, but finally settled at Chicago. There John was graduated from St. Mary's College in 1853, and, proceeding to Rome, studied in the Urban College. He was ordained in 1858 and appointed pastor of St. Luke's, but took an active part in erecting churches on the suburbs of Chicago. He was president of the University of St. Mary's of the Lake for four years, and was then for three years professor of Hebrew and philosophy at the seminary. In October, 1870, he was named pastor of the cathedral, and in 1877 vicar-general of the diocese. During the illness of Bishop Duggan his position was one of difficulty and trial, and he appealed to Rome before it was generally recognized that the unfortunate bishop was not responsible. On the death of Bishop Foley the Rev. Mr. McMullen became administrator of the diocese, but in July, 1881, the pope selected him to fill the important see of Davenport. He was consecrated bishop on July 25, 1881. His incessant toil in making the visitations of his diocese, during which he confirmed six thousand persons, and his endeavors to meet all the wants which he discovered, broke down his health, and physicians, unable to decide what his malady really was, recommended a change of climate. After a short stay at Los Angeles, California, Bishop McMullen returned to Davenport, where he was soon prostrated again, cancer in the stomach having declared itself. Incessant care and anxiety, with litigation which he found necessary, had told fatally on his constitution. He lingered for a few months, bearing his sufferings with heroic firmness. Fortified by all the sacraments, Bishop McMullen expired at four o'clock on the morning of July 4, 1883. From his entrance into the diocese Dr. McMullen had won the esteem of the Protestant community and the loving veneration of his own flock for his life-long devotion to works of piety and charity.

RIGHT REV. HENRY COSGROVE,

Second Bishop of Davenport.

HENRY COSGROVE was born in Williamsport, Pa., on the 19th of December, 1834. His parents, John and Bridget Cosgrove, had emigrated to this country some years before, but, when their son was eleven years of age, removed to the West and settled at Dubuque. There Henry was often an acolyte in the cathedral when Bishop Loras officiated, and when he was fifteen he began his studies for the priesthood under Very Rev. Mr. Crétin. After going through his higher and theological course at St. Mary's, Perry County, and the seminary at Carondelet, Henry Cosgrove was ordained by Bishop Smythe, being the first to receive holy orders at his hands. On the 6th of September, 1857, eleven days after his ordination, the young priest was sent to Davenport as assistant to Rev. A. Trévis, of St. Marguerite's; but for a year he was in full charge, the pastor being absent in Europe. In 1862 he became pastor, and proceeded to make his church and school meet the wants of the large congregation that had grown up in the parish. In 1865 he enlarged the church, and in 1869 erected a large and handsome brick school-house. Ever devoted to the spiritual wants of his flock, the Rev. Mr. Cosgrove found them equally devoted to him and ready to carry out all his projects. On the 28th of August, 1882, they surprised him by a celebration of his silver jubilee, many of the priests of the diocese joining in the popular ovation. When Dr. McMullen was made bishop he selected St. Marguerite's Church as his cathedral, and appointed Rev. Mr.

Cosgrove vicar-general of the diocese. In that position he gave Bishop McMullen most important and constant aid. Recognizing this, and regarding him as one of the most devoted and useful priests in the West, Bishop McMullen left a sealed letter to be opened after his death, in which the Very Rev. Henry Cosgrove was appointed administrator *sede vacante*. The bishops of the province proposed him to the Holy See as successor of Bishop McMullen, and the clergy of the diocese almost unanimously solicited his appointment. The Holy Father issued the bulls, and he was consecrated on the 14th day of September, 1884, and as Bishop of Davenport attended the Third Plenary Council. Bishop Cosgrove was the first native of the United States who has filled a see west of the Mississippi River. His diocese in the commencement of the year 1885 contained seventy-nine priests, who had under their care one hundred and thirty-four churches. The Catholic population had been estimated in 1883 at 45,690, and in 1885 there were nearly five thousand children in the Catholic parochial schools.

DIOCESE OF DETROIT.

RIGHT REV. FREDERIC RÉSÉ,

First Bishop of Detroit.

FREDERIC RÉSÉ was born at Hildesheim, in the kingdom of Hanover, in 1797, and during the wars of the French Revolution was drawn into the military service. As a dragoon he fought under Blücher at Waterloo. With the return of peace he sought a far different career. Proceeding to Rome, he became a student at the College of the Propaganda, resolved to devote himself to the missions. His first experience was in Africa, but he soon selected the American field. Bishop Fenwick, who wished German priests, gladly accepted him for his state, and he came to the diocese of Cincinnati with that prelate in 1825. He entered on the mission work with zeal and energy. As secretary he rendered great services to the bishop, and was sent by him to Europe in 1827 to obtain priests for his extended diocese. It was due to this urgent appeal, especially in behalf of the scattered German Catholics in the United States, that the Leopold Society was founded in Austria. After sending over several priests and aid for the missions the Rev. Mr Résé returned to Ohio in 1828, and resumed his work in that State and Michigan. He was soon made vicar-general of the diocese; and when it was resolved to erect Detroit into an episcopal see, no one seemed more worthy than the zealous German priest. He was consecrated October 6, 1833, and soon after took his seat in the Second Provincial Council of Baltimore. His diocese comprised Michigan and Northwest Territory, now Wisconsin. It contained fourteen priests and some ten or twelve churches. Dr. Résé established a college at Detroit and introduced the Franciscan Sisters known as Poor Clares, who opened academies at Detroit and Green Bay. He made efforts to revive the faith of the Catholic Indians, and established schools among them. But his administration was not on the whole prosperous; he lost self-control and resolved to resign his see. When the Third Provincial Council met in April, 1837, Bishop Résé addressed the archbishop and his suffragans, tendering his resignation of the see of Detroit, and asking their influence to have it accepted. He retained, however, the title of Bishop of Detroit, and, proceeding to Europe, resided for some years in Rome, but in 1848 returned to his native place, where he died December 27, 1871.

RIGHT REV. PETER PAUL LEFEVERE,

Bishop of Zela and Administrator of Detroit.

PETER PAUL LEFEVERE was born at Roulers, in the diocese of Bruges, April 30, 1804. After a classical course in his own Belgian province of West Flanders he studied theology at Paris, and came to the United States in 1828 and was ordained by Bishop Rosati at St. Louis in 1831. He was first stationed at New Madrid, but was soon sent to the northern part of Missouri, his mission district extending into Iowa and Illinois. We find the zealous Belgian priest for several years at St. Paul's Church, Salt River, Ralls County, extending his services to Pike, Lincoln, Monroe, Marion, Lewis, Clarke, and Shelby counties. Ere long Rev. Mr. Lefevere was erecting churches at Cincinnati town, Louisville, Sandy Creek, and Wyaconda. In 1840 he attended the Fourth Provincial Council of Baltimore as theologian of the Bishop of Vincennes, and subsequently visited Europe to appeal for aid for the missions. Meanwhile his name had been forwarded to Rome for coadjutor to Bishop Résé, of Detroit, and administrator of the diocese. His bulls awaited his return. He was consecrated by Bishop Kenrick in Philadelphia, November 21, 1841. The diocese had been for four years without a bishop, and contained twenty thousand Catholics, for whom there were some twenty churches attended by seventeen priests. Bishop

Lefevere began to restore order in the long-widowed diocese. In 1844 he laid the corner-stone of the cathedral of St. Peter and St. Paul, and dedicated it June 29, 1848. Meanwhile Wisconsin was taken from the diocese of Detroit in 1844, when a see was erected at Milwaukee. The State of Michigan, thus left under his care, contained thirty-seven churches and chapels, fourteen priests, sixteen academies and schools, with several Indian missions, all with schools. In 1845 the Sisters of Charity, who already directed an academy, opened also a hospital; the next year the bishop founded the theological seminary of St. Thomas. In 1848 the Sisters of the Immaculate Heart of Mary opened an academy at Monroe, and the Sisters of the Holy Cross one at Bertrand. Three years after Bishop Lefevere added to the teaching orders in his diocese the Ladies of the Sacred Heart and the Christian Brothers, who were soon followed by the Sisters of Notre Dame. In 1853 the northern peninsula of Michigan, lying along the southern shore of Lake Superior, was formed into an apostolic-vicariate. The diocese of Detroit, thus again reduced, contained sixty churches, thirty-four priests, an ecclesiastical seminary, three academies for young ladies, twenty-four Catholic schools, and an hospital, with a Catholic population of 85,000.

Bishop Lefevere was anxious to establish in Europe a seminary that would train candidates for the American mission. The project was not generally supported, but he persevered, and, with the aid of the great Bishop Spalding, of Louisville, was able to see his plan carried into operation by the establishment of the American College at Louvain, which has furnished so many excellent priests. He introduced the Redemptorists once more into his diocese, and continued year by year to improve the condition of the flock confided to him. After taking part in the consecration of Bishop Mrak, February 7, 1869, Dr. Lefevere was taken seriously sick, and expired on the 4th of March. During Bishop Lefevere's long and able direction of the Church in Michigan Catholicity had grown rapidly in the southern peninsula, so that he left eighty churches with eighty-eight priests in place of the twenty churches and seventeen priests that he found on his arrival. He extended the system of parochial schools, and left a hospital, a house for the insane, and orphan asylums, for a Catholic population estimated at 150,000.

RIGHT REV. CASPAR H. BORGESS,
Second Bishop of Detroit.

CASPAR HENRY BORGESS was born on the 1st of August, 1826, at Holdrup-bei-Damme, in the Grand Duchy of Oldenburg. He came to the United States at the age of thirteen. After preliminary studies in Philadelphia and Cincinnati he entered St. Xavier's College, from which he passed to the seminary. He was ordained by Archbishop Purcell on the 8th of December, 1848, and said his first Mass in the church of the Holy Trinity. He was then made pastor of the church of the Holy Cross in Columbus. After ten years' service at this church and its missions the Rev. Mr. Borgess was made rector of the cathedral of Cincinnati and chancellor of the diocese. The important functions thus imposed upon him he discharged for eleven years, till the venerable Pontiff Pius IX., on the 8th of February, 1870, appointed him Bishop of Calydon and administrator of the diocese of Detroit. He was consecrated on the 24th of April, in the cathedral at Cincinnati, by Bishop Rosecrans, assisted by Bishops Luers and Feehan. The new coadjutor assumed direction of the diocese, and in December, 1871, became by succession second Bishop of Detroit. Under his able management the Jesuit Fathers have established a college at Detroit, and the Franciscans a central house and scholasticate; the Little Sisters of the Poor have opened a Home for the Aged. Bishop Borgess had at the commencement of the year 1885 79 churches, 104 priests, a college, 3 academies, 45 parochial schools under Brothers of the Christian Schools, Franciscan Brothers, Sisters of the Immaculate Heart of Mary, Sisters of Notre Dame, of St. Dominic, of Christian Charity, Sisters of Providence, Sisters of St. Agnes, Polish Franciscan Sisters, Ladies of the Sacred Heart, with more than 10,000 pupils, and a Catholic population of 102,655—the annual baptisms being 5,346.

RT. REV. CASPAR H. BORGESS.
Born at Holdrup-bei-Damme, Germany, Aug. 1, 1824.
Ordained Dec. 8, 1848 ; Consecrated Bishop of
Calydon and Administrator of Detroit, April 24, 1870 ;
Bishop of Detroit, December 27, 1871.

RT. REV. TOBIAS MULLEN, D.D.
Born at Flushtown, Ireland, March 4, 1818.
Ordained Sept. 1, 1844 ; Consecrated Bishop
of Erie, August 2, 1868.

RT. REV. JOHN HENNESSY, D.D.
Born in County Limerick, Ireland.
Ordained Nov. 1 1850 ; Consecrated Bishop of
Dubuque, Sept. 30, 1866.

RT. REV. JOSEPH DWENGER, D.D.
Born at St. Johns, Ohio, 1837.
Ordained Sept. 4, 1859 ; Consecrated April 14, 1872.

DIOCESE OF DUBUQUE.

RIGHT REV. MATTHIAS LORAS,

First Bishop of Dubuque.

MATTHIAS LORAS was born in Lyons, France, in July, 1792, of a family eminent for their piety and social position. His father fell a victim to the infidel revolutionists soon after his birth, but, trained by his mother, young Matthias studied for the priesthood, and was ordained about 1817. Notwithstanding his youth he was soon after made superior of the seminary of Largentière, and resigned the position only to join a band of excellent priests who gave missions in the parishes. When Bishop Portier, in 1829, visited France to seek missionaries, Rev. Mr. Loras offered his services and reached Mobile with the bishop January 3, 1830. For seven years he was pastor of the cathedral and vicar-general of the diocese; but when the Holy See, on the 28th of July, 1837, erected Iowa and Minnesota into a diocese, Rev. Mr. Loras was appointed the first bishop, and was consecrated by Bishop Portier on the 10th of December. In the diocese assigned to him there was but one half-finished church and one priest. Bishop Loras proceeded first of all to France, where he obtained two priests and four seminarians, and with these started for Dubuque, and was installed as bishop April 29, 1839. He at once began with his few priests to build churches and schools, calling the Sisters of Charity to aid as teachers. He made a thorough visitation of his diocese, finding many Canadians and half-breeds, whom he brought back to their religious duties. He also established missions among the Sioux, Foxes, and Winnebagoes. Under the care of Bishop Loras the community of Sisters of Charity of the Blessed Virgin, founded in Philadelphia by Very Rev. T. C. Donaghoe, was greatly developed, rendering essential service to the diocese of Dubuque. Bishop Loras encouraged and guided Catholic immigration, so as to afford the incoming settlers every facility for practising their religion and bringing up their children in the faith. Thus he built up the Church by personal supervision, spending much of his time in going through the diocese, not as on a visitation, but personally beginning the erection of a needed church or school, or aiding to complete it for dedication. This work he continued till Minnesota was formed into a separate diocese in 1851. Besides this mission work Bishop Loras established a theological seminary, introduced the Trappist monks and Visitation nuns.

Bishop Loras sat in the Plenary Council of Baltimore and the four preceding Provincial Synods.

In 1857 he established a hospital, and during his long career was eminent for his charity and love of the poor and afflicted. How Catholicity developed in Iowa under his prudent and constant supervision may be seen in the fact that in the Iowa part of his diocese, where, upon his arrival, he found one priest and one church, he left sixty churches, forty priests, several religious orders, many academies for higher education, and schools and a Catholic population of 54,000.

His constant labors called at last for one to hold up his hands in his ministry, and in 1857 the Right Rev. Clement Smyth was consecrated coadjutor. In February of the ensuing year Bishop Loras was stricken down with illness, and though medical skill seemed at first to control the disease, his recovery was but delusive. On the 18th of February he retired to his room in the evening, and was soon after found insensible on the floor, stricken with paralysis. The good bishop lingered till the next morning, when he expired.

RIGHT REV. CLEMENT SMYTH,

Second Bishop of Dubuque.

TIMOTHY SMYTH was born at Finlea, in the county of Clare Ireland, on the 24th of January, 1810. After studying in his native place and at Limerick he entered Trinity College, Dublin, where he was graduated. Renouncing the pursuits open to him, he joined the Presentation Brothers at Youghal, but, feeling called rather to the contemplative than the active life, he sought admission among the Trappists at Mount Melleray. His wish was gratified, and he became Brother Clement. With the permission of his abbot he some years after established a poor-school at the abbey; but though he desired to remain a lay member, he was ordered to commence studies for the priesthood. He was ordained in 1844, and five years later was sent with a Brother to found a house of his order in America, the distressed condition of Ireland giving no hope of extension in that island. Bishop Loras welcomed the Cistercians, and Father Smyth founded a New Melleray near the city of Dubuque. Church, monastery, and poor-school soon rose, and a community of forty-seven members were in time edifying all by their strict monastic discipline. The will of the Sovereign Pontiff drew Father Smyth from his seclusion, and the Trappist prior was consecrated Bishop of Thanasis, May 3, 1857. Assuming the duties with zeal, Bishop Smyth completed the cathedral and was active in visitations of the diocese. He succeeded Bishop Loras in the see of Dubuque in February, 1858. Bishop Smyth rarely went beyond the limits of his diocese, and then only at the call of duty, as on the occasion of his visit to Europe in 1862. After a short but painful illness, which he bore with Christian courage, he expired on the 23d of September, 1865.

RIGHT REV. JOHN HENNESSY,

Third Bishop of Dubuque.

JOHN HENNESSY was born in Ireland, but made this country his home, with the high ambition of laboring to keep fresh in all hearts the faith of his ancestors. He began his labors as a missionary priest in the diocese of St. Louis in 1850 as pastor of the church of St. John the Baptist at New Madrid, Mo., and for a few years subsequently of St. Peter's at Gravois, in St. Louis County. While still retaining this charge the Rev. Mr. Hennessy was appointed professor of dogmatic theology and Holy Scripture in the theological seminary at Carondelet, and in 1857 became superior of that institution, his learning and experience fitting him for the position. He was subsequently attached to the cathedral, and towards the close of the civil war was pastor of St. Joseph's Church in the now episcopal city of St. Joseph's. Having been elected Bishop of Dubuque on the 24th of April, 1866, he was consecrated on the 30th of September in that year. The important diocese confided to Bishop Hennessy comprised the whole State of Iowa, with a rapidly growing Catholic population which already exceeded a hundred thousand souls, with about sixty priests and seventy-nine churches.

Early in his administration Bishop Hennessy founded the Mercy Hospital at Davenport on property secured by Rev. Mr. Pelamourgues. He endeavored to establish a college, but it was not till 1873 that St. Joseph's College was opened. It is now in a flourishing condition.

The same year the Fathers of the ancient order of St. Benedict, with Father Augustine Burns as superior, founded St. Malachy's Priory at Creston, in Union County, the first English-speaking community of Benedictines in the United States.

In 1881 the diocese, which had increased greatly, was divided, and a new see established at Davenport. The diocese of Dubuque thus reduced comprised the portion of the State of Iowa lying north of the counties of Harrison, Shelby, Audubon, Guthrie, Dallas, Polk, Jasper, Poweshiek, Iowa, Johnson, Cedar, and Scott.

By 1884 the episcopal city of Dubuque had a fine cathedral, dedicated to St. Raphael, and twenty-six other churches; the Mercy Hospital and Marine Hospital, both under the care of the Sisters of Mercy; an asylum for orphans of German parentage, St. Joseph's College, convents of Visitation and Presentation nuns and of Franciscan Sisters, with several academies and parochial schools. The total number of priests was one hundred and fifty, the churches nearly equalling that number, giving the sixty thousand Catholics of the diocese every advantage for hearing Mass and approaching the sacraments; while the care of the growing youth, on whose fidelity to the faith so much depended, was evinced by the fact that more than seven thousand six hundred attended Catholic schools. Bishop Hennessy was one of the Fathers of the Third Plenary Council of Baltimore in 1884.

DIOCESE OF ERIE.

RIGHT REV. JOSUE M. YOUNG,

Second Bishop of Erie.

JOSHUA MOODY YOUNG was born at Shapleigh, Maine, October 29, 1808, and was brought up in the Protestant doctrines which his parents professed. After passing through the district schools he entered the printing-office of the *Eastern Argus* at Portland in 1823. Here he met a Catholic, whom he attacked in the usual way on the score of religion; but he found his fellow-printer to be a man able to give an account of his faith, and one who lived up to it. Young began to read Catholic books, and the good seed germinated. After editing a paper at Saco he returned to Portland about the time of Bishop Fenwick's visit in 1827. He sought through his friend an introduction to the bishop, and received a series of instructions from that learned prelate. He was baptized in 1828, taking the name of Josue Maria, and soon proceeded to Cincinnati with the view of entering the priesthood. After a time spent there he was sent to Mount St. Mary's, and was ordained in 1837. The Rev. Mr. Young was for seven years a laborious missionary, much of the time at Lancaster, Ohio. On the erection of the see of Erie in 1852 Bishop O'Connor was appointed to the new diocese; but Rev. Mr. Young was reluctant to replace him at Pittsburgh, and Bishop O'Connor returned to his former see. Rev. Mr. Young was consecrated Bishop of Erie April 23, 1854, by Archbishop Purcell, and began to organize the diocese confided to his care. He founded an hospital at Erie, erected a fine school, which he placed under the charge of the Franciscan Brothers and Sisters of St. Joseph. Other academies and schools and an infirmary, as well as churches, erected in various parts of the diocese, proved his activity and zeal. He was, too, an ardent supporter of the temperance cause, and by example and precept endeavored to withdraw his flock from intoxicating drinks. By his influence all his brothers and sisters except one embraced the Catholic faith, although at first his becoming a Catholic and a priest caused a mysterious horror in the family. In the midst of his active administration Bishop Young was suddenly stricken down with heart-disease, and survived only long enough to receive the last sacraments before his death, September 18, 1866.

RIGHT REV. TOBIAS MULLEN,

Third Bishop of Erie.

TOBIAS MULLEN was born in the parish of Urney, County Tyrone, Ireland, the youngest of the six sons of James Mullen and Mary Travers. His earliest days were spent on a farm, and after attending the schools in the neighborhood of his home he made classical studies at Castlefin. About 1840 he was examined with others by Bishop McLaughlin, and passed so successfully that he was directed to prepare for the Irish College in Paris. Before the young man was ready to start he attended another examination of all the students of the diocese, and, passing this with honor, he was sent to Maynooth. While there young Mullen, with four other students, having listened to an appeal from Bishop O'Connor, of Pittsburgh, they all resolved to devote themselves to the American missions under the direction of that prelate. After prosecuting his theological studies for some time in Pittsburgh he was ordained on the 1st of September, 1844, by Bishop O'Connor, and served for about two years as assistant at the cathedral in Pittsburgh. Rev. Mr. Mullen was afterwards charged with the care of congregations at Johnstown and in Jefferson County. Nine years after he was appointed pastor of St. Peter's, Allegheny City. Here he remained thirteen years, and for a considerable period was vicar-general of the diocese under Bishop Domenec.

Rev. Mr. Mullen was appointed Bishop of Erie on the death of Bishop Young, and was consecrated August 2, 1868. The development of the oil-springs discovered more than two centuries ago by the Franciscan De la Roche caused an influx of people into this diocese, bringing many Catholics; but the population was not always permanent, and churches erected for large congregations became in a few years scantily attended. Yet during the administration of Bishop Mullen the population has increased from thirty to forty five thousand, and the churches from fifty-five to eighty-four. On his installation the diocese had but thirty-five priests; it has now sixty secular clergymen and seven Benedictine Fathers. The Congregation of the Most Holy Redeemer has, within a few years, established a preparatory college at Northeast. There are academies for young ladies under Benedictine nuns, under Sisters of St. Joseph, and parochial schools under their care and that of the Sisters of the Humility of Mary. There are in the fifty-eight parochial schools 5,687 pupils. Besides this the diocese has two hospitals and an asylum.

DIOCESE OF FORT WAYNE.

RIGHT REV. JOHN HENRY LUERS,

First Bishop of Fort Wayne.

JOHN HENRY LUERS was born near the city of Münster, Germany, September 29, 1819, and emigrated with his family to the United States in 1833. He was soon placed as a clerk in a store at Piqua, Ohio; but he desired to become a priest. An accidental meeting with Bishop Purcell encouraged the hopes of the young man and enabled him to enter the Lazarist Seminary of St. Francis Xavier. He was ordained priest November 11, 1846, and was stationed in the parish of St. Joseph, where a half-finished church needed an active hand. The Rev. Mr. Luers completed the sacred edifice, and beside it erected a substantial school-house, into which he gathered the children of the parish after making a careful census. Here he labored for years, seeking the salvation of his flock.

When the see of Fort Wayne was erected the Rev. Mr. Luers was chosen bishop, to his own great surprise, and was consecrated January 10, 1858. His diocese contained a small frame building for his cathedral and nineteen other churches, attended by fourteen priests, though the diocese comprised thirty-eight counties. Bishop Luers began the erection of a cathedral, but he was more anxious to preserve the religion of his flock, and by constant visits to parts where Catholics had settled he encouraged the erection of parochial churches. Bishop Luers obtained priests to meet their wants, and, holding a synod, established sound regulations. On a visit to Rome in 1864 he was commissioned by Pope Pius IX. with the task of drawing up a constitution and rules for the Sisters of the Holy Cross. The Congregation of Priests of the Holy Cross found in him a warm and earnest friend, and that community, under the guidance of the venerable Father Sorin, has grown to be one of the most important bodies of regular priests in the country, the University of Notre Dame being one of our greatest Catholic institutions. Bishop Luers attended the Provincial Councils of Cincinnati and the Plenary Council of Baltimore. In June, 1871, he went to Cleveland to ordain some of the seminarians, and while on his way to the episcopal residence on the morning of the 28th, before taking a train to another diocese, the charitable bishop was stricken down with apoplexy. He was carried to the bishop's house and expired a few moments after receiving the last sacraments.

RIGHT REV. JOSEPH DWENGER,

Second Bishop of Fort Wayne.

JOSEPH DWENGER was born in 1837 at St. John's, near Minster, Ohio, of parents who had recently emigrated from Ankum, in Hanover. He lost his father at the age of three, and on his mother removing to Cincinnati he was sent to the school of the Holy Trinity. At the age of twelve he lost his mother also, but the Rev. Mr. Kunkler took the talented orphan boy and placed him with the Fathers of the Precious Blood. Young Dwenger began his studies for the priesthood, and completed them in the Seminary of Mount St. Mary's of the West. He was ordained priest in the chapel of that institution by Archbishop Purcell on the 4th of September, 1859. How highly he was esteemed may be inferred from the fact that he was appointed professor and director in the seminary of the Precious Blood, and retained the position for three years. He was then placed in charge of the congregations at Wapakoneta and St. Mary's, and showed himself a zealous missionary priest, ever anxious for the welfare of his flock. He was also secretary and consultor in his order, and connected with the seminary at Carthagena. From 1867 to 1872 he was employed in giving missions in Ohio, Kentucky, and Indiana. Having been selected to succeed Bishop Luers, he was consecrated by Archbishop Purcell, assisted by Bishops Toebbe and Borgess, on the 14th of April, 1872, and was the youngest member of the hierarchy. The development and proper organization of the parochial schools has been the great object of his attention. He established a Diocesan School Board, which introduced into the schools uniformity of teaching and grading as well as in text-books, and has since exercised a wise supervision over them. The reports are annually printed, and stimulate the faithful to support the schools. In 1884 there were sixty schools with eight thousand pupils—nearly nine per cent. of the total Catholic population of 85,000. His diocese had also the university of Notre Dame, under the Priests of the Holy Cross, with Sisters of the same origin; Priests and Sisters of the Precious Blood, Sisters of the Third Order of St. Francis attending schools and hospitals, Poor Handmaids of Christ similarly employed, Sisters of Providence, and Sisters of Notre Dame.

On the occasion of the American pilgrimage to Rome Bishop Dwenger accompanied it as superior. He attended the Third Plenary Council, and visited Rome soon after its close.

DIOCESE OF GALVESTON.

RIGHT REV. CLAUDE MARY DUBUIS,

Second Bishop of Galveston.

CLAUDE MARY DUBUIS was born in France about the year 1817. He was one of the early missionaries whom Bishop Odin drew to Texas. He was stationed in 1847 in the difficult mission of Castroville, where he suffered greatly, living in a wretched hut till he and his fellow-missionary built a house with their own hands. An accident for a time placed his life in danger, but a constitution of iron enabled the zealous priest to endure all, where others sank under their trials. His associate, the Rev. Mr. Chazelle, died of typhus, while he himself was so ill that he was able to say Mass only by resting from time to time before he could administer the Holy Viaticum to his fellow-priest. He persevered, however, and even established a school. About 1850 he was transferred to San Antonio, and was for many years pastor of San Ferdinand's Church, and, with the aid of curates, attended a large and scattered flock. Here, too, he showed zeal for education, aiding greatly the Ursulines in establishing a convent. On the promotion of Bishop Odin to the see of New Orleans the Rev. Mr. Dubuis was chosen as his successor, and was consecrated November 23, 1862, taking possession of his see during the difficult period when the South was ravaged by contending armies. When peace was restored Bishop Dubuis endeavored to repair the losses which religion had sustained, and by 1874 the diocese contained fifty-five churches and chapels, with eighty-three priests and about 100,000 Catholics. On the 3d of September in that year the diocese of San Antonio and the vicariate-apostolic of Brownsville were created; but Bishop Dubuis' health made him solicit a coadjutor, and the Right Rev. P. Dufal, who had been consecrated Bishop of Delcon in 1860 and

Vicar-Apostolic of Eastern Bengal, was transferred May 14, 1878, to Texas as coadjutor with the right of succession; he resigned, however, in 1880, but Bishop Dubuis retired to France, and the next year resigned the see of Galveston.

RIGHT REV. NICHOLAS A. GALLAGHER,

Bishop of Canopus and Administrator of Galveston.

NICHOLAS A. GALLAGHER was born at Temperanceville, Belmont County, Ohio, on the 19th of February, 1846, and, after pursuing literary and divinity studies at Mount St. Mary's of the West, was ordained priest at Columbus on Christmas day in the year 1868. He was known for many years as a zealous and talented priest of the diocese of Columbus, where his piety and executive ability, as well as his devotedness to his sacred calling, made him remarked by all. From 1869 to 1872 he was attached to St. Patrick's Church, under Bishop Rosecrans, and from it attended the chapel of St. Joseph's Cathedral before the solemn opening of that church itself. He was next president of St. Aloysius' Seminary, near Columbus, and when St. Joseph's became the bishop's residence Rev. Mr. Gallagher was appointed pastor of St. Patrick's and vicar-general. During the vacancy of the see from October, 1878, to August, 1880, he was administrator of the diocese. The Holy See selected this able clergyman to regulate the affairs of the diocese of Galveston as administrator, appointing him Bishop of Canopus. He was consecrated at St. Mary's College, Galveston, on Sunday, April 30, 1882, by the Right Rev. Edward Fitzgerald, Bishop of Little Rock. He then assumed the administration of the diocese, of which Dr. Dubuis still retained the title of bishop. During the short period since his consecration Bishop Gallagher, laboring assiduously, has done much to restore order and meet the difficulties of the diocese confided to him. In the portion of Texas under his charge there were in 1884 forty priests, with fifty churches and chapels, and, as is estimated, some eight-and-thirty thousand Catholics. There are several female academies under the Ursuline nuns and other religious, and two charitable institutions, but much has yet to be accomplished in the direction of parochial schools. This task and the keeping pace with increasing immigration make the position of Bishop Gallagher one of trial.

RT. REV. N. A. GALLAGHER, D.D.
Born at Temperanceville, Ohio, Feb. 19, 1846.
Ordained Dec. 25, 1868; Consecrated Bishop of Canopus and Administrator of Galveston, April 30, 1882.

RT. REV. EUGENE O'CONNELL, D.D.
Born near Kells, Ireland, June 18, 1815.
Ordained 1842; Consecrated Bishop of Flaviopolis, Feb. 3, 1861; Bishop of Grass Valley, March 22, 1868; resigned, 1884.

RT. REV. HENRY J. RICHTER, D.D.
Born at Neuen Kirchen, Germany, April 9, 1838.
Ordained June 10, 1865; Consecrated Bishop of Grand Rapids, April 22, 1883.

RT. REV. PATRICK MANOGUE, D.D.
Born at Desart, Ireland, in 1831.
Ordained in 1861; Consecrated Bishop of Ceramos and Coadjutor, Jan. 16, 1881; Bishop of Grass Valley, 1884.

DIOCESE OF GRAND RAPIDS.

RIGHT REV. HENRY JOSEPH RICHTER,

First Bishop of Grand Rapids.

HENRY JOSEPH RICHTER was born on the 9th of April, 1838, at Neuen Kirchen, in the Grand Duchy of Oldenburg. After studying in the local schools he came to the United States in 1854 and entered St. Paul's School, in Cincinnati, in the succeeding year. This was followed by five years of steady application in St. Xavier's, the college at Bardstown, and Mount St. Mary's. He went to Rome in 1860, entering the American College, and winning his doctor's cap in 1865, was ordained on the 10th of June by Cardinal Patrizi. Returning to Cincinnati in October, he was made vice-president of Mount St. Mary's Seminary, where he filled the chairs of dogma, philosophy, and liturgy till 1870. He then founded the church of St. Laurence, and made it a thriving parish; was director of the Academy of Mount St. Vincent, and one of the Committee of Investigation of the diocese. When His Holiness Leo XIII. established the diocese of Grand Rapids on the 19th of May, 1882, the Rev. Dr. Richter was selected for the new see. He was consecrated and enthroned in St. Andrew's, Grand Rapids, on the 22d of April, 1883, by the Right Rev. William Henry Elder, Coadjutor of Cincinnati.

The diocese confided to Bishop Richter contained thirty-three churches with resident pastors, seventeen parochial schools with 2,867 scholars, out of a population of forty or fifty thousand Catholics. There were also two hospitals and an orphan asylum. There is a community of Franciscans at the Indian settlement of Cross Village; and Sisters of Charity, of Providence, of Notre Dame, of the Immaculate Heart of Mary, with Franciscan and

Dominican Sisters, in charge of academies, schools, and charitable institutions.

The total number of churches in the diocese in 1884 is given as ninety, with fifty-two priests, for a population of nearly sixty thousand.

DIOCESE OF GRASS VALLEY.

RIGHT REV. EUGENE O'CONNELL,

First Bishop of Grass Valley.

EUGENE O'CONNELL was born in the parish of Kingscourt, in the diocese of Meath, Ireland, and studied in the diocesan seminary of Navan, and subsequently at Maynooth, where he was ordained in 1842. He remained at Navan as professor for several years, and then joined the community at All Hallows' College, where he rendered very great service. Here he spent several years, leaving it for a time to act as missionary in California. There he was appointed president of Santa Iñez College and president of St. Thomas' Theological Seminary. When it was resolved to divide the diocese of San Francisco by erecting the vicariate-apostolic of Marysville, the Rev. Eugene O'Connell was selected. He was consecrated Bishop of Flaviopolis in the college of All Hallows on the 3d of February, 1861, by the Most Rev. Dr. Cullen. The next month he set out for his vicariate, which comprised the portion of California north of the thirty-ninth degree and the Territory of Nevada. In this district he found only four priests. He made Marysville his residence and took charge of it as his personal mission, attending with one priest the stations in California; while Nevada at first gave greater hopes. Virginia City soon had two churches, one under the Rev. P. Manogue, the other directed by the Passionist Fathers. Bishop O'Connell established the Sisters of Notre Dame at Marysville, and Sisters of Mercy at Grass Valley, in August, 1863. Churches were soon established at Downieville, Forest Hill, Grass Valley, Mendocino, and Weaverville, whence priests attended a number of stations. Orphan asylums were the bishop's next object. On the 3d of March, 1868, Pope Pius IX. established the diocese of Grass Valley, comprising the territory between the Pacific and the Colorado, between the 39th and 42d degrees. Some years after Bishop O'Connell, worn out by his labors in the large and toilsome field, obtained as a coadjutor the Right Rev. P. Manogue. and in 1884 he resigned the see and was transferred to Joppa. The progress of Catholicity in that portion of the country has been slow, and Nevada, prematurely made a State, has declined rapidly in population.

RIGHT REV. PATRICK MANOGUE,

Second Bishop of Grass Valley.

PATRICK MANOGUE was born in 1831 at Desert, County Kilkenny, Ireland, and arrived in this country in his boyhood, after preliminary studies at Callan. He was thrown into the midst of a New England community, where he found men of all ideas, all claiming to be the organs of perfect religions, and all agreeing in one single point—an insensate ignorance of everything relating to the Catholic Church, and consequently a deep-seated prejudice against it. Called on constantly to explain and defend his faith, he resolved to become a priest, and entered the university of St. Mary's of the Lake, Chicago. After pursuing a classical and philosophical course in that institution he was sent to Paris, and made his theological studies in the great seminary of St. Sulpice. He was ordained priest in 1861 by Cardinal Morlot in the parish church of St. Sulpice. He soon after joined the California mission, and about 1864 was one of the first priests sent to Nevada. He erected St. Mary's, a very fine church, in Virginia City, and established a house of Sisters of Charity. He continued his mission labors here for many years, acting for no fewer than fifteen as vicar-general of the diocese of Grass Valley, and obtaining favorable comments from all for his zeal and energy. The diocese is a large and thinly settled one, and when the priest first selected as coadjutor to Bishop O'Connell shrank from the onerous duty, the Holy See, July 27, 1880, selected the hard-working and unambitious but able priest of Virginia City.

He was consecrated Bishop of Ceramos on the 16th of January, 1881, by Archbishop Alemany in St. Mary's Cathedral, San Francisco. The ill-health and infirmities of Right Rev. Dr. O'Connell devolved much of the administration on the coadjutor, till by his resignation in 1884 the Right Rev. Dr. Manogue became second Bishop of Grass Valley. His diocese contains only from seven to ten thousand Catholics, with thirty-five priests and thirty-seven churches. Sisters of Notre Dame, of Charity and Mercy, as well as Dominican nuns, conduct academies, schools, asylums, and an hospital. Zealous priests have begun an earnest work at the Indian Reservation to save the last remnant of the Mission Indians.

DIOCESE OF GREEN BAY.

RIGHT REV. JOSEPH MELCHER,

First Bishop of Green Bay.

JOSEPH MELCHER was born in Vienna in the year 1807. After pursuing his preliminary studies in that capital he went to Modena to complete his course, and there won the doctor's cap. After his ordination in 1830 he became one of the chaplains at the court of Austria, but he longed to devote himself to the laborious life of a missionary beyond the limits of Europe. When Bishop Rosati visited Vienna to solicit German priests for his diocese, the Rev. Mr. Melcher offered his services, and came to the United States in 1843. He was stationed at Little Rock, Arkansas, and remained there till the next year, when that State was erected into a separate diocese. Rev. Mr. Melcher was then recalled to St. Louis and appointed pastor of St. Mary's Church, in which position he remained till he was called to the episcopate. He had also for many years held the responsible position of vicar-general of the diocese. On the erection of the see of Green Bay, March 3, 1868, he was chosen its first bishop and was consecrated in the cathedral, St. Louis, July 12, 1868. His diocese comprised the part of Wisconsin from the east bank of the river of that name to Lake Michigan, and running north from the Fox and Manitowoc rivers to the State line. He found sixteen priests for a population of more than forty thousand Catholics from various countries. He proceeded to organize his diocese, and so successfully that in the report furnished by him in 1873 he could claim sixty-five churches and chapels, attended by fifty-six priests, two thousand children in the Catholic schools, in a total Catholic population of sixty thousand. Bishop Melcher died piously, at Green Bay, on the 20th of December, 1873.

RIGHT REV. FRANCIS XAVIER KRAUTBAUER,

Second Bishop of Green Bay.

FRANCIS XAVIER KRAUTBAUER was born on the 12th of January, 1824, at Bruck on the Oberpfalz, diocese of Ratisbonne, and after pursuing his studies in his native country, and being raised to priestly orders on the 16th of July, 1850, he came to America in the following autumn to devote himself to missionary work among his countrymen. From 1851 to 1859 we see him laboring in a poor parish at Rochester, then in the diocese of Buffalo. He showed his zeal for Catholic education by establishing a school for children of both sexes, placing the girls under School Sisters of Notre Dame, and deeming it sounder policy to retain his congregation in a little frame church till the school was erected and paid for, rather than cripple the parish by erecting a fine church beyond its means. In 1859 Rev. Mr. Krautbauer went to Milwaukee to become chaplain and director at the church of Our Lady of the Angels, connected with the mother-house of the School Sisters of Notre Dame. Here he remained for more than ten years, his influence being felt in the community of Sisters, who profited by his counsels. Having been selected to succeed Bishop Melcher, Dr. Krautbauer was consecrated June 29, 1875, and took possession of the see of Green Bay. The diocese contained sixty-three priests and ninety-two churches, the Servites representing the religious orders, with Servite nuns, Ursulines, School Sisters of Notre Dame, Sisters of the Third Order of St. Francis and St. Dominic, Sisters of St. Agnes. The population comprised English-speaking Catholics, with others of German, French, Hollandish, Bohemian, Walloon,

Polish, and Indian tongues. Many congregations contained representatives of several languages. Bishop Krautbauer labored earnestly to extend the school system, and by 1884 could number 96 priests, 111 churches, and 15 chapels, with 44 parochial schools in which 5,292 children were saved from the soul-withering influence of the public-schools, where religious teaching is excluded. The resources of the diocese by the policy of Bishop Krautbauer have been greatly enhanced, although the population had not increased in the same ratio as the priests and institutions.

Bishop Krautbauer continued his zealous labors to the end. On the 16th day of December, 1885, he was found dead in his bed.

DIOCESE OF HARRISBURG.

RIGHT REV. JEREMIAH F. SHANAHAN,

First Bishop of Harrisburg.

JEREMIAH F. SHANAHAN was born in Susquehanna County, Pennsylvania, and pursued all his studies in his native State, from his earliest rudiments to the close of his ecclesiastical course. He was ordained priest by Right Rev. John Nepomucene Neumann, Bishop of Philadelphia, in July, 1859. The extent of his learning, his administrative powers and piety, led to his appointment as rector of the Preparatory Seminary at Glen Riddle, where boys who evince the piety and zeal likely to produce a vocation are trained in classical and general learning to fit them for entrance into the diocesan seminary, in case God calls them to the priesthood. Under his fostering care the establishment at Glen Riddle sent many students to the seminary, who in time were ordained to the priesthood. He was selected as first bishop of the new see of Harrisburg, established in 1868, and was consecrated in the cathedral of St. Peter and St. Paul, by Archbishop Wood, assisted by Bishop McGill, of Richmond, and Bishop Domenec, of Pittsburgh, on Sunday, July 12, 1868.

The diocese of Harrisburg was another taken from that of Philadelphia, which once embraced the whole States of Pennsylvania and Delaware, and a district in New Jersey. The part of Pennsylvania confided to the care of Bishop Shanahan comprised the counties of Dauphin, Lebanon, Lancaster, York, Adams, Franklin, Fulton, Cumberland, Perry, Juniata, Mifflin, Centre, Clinton, Union, Snyder, Northumberland, Montour, and Columbia. The diocese lying along the southern part of the State was not insignificant in extent, but, though it comprised within its limits two of the oldest Catholic missions in the State, the Catholic population was comparatively small. Conewago and Lancaster had at a very early day been visited by the Jesuit missionaries from Maryland, and those zealous missionaries of colonial days established residences and churches there before the American Revolution, Father William Wapeler being the pioneer priest at both places, as early as 1741. When Bishop Shanahan began to organize his diocese he found about twenty-five thousand of the faithful, with forty churches and twenty-two priests. There were convents with academies at McSherrystown, Lebanon, and Lancaster, but there were only seven parochial schools. Harrisburg, though the capital of the State, contained but two churches, and the newly-consecrated bishop took up his residence at St. Patrick's, acting as rector. The diocese does not increase much by immigration, but develops by the natural growth of the Catholic body. Accordingly the great care of the bishop was to do all in his power to save for religion and society the rising generation. He introduced the Sisters of Mercy, of St. Joseph, of Christian Charity, of the Holy Cross, and the Seton Sisters of Charity from New York. The result has been consoling. By 1884 the diocese contained seven academies for the higher education of girls, twenty-nine parochial schools, attended by more than four thousand pupils; there were two asylums to save orphans from misery and loss of faith. Eleven new churches had been erected, and he had forty-five priests, nearly one for every church in his diocese.

DIOCESE OF HARTFORD.

RIGHT REV. WILLIAM TYLER,

First Bishop of Hartford.

WILLIAM TYLER was born on the 5th of June, 1806, at Derby, Vermont, his father being a substantial farmer, his mother a sister of the famous convert, Rev. Daniel Barber. She followed the example of her relatives, and soon after their conversion, in 1816, was received into the Church with her three sons and four daughters. When about fifteen William entered the classical school established at Claremont by Rev. Virgil Barber. Showing a vocation for the priesthood, he was taken into his house by Bishop Fenwick, and began his theological course, receiving ordination in Pentecost week, 1828.

His first appointment was in the cathedral, Boston, where his zeal and piety, as well as his charity, won all hearts, his only absence being a short missionary service at Aroostook. He was in time made vicar-general of the diocese, and on its division in 1843 he was selected as the first to wear the mitre as Bishop of Hartford. He was consecrated on the 17th of March, 1844, by Bishop Fenwick, and proceeded to his diocese, which embraced Rhode Island and Connecticut, and contained only six priests. He took up his residence at Providence, making the church of St. Peter and St. Paul his cathedral. The health of Bishop Tyler was never strong, and he loved retirement and prayer; but he was zealous in his missionary and episcopal duties, and gradually increased the numbers of his clergy and churches, accomplishing all the more by means of allowances from the Leopoldine Society. He attended the Sixth and Seventh Councils of Baltimore, presenting to the Fathers of the latter synod a certificate that he could not long survive, and asking permission to resign his see.

The appointment of a coadjutor was recommended by the Fathers of the council, but Bishop Tyler returned to his diocese only to be stricken down by a rheumatic fever. He was for a time delirious, but recovered his faculties, and, receiving the last sacraments, gave the final directions as to the affairs of the diocese, and, closing his eyes to all earthly things, murmured pious ejaculations and prayers till his soul departed, June 18, 1849.

RIGHT REV. BERNARD O'REILLY,

Second Bishop of Hartford.

BERNARD O'REILLY was born in the County Longford, Ireland, in 1803, and after a pious education declared as he reached his majority that he felt called by God to serve him in the priesthood and on the American mission. Sailing for America January 17, 1825, the young Levite entered the College of Montreal, and, completing his theological studies at St. Mary's College, Baltimore, he was ordained in New York, October 13, 1831. He was appointed to St. James' Church in Jay Street, Brooklyn, and was a faithful pastor during the cholera of 1832, being twice prostrated by the disease while attending his flock. In December, 1832, he was made pastor of St. Patrick's Church, Rochester, his district extending from Auburn to Niagara. When the see of Buffalo was erected, in 1847, Bishop Timon summoned him to that city and appointed him vicar-general. The hospital of the Sisters was his especial care, and he ably defended it against the aspersions of the Rev. John C. Lord, a Presbyterian clergyman. The Council of Baltimore in 1849 recommended him as coadjutor to Bishop Tyler, but on the sudden death of that prelate he was consecrated Bishop of Hartford, on the 10th of November, 1850, the ceremony taking place in St. Patrick's Church, Rochester. He took up the administration with zeal and energy, but found that his little flock excited great hostility from the population among whom they were scattered. When the bishop introduced the Sisters of Mercy into his diocese in 1855, the good religious were threatened by a mob; but he fearlessly faced the furious crowd, declaring that it was their home, and that they should not leave it for an hour. "I shall protect them while I have life, and, if needs be, register their safety with my blood." He increased his clergy to forty-two and his churches to forty-six, established five academies and three orphan asylums, and beheld his flock advance to seventy thousand. To carry out more extensive plans for the spiritual good of his flock Bishop O'Reilly sailed to Europe on the 5th of December, 1855. He secured a religious community to direct schools for boys in his diocese, and, paying a visit to his aged parents, embarked for New York on the steamer *Pacific*, January 23, 1856. No tidings of the vessel or her passengers ever reached either shore. The good bishop in the midst of his labors had been summoned to his reward.

RIGHT REV. FRANCIS PATRICK McFARLAND,

Third Bishop of Hartford.

FRANCIS PATRICK MCFARLAND was born at Franklin, Pennsylvania, April 16, 1819, and was early trained to piety by his parents. Evincing talent and a desire to minister at God's altar, he entered Mount St. Mary's College, and, on the completion of the period assigned for the ecclesiastical studies, was ordained priest in St. Patrick's Cathedral, New York, by Bishop Hughes, May 18, 1845. After acting as professor at St. John's College, Fordham, he was appointed to the mission of Watertown, and subsequently made pastor of St. John's Church, Utica. Here he remained several years, building up the Catholic body by his zeal for the education and training of the young, and his constant care of the spiritual wants of his whole flock.

When it became evident that Bishop O'Reilly had perished at sea the Rev. Mr. McFarland's name was proposed for the vacant bishopric. He was consecrated on the 14th of March, 1858, and, like his predecessors, made Providence his residence. Under his administration the progress of the faith continued, so that in 1872 the diocese, which could boast a population of two hundred thousand Catholics, with more than a hundred churches and priests, ten academies, forty-five parochial schools, and pupils exceeding five thousand, was divided. A new see was erected at Providence, with Rhode Island and part of Massachusetts as a diocese. Bishop McFarland removed to Hartford, and began the erection of a cathedral with an episcopal residence and a convent for Sisters. His health, however, failed, and though he visited the South, the zealous bishop was unable to remain away from his diocese; he returned to linger and die on the 12th of October, 1874. His administration had been that of a kind and gentle father, winning the love of his flock and the respect of the whole community by his virtues, his learning, and his modesty. At his death Connecticut alone had 89 churches and 76 priests.

RIGHT REV. THOMAS GALBERRY, O.S.A.,

Fourth Bishop of Hartford.

THOMAS GALBERRY first saw the light at Naas, in the County Kildare, Ireland, in 1833; but three years after his birth his parents came to this country and settled in Philadelphia. Here he received his early training, and at the age of sixteen entered Villanova College. On his graduation, in 1851, he resolved to renounce the world, and the next year received the habit of the Hermits of St. Augustine at Villanova. After a fervent novitiate he began his divinity studies, and was ordained priest by Bishop Neumann, December 20, 1856. Father Galberry was for two years a professor at Villanova, then pastor of St. Dennis' Church, West Haverford. At the opening of the year 1860 he was sent to Lansingburg, New York, a mission long in the hands of the Augustinians. Here he erected a fine Gothic church at a cost of more than thirty-three thousand dollars, and near it a house for the Sisters of St. Joseph. On the 30th of November, 1866, he was made superior of the Commissariate of Our Lady of Good Counsel, the mission of his order in the United States. While holding this important office he took charge at Lawrence, Mass., completing the church in that place, and, having been elected president of Villanova College, erected a new edifice and reorganized the university course. When the Augustinians in the United States were formed into the province of St. Thomas of Villanova, in 1874, Father Galberry was elected provincial, but was soon after appointed by the Pope Bishop of Hartford. Reluctant to sever his life from his religious brethren, he forwarded his resignation to Rome, but was required to obey. He was accordingly consecrated by Archbishop Williams, March 19, 1876. On assuming the mitre of Hartford he entered on his duties with his wonted zeal and devotion, seeking to spread through his flock solid and deep piety and attachment to the faith, as he had while superior of his order extended the Third Order of St. Augustine with great spiritual fruit. He was not, however, long to rule the diocese of Hartford. In October, 1878, feeling that his health was breaking, he hoped that a visit to Villanova would enable him to recruit his strength and obtain the care of physicians who knew his constitution. His case, however, was far more critical than he supposed. Before the rapidly-moving cars reached New York Bishop Galberry was seized with a hemorrhage, and as the Grand Central Station was entered he was conveyed to a hotel and medical aid was summoned. It was beyond the power of science to arrest the malady. The faithful bishop prepared to surrender a life which he had spent in the service of religion and his fellow-men, and was attended by several of the city clergy. He died calmly about seven o'clock in the evening of October 10, 1878, greatly lamented by his fellow-religious and by the diocese of Hartford, which had just begun to appreciate his worth.

RIGHT REV. LAWRENCE S. McMAHON,

Fifth Bishop of Hartford.

LAWRENCE S. MCMAHON was born in the British province of New Brunswick in 1835, but was brought to the United States in his fourth year. His early studies were made in the public schools of Boston, but he subsequently entered the College of the Holy Cross at Worcester, Mass., and remained there till the destruction of that institution by fire suspended its work for a time. He made the rest of his course in Montreal and Baltimore. Desirous of devoting himself to the service of the Almighty, he went to France and began his theological course at the college of Aix, but completed it at Rome, March 24, 1860. He was ordained that same year in the Basilica of St. John Lateran by the cardinal vicar. On his return to the United States he was first stationed in the cathedral at Boston, but in 1863 accompanied the Twenty-eighth Massachusetts regiment to the field as chaplain. After the war he was appointed the first pastor of Bridgewater, from which parish he was, on the 1st of July, 1865, transferred to New Bedford. Here he erected the elegant Gothic church dedicated to St. Lawrence, collecting means as he advanced, so that he escaped any large indebtedness. His next step was to establish an hospital for the care of the sick, under the charge of the Sisters of Mercy— the first institution of the kind in New Bedford—and he also acquired land for other pious establishments. When the see of Providence was erected, in 1872, Bishop Hendricken made Rev. Mr. McMahon his vicar-general, and the next year the zealous priest received from Rome the degree of Doctor of Divinity. After fourteen years' mission work at New Bedford he was chosen for the see of Hartford, and was consecrated by Archbishop Williams on the 10th of August, 1879. He completed the cathedral, and governs the diocese with zeal and prudence. The diocese contained, in 1884, 136 priests, 116 churches, and a Catholic population estimated at 180,000.

RT. REV. F. X. KRAUTBAUER, D.D.
Born at Bruck, Jan. 12, 1824.
Ordained July 16, 1850; Consecrated Bishop of
Green Bay, June 29, 1875. Died Dec., 1885.

RT. REV. LAWRENCE S. McMAHON.
Born in New Brunswick in 1835.
Ordained in 1860; Consecrated Bishop of
Hartford, Aug. 10, 1879.

RT. REV. JEREMIAH F. SHANAHAN.
Born in Susquehanna Co., Pa.
Ordained July, 1859; Consecrated Bishop of
Harrisburg, July 12, 1868.

RT. REV. JOHN B. BRONDEL, D.D.
Born at Bruges, Belgium, Feb. 23, 1842.
Ordained Dec. 17, 1864; Consecrated Bishop of Vancouver's Island, Dec. 14, 1879; Vicar-Apostolic of Montana in 1883; Bishop of Helena, March 7, 1884.

DIOCESE OF HELENA.

RIGHT REV. JOHN B. BRONDEL,

First Bishop of Helena.

JOHN B. BRONDEL was born at Bruges, in the Belgian province of West Flanders, on the 23d of February, 1842, and received his first instructions from the Xaverian Brothers, a community but recently formed in his native city. He then for ten years followed the French and Latin courses at the College of St. Louis, the episcopal seat of learning. Choosing the career of a missionary, he made his philosophical and theological studies in the American College at Louvain, and was ordained priest by His Eminence Cardinal Sterckx at Mechlin on the 17th of December, 1864. He had been received by Bishop Blanchet for the diocese of Nesqually, and set out for it by the way of Panama, reaching Vancouver on All-Hallow Eve, 1866. After spending a year at the college, combining the duties of a professor with those of a missionary, he was stationed for ten years at Steilacoom, on Puget Sound, and after a year at Walla Walla returned to it. During his pastorship he built churches at Olympia and Tacoma. Having been elected Bishop of Vancouver's Island, he was consecrated by Archbishop Seghers on the 14th of December, 1879. He directed this difficult diocese till the Holy See assigned to Bishop Brondel the task of organizing the Church in Montana preparatory to the establishment of an episcopal see. The Territory had been erected into a vicariate-apostolic as early as 1868, and the Very Rev. A. Ravoux had been elected to preside over it, but he declined the appointment. The vicariate was administered by neighboring bishops, but was re-erected on the 7th of April, 1883, and Bishop Brondel was the first vicar-apostolic. On the 7th of March, 1884, His Holiness Pope Leo XIII. erected the see of Helena and transferred Bishop Brondel to it. The church of the Sacred Heart became his cathedral, and he endeavored to secure missionaries who would accomplish among other tribes what the Jesuit Fathers had effected among the Flatheads and Pends d'Oreilles. The population of the diocese is about ten thousand, the white Catholics being widely scattered, and beside the thirteen Jesuit Fathers he had only five secular priests.

DIOCESES OF KANSAS CITY AND ST. JOSEPH'S.

RIGHT REV. JOHN JOSEPH HOGAN,

First Bishop of Kansas City and First Bishop of St. Joseph's.

JOHN J. HOGAN was born May 10, 1829, in the parish of Bruff, diocese of Limerick, Ireland. At the age of five he was sent to the neighboring village school of Holy Cross. At ten he was placed under the care of a private tutor in his father's house, where for four years he devoted himself to acquiring Latin, Greek, and French. After four years more spent in classical schools young Hogan came to the diocese of St. Louis, Missouri, to enter the theological seminary, and at the close of the regular course was ordained priest in April, 1852. The young priest's first mission was at Old Mines, where he spent a year and a half, and was then transferred to Potosi, where he became pastor. In 1854 he was called to St. Louis, and besides duty as assistant at St. John's Church officiated as chaplain to the Male Orphan Asylum and confessor to the Sisters. While thus engaged he was commissioned to organize a new parish, and erected St. Michael's Church, of which he became rector, signalizing his pastorship by at once commencing the parochial schools. Northwest Missouri, a wide district of country, without altar or priest, required an active and zealous missionary. He cheerfully left the parish which he had created to undertake the difficulties and hardships of an unprovided district. The resolute energy of the priest appears in the missions founded by him at Martinsburg, Mexico, Sturgeon, Allen—now called Moberly—Macon City, Brookfield, Chillicothe, and Cameron. Shortly before the civil war he undertook to establish a settlement in southern Missouri, on the borders of Arkansas, but was unsuccessful, the fiery tide of conflicting armies having rolled too frequently forward and backward over the peaceful labors of the ruined settlers. The diocese of St. Louis had long comprised the whole State of Missouri, but it was evident that, by assigning a portion of the territory to a local bishop, the interests of religion would be better subserved. Soon after the restoration of peace plans were made for the erection of a new see, which was created by Pope Pius IX. on the 3d of March, 1868, at St. Joseph, in Buchanan County, the diocese comprising the portion of Missouri lying between the river of that name and the Chariton. To this see the laborious missionary was appointed, receiving episcopal consecration on the 13th of September, 1868, at the hands of Archbishop Kenrick, in St. John's Church, St. Louis, the assistant bishops being the Right Rev. John B. Miége and Right Rev. P. A. Feehan, the eloquent sermon on the occasion being preached by Bishop Hennessy, of Dubuque. The diocese included part of Dr. Hogan's former missions, so that he was personally known. When he was installed it contained fourteen thousand Catholics, with eleven churches attended by nine priests; but education had received a solid basis in the establishment of the Ladies of the Sacred Heart and the Christian Brothers at St. Joseph. Under the bishop's impulse a new energy was infused into the Catholic body, priests were obtained for growing congregations, churches rose, the Benedictine Fathers came to found a priory at Conception, in Nodaway County, and the Franciscans at Mount St. Mary's, in Chariton County. Benedictine nuns, Sisters of St. Joseph and of the Perpetual Adoration, help to carry on the needed parochial schools. By 1880 the Catholics of the diocese, considerably increased in numbers, had thirty churches and twenty-six priests.

On the 10th of September in that year the Holy See erected another diocese, comprising the portion of the State south of the Missouri River and west of Moniteau, Miller, Camden, Laclede, Wright, Douglas, and Ozark counties. The episcopal see was fixed at Kansas City, and to it Bishop Hogan was transferred, retaining the charge of his former diocese as administrator. This new diocese contained forty-two churches and thirty priests, and some twelve thousand Catholics. The Sisters of St. Joseph had opened at St. Joseph's a convent, attending an hospital, an asylum, and schools. Chillicothe, Brookfield, Sedalia, Conception, Maryville, Boonville, Springfield, Independence, and Tipton, all had schools.

The Redemptorist Fathers soon made Kansas City the centre of their Western missions, establishing there a novitiate and preparatory college; the Benedictine priory became the abbey of New Engelberg, with the Right Rev. Frowenus Conrad mitred abbot; a hospital was established at Kansas City, and orphan asylums there and at St. Joseph's; and Little Sisters of the Poor opened in the former city a house for those who were left in poverty in an advanced age. In May, 1882, he laid the corner-stone of the cathedral of the Immaculate Conception, a fine Corinthian church, capable of holding four thousand people. By 1884 the two dioceses under the care of Bishop Hogan had a Catholic population of 40,000, with seventy-five churches and eighty priests. The whole development was coeval with the bishop's labors; and he has never relaxed his efforts, aiming to give his people every facility for the practice of their religion and for the Catholic education of their children, and constantly keeping in view the training-up of candidates for the priesthood to maintain the work and meet the ever-increasing audacity of infidelity, which thrives in a land of godless schools.

DIOCESE OF LA CROSSE.

RIGHT REV. KILIAN FLASCH,

Second Bishop of La Crosse.

KILIAN FLASCH was born on the 16th of July, 1831, at the village of Retzstadt, in the diocese of Würzburg, Bavaria. He was brought up on his father's farm, attending the neighboring schools till his parents emigrated to America, in 1847. He soon after entered the College of Notre Dame, Indiana, from which he passed to the pro-seminary at Milwaukee, and, persevering in his resolve to devote his life to the apostolate of the Christian priesthood, he became a student in the Salesianum, or Seminary of St. Francis, at its opening in 1856. After pursuing a solid course of divinity studies in that thorough seminary he was ordained priest, December 16, 1859. His pious parents lived to see with joy their son a priest and three daughters enter the Sisterhood of Notre Dame, his mother attaining an age of nearly fourscore and ten to receive his episcopal blessing. The young priest was stationed at Laketown for about ten months, but in October, 1860, was recalled to the Salesianum, where, as master of discipline and professor, he remained till May, 1867, when ill-health required a change. He sought rest, however, in mission work, taking charge of a small parish and an orphan asylum at Elm Grove, near Milwaukee. In November, 1874, he became spiritual director at the seminary and professor of moral theology, and in 1879, on the retirement of Rev. Mr. Wapelhorst, Rector of the Salesianum. When Bishop Heiss was made coadjutor of Milwaukee this learned and experienced priest was selected for the see of La Crosse, and was consecrated by his predecessor, August 24, 1881. He was installed in his cathedral a week later, and has since labored for the flock committed to his care, now numbering 54,500, with 119 churches attended by 71 priests. The Jesuit Fathers have established a thriving college at Prairie du Chien; the Franciscan Sisters of the Perpetual Adoration have a large community, taking charge of two orphan asylums, a hospital, and eighteen parochial schools, other schools being conducted by Sisters of Notre Dame, St. Dominic, St. Joseph, and Sisters of Charity.

DIOCESE OF LEAVENWORTH.

RIGHT REV. JOHN B. MIÉGE,

Bishop of Messenia and Vicar-Apostolic of Kansas.

JOHN BAPTIST MIÉGE was born September 18, 1815, at Chevron, in Upper Savoy, of a pious and prominent family which had seen many of its members in dignities of Church or state. He was educated mainly by his elder brother, Urban, who for nearly forty-two years presided over the Episcopal Seminary of Montiers. His early inclinations pointed to the sacerdotal state, but on completing his studies, at the age of nineteen, he announced to his brother his wish to enter the army. Urban urged him to make a thorough course of philosophy before taking the step, and two years later John Baptist said to him: "Brother, with your consent I would like to enter the Society of Jesus." He was received into the novitiate at Mélan, October 23, 1836, and, after some years spent as a successful teacher of the young, studied theology under Perrone, Passaglia, Patrizzi, and Ballerini. He was ordained at Rome in 1847, and on the dispersion of the Italian houses of the society in the following year asked to be sent to the American mission. Reaching St. Louis near the close of 1849, he became pastor of St. Charles' Church, professor of moral theology at Florissant, and subsequently at the University of St. Louis. In 1850 he received a package containing his appointment as Vicar-Apostolic of the Indian Territory east of the Rocky Mountains. He firmly but respectfully returned the documents to Archbishop Kenrick, through whom they had been forwarded. In time a formal order arrived from Rome requiring his submission, but promising that he should not be raised to any see in the United States, and that as titular bishop he might remain a member of the Society. He was consecrated Bishop of Messenia by Archbishop Kenrick on the Feast of the Annunciation, 1851, in St. Xavier's Church, St. Louis. The vicariate assigned to his care was then held mainly by Indian tribes, few white settlers having entered it. The States of Kansas, Nebraska, Colorado, and Indian Territory have since been formed from the territory. He proceeded to St. Mary's Mission, which he made his residence, and entered on the work of a missionary priest, to explore his vicariate and ascertain its wants, and form plans for the development of religion. In 1853 he visited Rome to report its condition, acting also as procurator of his order at a General Congregation. When he took possession of the vicariate it contained missions of his order among the Pottowatamies and Osages, Ladies of the Sacred Heart directing a girls' school at the former. Bishop Miége soon had an Osage school, under Sisters of Loretto; the Catholics in his whole district numbering about five thousand. For these he gradually provided more priests and churches. As the district soon invited settlers, who poured in from the north and the south, the Territories of Kansas and Nebraska were laid off, and here began a struggle which culminated in a civil war between the two sections. In August, 1855, Bishop Miége fixed his residence at Leavenworth, where he found seven Catholic families. That year he could report six churches, three building, eleven stations, and eight priests. The next year the Benedictine Fathers began a mission at Doniphan, and in a few years Dom Augustine Wirth opened a college at Atchison. As settlers increased churches sprang up, so that in 1857 Nebraska was formed into a separate vicariate, and Bishop Miége's jurisdiction was confined to the Territory of Kansas. Before the close of the civil war Kansas had nineteen priests—seculars, Jesuits, Benedictines, and Carmelites—and, beside the Sisterhoods already noted, Sisters of Charity, who opened at Leavenworth an academy, an hospital, and an asylum. After that the growth of religion was rapid, and in 1871 Bishop Miége obtained his wish in the consecration of a coadjutor, Dom Louis Fink, who, as prior of the Benedictines at Atchison and vicar-general of the diocese, was fully conversant with the vicariate. When, in 1874, Bishop Miége was permitted to resign the charge of vicar-apostolic, he left in the State thirty-five thousand Catholics, forty-eight priests, and seventy-one churches, including a magnificent cathedral. To meet the debts incurred in the new buildings Bishop Miége made a successful tour through California and Spanish America.

In July, 1874, he returned as a simple Jesuit Father to the university in St. Louis. As spiritual director of the young students of the order at Woodstock he passed a few quiet years, and, after opening a college of his order at Detroit in 1877, returned to that house of studies. Prostrated by paralysis in 1883, he lingered in great suffering till his death, July 20, 1884.

RIGHT REV. LOUIS MARIA FINK,

First Bishop of Leavenworth.

MICHAEL FINK was born in Triftersberg, Bavaria, on the 12th of June, 1834, and, after studying in the Latin school and gymnasium at Ratisbon, came to this country at the age of eighteen. Called to a religious life he sought admission among the Benedictines of St. Vincent's Abbey, in Westmoreland County, Pennsylvania. He was received by the founder, Abbot Wimmer, and made his profession on the 6th of January, 1854, taking the name of Louis Maria. After completing his theological studies he was ordained priest on the 28th of May, 1857, by Bishop Young, of Erie. The first missionary labors of the young Benedictine priest were at Bellefonte, Pa., and Newark, N. J. He was then made pastor of a congregation in Covington, Ky., where he completed a fine church. He introduced into the parish Benedictine nuns to direct a girls' school, which was one of his earliest cares. Appointed to St. Joseph's, Chicago, he aroused a spirit of faith in his flock at that place and gathered so many around the altar that a new church was required, which he erected at a cost of eighty thousand dollars, planting a large and well-arranged school-house beside it. As prior of the house of his order in Atchison, Kan., he showed the same zeal and ability; and when Bishop Miége wished to obtain a coadjutor to whom he could resign his charge, that prelate solicited the appointment of the prior

RT. REV. JOHN J. HOGAN, D.D.
Born at Bruff, Ireland, May 10, 1829.
Ordained April, 1852 ; Consecrated Bishop of St. Joseph, Sept. 13, 1868; made Bishop of Kansas City, Sept. 10, 1880.

RT. REV. LOUIS MARIA FINK.
Born at Triftersberg, Bavaria, June 12, 1834.
Ordained May 28, 1857 ; Consecrated Bishop of Eucarpia and Coadjutor, June 11, 1871 ; Bishop of Leavenworth, May 22, 1877.

RT. REV. KILIAN FLASCH, D.D.
Born at Retzstadt, Bavaria, July 16, 1831.
Ordained Dec. 16, 1859 ; Consecrated Bishop of La Crosse, Aug. 24, 1881.

RT. REV. EDWARD FITZGERALD, D.D.
Born in Limerick, Oct. 13, 1833.
Ordained Aug. 22, 1857; Consecrated Bishop of Little Rock, Feb. 3, 1867.

of St. Benedict. On the 11th of June, 1871, he was consecrated by Bishop Foley Bishop of Eucarpia in St. Joseph's Church, Chicago, which he had erected. Bishop Fink not only aided Bishop Miége in the episcopal labors of the vicariate, but in his absence had the entire charge. In 1874 Bishop Miége resigned the vicariate, and resumed his position in the Society of Jesus as a simple Father. Bishop Fink became Vicar-Apostolic of Kansas till the erection of the see of Leavenworth, May 22, 1877, when he was transferred to it. The diocese is a large and important one, and Bishop Fink in pastorals and otherwise shows his zeal for Catholic progress. His diocese is well provided with educational establishments for its 80,000 Catholics. St. Benedict's College is connected with the Benedictine Abbey at Atchison; the Jesuit Fathers direct St. Mary's College at St. Mary's; there are besides 3 academies and 48 parochial schools, with 4,000 pupils, under Benedictine and Franciscan Sisters, Sisters of St. Joseph and of Charity, and of St. Agnes. The diocese also possesses orphan houses and hospitals under the charge of the Sisters of Charity.

DIOCESE OF LITTLE ROCK.

RIGHT REV. ANDREW BYRNE,

First Bishop of Little Rock.

ANDREW BYRNE was born at Navan, in Ireland, once famous for its shrine of Our Lady, on the 5th of December, 1802. After careful studies he entered the diocesan seminary in his native place, and while there responded to a call from Bishop England for laborers in his diocese. Young Byrne accompanied the bishop to Charleston in 1820, and, completing his course under him, was ordained November 11, 1827. After spending some years in laborious missions in the Carolinas the Rev. Mr. Byrne became pastor of St. Mary's, Charleston, in 1830, and was for several years vicar-general of the diocese. After attending the Second Provincial Council of Baltimore as theologian to Bishop England, he came to New York in 1836 and was pastor of St. James' and the Nativity, establishing subsequently St. Andrew's Church. In all these positions he had displayed untiring devotion to his priestly duties, a kind and benevolent heart, zeal in the confessional, and eloquence in the pulpit. On the erection of the see of Little Rock in 1843 he was nominated as bishop, and was consecrated, with Bishop McCloskey and Bishop Quarter, on the 10th of March, 1844, in St. Patrick's Cathedral, New York. He proceeded to his diocese, which comprised the State of Arkansas and Indian Territory, only to find that Catholics were few, widely scattered, and destitute of all spiritual aid. He twice visited Europe to obtain priests and some sisterhood to direct schools and charitable institutions. He was the first to introduce into this country the Sisters of Mercy, and labored assiduously for his diocese; but Catholic progress was comparatively slow. He found but seven hundred Catholics, with four priests and as many churches. At his death he left thirteen churches and nine priests. For several years his diocese afforded little or nothing for his support, but he was never discouraged. He attended the Sixth Provincial Council of Baltimore and the first of New Orleans, and died at Helena June 10, 1862.

RIGHT REV. EDWARD FITZGERALD,

Second Bishop of Little Rock.

EDWARD FITZGERALD was born in Limerick, Ireland, on the 13th of October, 1833; descended on his father's side from one of the old landed families, and on his mother's from the German Palatines, who settled in Ireland to avoid Catholicity, but gave many children back to the Church. Coming to this country with his family in 1849, he entered the college at the Barrens, Mo., in the ensuing year to prepare for his entrance into a theological seminary. After five years of ecclesiastical study at Mount St. Mary's of the West and its prototype at Emmittsburg he was ordained for the diocese of Cincinnati, August 22, 1857, and was at once sent on a mission of unusual difficulty for a newly-ordained priest. He was made pastor of the church at Columbus, Ohio, then under interdict, and in a state of rebellion against Archbishop Purcell. Rev. Mr. Fitzgerald restored peace, and brought the erring to a sense of duty. For nine years he labored assiduously, building up Catholicity in that city, soon to become a bishop's see.

After the close of the Civil War, when it was possible to begin to repair the losses, Rev. Mr. Fitzgerald was appointed to the diocese of Little Rock. It was a sacrifice of no ordinary character to undertake, without resources, to restore or advance the interests of the Church in a State like Arkansas, where the little Catholic beginnings had almost been swept away; yet he accepted the onerous task, and was consecrated February 3, 1867. When he reached the diocese there were but five priests left in the whole State, and of the institutions naught remained but three houses of Sisters of Mercy. The Catholic population in the State and in Indian Territory was estimated at sixteen hundred. Bishop Fitzgerald found much to be done, and absolutely no resources, but he endeavored to attract Catholic immigrants to the State. For a time Germans and Poles came to settle in Arkansas, so that in 1884 the Catholic body had risen to about seven thousand; but there is very slight increase now. The annual baptisms are about 375. In such dioceses, especially where the flocks are too few and too poor to maintain separate pastors, the hope of religion rests on those orders which, vowed to poverty and obedience, labor more earnestly because they are sustained by the spirit of their institute and the co-operation of brother religious. Bishop Fitzgerald called to his aid the ancient order of St. Benedict, who founded a priory in Logan County, and take charge of several missions; and also the Fathers of the Holy Ghost, whose monastery is at Marienstatt, in Conway County. These religious make their house a centre for missions in several counties. There were in all, in 1884, 23 priests in the diocese, which has 34 churches and 4 convent chapels. Besides the Sisters of Mercy, who so heroically clung to the diocese, Sisters of Charity, Sisters of St. Joseph, and Benedictine nuns are also laboring there, and this diocese can report 16 parochial schools with 1,143 pupils. Bishop Fitzgerald was one of the Fathers of the Vatican Council, and at the time of the conference of the bishops of the United States at Rome, in 1883, was selected to represent the province of New Orleans. He also attended the Third Plenary Council of Baltimore in 1884.

DIOCESE OF LOUISVILLE.

RIGHT REV. BENEDICT JOSEPH FLAGET,

First Bishop of Bardstown and Louisville.

BENEDICT JOSEPH FLAGET was born November 7, 1763, at Contournat, in Auvergne, France, of a family of pious farmers; his father died before his birth, and his mother did not long survive. Trained by a good aunt, young Flaget entered the college at Billom, and in time passed to the University of Clermont to study for the priesthood, as his elder brother had already done. The famous seminary of St. Sulpice attracted him, and, completing a thorough course there, Benedict Joseph was ordained priest and joined the community. He was for some years professor of dogmatic and subsequently of moral theology in the seminary at Nantes, till the French Revolution broke up all institutions of the kind. The good priest then sought refuge with his family at Billom, but he felt called to the American missions, and with the consent of his superior, Rev. Mr. Emery, sailed for Baltimore in 1792. Bishop Carroll welcomed the learned clergyman and sent him to Vincennes, where a French priest was needed. Journeying by wagon and flat-boat, performing missionary duty wherever he could on the route, Rev. Mr. Flaget reached Vincennes December 21, 1792. Religion had declined so that with all his exhortation only twelve received Holy Communion on Christmas day. He labored earnestly to revive religion at Vincennes and other little centres of population where the people had for years been deprived of all spiritual succor. Recalled to Baltimore in April, 1795, he descended the Mississippi in a boat to New Orleans and embarked from that city for Baltimore. Rev. Mr. Flaget was then for three years chief prefect and one of the professors of Georgetown College, having the honor to welcome Washington to the institution. In 1798 he visited Cuba with the view of establishing a house of the Sulpitian body on that island; but this design being frustrated, he returned to Baltimore with a number of young Cubans who desired to enter St. Mary's College. The next eight years were spent as professor in the college or in mission duties connected with the church and the parish attached to it. The arrival of the Trappists in America awakened in his heart a desire to fly from the world and all its vicissitudes, and seek peace in the silent cloisters of that austere order, but he never attained his wish.

When the diocese of Baltimore, which originally embraced all the thirteen United States, was divided in 1807, and new sees erected, Bishop Carroll recommended the Rev. Mr. Flaget for the see of Bardstown, Kentucky. The good priest at once begged Archbishop Carroll to obtain his release from the dreaded burden, and, failing to do so, went to Europe for the same object. Yielding at last to the will of the Sovereign Pontiff, he was consecrated in the cathedral, Baltimore, by Archbishop Carroll, assisted by Bishops Cheverus and Egan, on the 4th of November, 1810. Friends made up means to enable this bishop, apostolic in his poverty, to reach the diocese for which he had been consecrated. It comprised the State of Kentucky, then containing a thousand Catholics, with ten churches and three priests. Indiana and Michigan, with Tennessee, were also confided to his care. He took up his residence in a log-cabin sixteen feet square, and began his labors. The congregations in the diocese were frequently visited; a seminary was begun; confirmation given. All was not peace, however; there were dissensions to appease. Catholic doctrines were attacked, and the mild and gentle bishop was compelled to enter the arena, and, by his learning and solid reasoning, silence his opponent. His visitations to Indiana and Michigan revived religion far and wide, and those to Tennessee were the first mission efforts in that State. In 1817 he solicited the appointment of the Rev. Mr. David as his coadjutor, and that clergyman was consecrated in 1819. Relieved thus of some of his duties, devolving those nearest his cathedral on Bishop David, the venerable Dr. Flaget renewed his visitations. Besides his coadjutor he consecrated Bishop Fenwick, of Cincinnati, and went to Baltimore to consecrate Archbishop

Whitfield. In 1829 he attended the First Provincial Council of Baltimore, which had so long been desired by him. He was there received with great veneration as the holy survivor of Archbishop Carroll's associates in the episcopate. Subsequent to that council he, at different times, consecrated Bishops Kenrick, Purcell, Chabrat, and Bruté. Under his impulse and by his co-operation two religious communities of women, the Sisters of Loretto and Sisters of Charity, had risen up in his diocese, and the ranks of his clergy were swelled by the Dominicans and Trappists.

Bishop Flaget sought in vain to resign his episcopate. His reputation for sanctity, the blessings that God evidently gave his work, made the Sovereign Pontiffs refuse to deprive Kentucky of his presence as bishop. The Bishop of Bardstown visited Rome, where he was received with great respect and admiration, and while in France he was venerated as a saint. He returned to his diocese in the summer of 1839, after an absence of four years, and was welcomed with pious joy. Bishop Flaget immediately resumed his duties and made a thorough visitation of his diocese which lasted for two years. In 1841 the see of the diocese was removed from Bardstown to Louisville.

His first coadjutor, Bishop David, died in 1841, and in 1847 Bishop Chabrat, whose sight was rapidly failing, resigned to seek a cure in Europe. In 1848 the Rev. Martin John Spalding was appointed coadjutor, and on him the chief episcopal duties devolved, as the aged bishop never recovered from the fatigue of the day when his last coadjutor was consecrated.

Bishop Flaget introduced into his diocese the Sisters of the Good Shepherd in 1842; and in 1848 the Jesuit Fathers, to his great joy, consented to take charge of St. Joseph's, one of the two colleges he had founded. The Trappists in the same year returned to his diocese and founded an establishment, which grew and prospered with God's blessing. Relieved from the care of the diocese, Bishop Flaget spent his time in prayer or pious reading. In the summer of 1849 livid tumors appeared on his shoulder and lower limbs, and his health became such that, to his great sorrow, he was no longer able to offer the holy sacrifice of the Mass, and could only join in it in spirit from his room, and adore our Lord at the Consecration and at the Benediction of the Blessed Sacrament when the sound of the bell reached his ears. He bore all his sufferings with the utmost patience and cheerfulness. On the night of the 10th of February, 1850, he became restless and slightly delirious. At noon the next day Bishop Spalding, attended by the eleven priests of the city, administered the Holy Viaticum and Extreme Unction to the venerable prelate, who was in full possession of his faculties. He followed the profession of faith read by his secretary, and, after a few words expressing his ardent attachment to his clergy, religious, and people, he gave his last solemn episcopal benediction.

After this his lips moved in prayer, he pressed the crucifix to his lips, and at half-past five in the evening of the 11th calmly expired without a struggle.

"He died as he had lived," says Bishop Spalding, "a saint; and the last day was perhaps the most interesting and impressive of his whole life. Tranquilly, and without a groan, did he 'fall asleep in the Lord,' like an infant gently sinking to his rest."

No bishop in this country has ever been regarded as equalling Bishop Flaget in sanctity, in the spirit of prayer, in the ardor of his devotion, his firmness, patience, and constant devotion to all the duties of his state.

RIGHT REV. JOHN BAPTIST DAVID,

Bishop of Mauricastro and of Bardstown.

JOHN BAPTIST MARY DAVID was born near Nantes, France, in the year 1761. At the age of seven he began to study Latin and music under his uncle, a pious priest, and his greatest delight was to serve as altar-boy. At the age of fourteen he entered the college of the Oratorians, from which he passed to the diocesan seminary at Nantes. After receiving subdeacon's orders he spent some time in a pious family as tutor. In 1783, having been ordained deacon, he joined the Congregation of St.

Sulpice, and spent two years in retirement at Issy. After his ordination as priest, September 24, 1705, he became professor of philosophy, theology, and Holy Scriptures in the seminary at Angers, and remained there till it was closed by the infidel hordes of the French Revolution. Rev. Mr. David then retired to a private family, but in 1792 embarked with Rev. Mr. Flaget for America. Bishop Carroll confided to him several Catholic congregations in Maryland. Dr. David was the first to give retreats, reaping great fruit in a revival of piety. After being professor for two years at Georgetown College, and five in St. Mary's College, Baltimore, he was appointed ecclesiastical superior of the Sisters of Charity. In 1810 he accompanied Bishop Flaget to Bardstown and became superior of his theological seminary. In this position he became builder and farmer as well as theologian and director. His care extended to the Catholics around, and he founded the society of Sisters of Charity of Nazareth in a log hut, drawing up their rule, and by the bishop's orders becoming their spiritual director. To this day his community continues to render services to religion in the West. On the death of Bishop Egan he was nominated to the see of Philadelphia, but by his urgent appeals obtained permission to decline it. But Bishop Flaget besought the Pope to appoint Rev. Mr. David his coadjutor, and bulls were issued on the 4th of July, 1817. Dr. David yielded with great reluctance, and on August 15, 1819, was consecrated in the cathedral of Bardstown Bishop of Mauricastro and coadjutor of the Bishop of Bardstown. After his consecration he continued his austere life in the seminary, adding to his labors that of rector of the cathedral, ever ready for sick-calls or the confessional. He was never idle, and by his systematic use of time neglected none of his manifold duties. He met a Protestant controversialist named Hall in an oral discussion, and refuted him so clearly and with so much mildness that no one ever challenged him again. Besides this discussion he wrote several works in defence of the Faith, which rendered great service, and prepared "True Piety," a prayer-book which attained the most extended circulation. Bishop Flaget resigned his see in 1832, and Bishop David became for a time Bishop of Bardstown; but he would not accept the position, and the

Holy See reinstated Bishop Flaget, accepting Dr. David's resignation.

The weight of years at last compelled him to retire from the seminary, and he prepared for the close of his long and laborious career. He died at Bardstown on the 12th of July, 1841.

RIGHT REV. GUY IGNATIUS CHABRAT,

Bishop of Bolina and Coadjutor of Bardstown.

GUY IGNATIUS CHABRAT was born in the village of Chambre, France, on the 28th of December, 1787, his parents being Peter Chabrat, a merchant, and Louise Lavialle. After a pious youth, spent in the best schools of the day, he entered one of the Sulpitian theological seminaries, and in 1809 had received minor orders and the subdiaconate. At this time he volunteered to accompany Bishop Flaget to Kentucky, and embarked at Bordeaux with that holy bishop April 10, 1810. Continuing his ecclesiastical and spiritual preparation for the priesthood under Rev. Dr. David, he was ordained by Bishop Flaget at Christmas, 1811, and was the first who received the priesthood in the West, as Rev. Mr. Badin was in the East. Rev. Mr. Chabrat was at once placed on mission duty at St. Michael's, in Nelson Co., and St. Clare's, in Hardin Co., and for several years showed himself an active, prudent, and exemplary priest, residing at Fairfield and making excursions to other parts of the State. Bishop Flaget reposed great confidence in him, and about 1820 sent him to Europe to obtain aid for his diocese. After his return, in 1821, he was for a time superior of the Brothers of the Mission and pastor of St. Pius', in Scott County, and in 1824 was appointed superior of the Community of Loretto. From that time the direction of the Sisters and the pastoral care of the Catholics in the neighborhood exclusively engaged his attention.

Some years after, when Bishop Flaget tendered his resignation, he recommended the appointment of Rev. Mr. Chabrat as coadjutor to Bishop David, and the advice was taken. Bishop David, however, refused to accept the see, and Bishop Flaget was reinstated, and it was not till 1834 that bulls arrived appointing Rev. Mr. Chabrat Bishop of Bolina and coadjutor. He was consecrated on the 20th of July in the cathedral of Bardstown.

From 1835 to 1839, during the absence of Bishop Flaget, Bishop Chabrat administered the diocese, and even after the return of the venerable prelate the responsibility rested on him. But his long, active missionary service began to show its influence; for several years his health declined, and at last he was threatened with a loss of sight. Eminent oculists advised him to visit Europe. He accordingly asked to resign his coadjutorship, but the Fathers of the Council of Baltimore in 1846 were reluctant to advise that it should be accepted. The most skilful men in France in treating diseases of the eye gave Bishop Chabrat no encouragement, and he returned to America to close up his affairs. He then left the country for ever. On the certificate of able physicians he obtained in 1847, through the Papal Nuncio, the acceptance of the resignation of his coadjutorship. The Bishop of Bolina then returned to his father's house at Mauriac, preparing in seclusion for death. He became at last completely blind, but his health rallied and he lived more than twenty years, dying calmly in his native place, November 21, 1868, in his eighty-second year.

RIGHT REV. PETER JOSEPH LAVIALLE,

Third Bishop of Louisville.

PETER JOSEPH LAVIALLE was born at Lavialle, near Mauriac, France, in 1820, and early prepared to leave the world and enter the ecclesiastical state. While studying theology he was invited by his kinsman, Bishop Chabrat, to join the diocese of Louisville, and crossed the ocean in 1841 to complete his studies in the diocesan seminary of St. Thomas at Bardstown. After his ordination, in 1844, he was employed for some years in the cathedral of Louisville, and in 1849 took the chair of theology in the diocesan seminary of St. Thomas, and filled it with distinction till his appointment as president of St. Mary's College in 1856. Four years afterwards he was nominated to the see of New Orleans, but declined the appointment. When, however, at the promotion of Bishop Spalding to the see of Baltimore, bulls were sent to Rev. Mr. Lavialle appointing him Bishop of Louisville, he was compelled to accept. He was consecrated September 24, 1865, and assumed the duties with conscientious responsibility. He made several visitations of his diocese, attending to all details, and encouraging priests and people in erecting churches and schools, as well as laboring to suppress all abuses and remove all obstacles. His health was, however, extremely feeble, and in 1867 he retired for a time to St. Joseph's Infirmary, kept by the Sisters of Charity, and then went to Nazareth, where the Sisters did all in their power to minister to his comfort; but the disease was too powerful for his feeble constitution to meet. He sank gradually, and died a peaceful and happy death on Passion Sunday, the 11th of May, 1867, in the residence of the ecclesiastical superior of the Sisters of Charity of Nazareth.

Of this prelate the Hon. Ben. J. Webb says: "Bishop Lavialle was a man to whom no one accorded the possession of extraordinary natural talents. He was not eloquent in the pulpit, neither was he forcible as a writer. Judged by the standard of the world, he was a plain man with practical ideas. But he was in reality much more than all this. He was a man of God, and he labored, not with dependence upon his own strength, but with the assurance that what was lacking to him therein would be supplied by Him from whom was derived his commission."

RIGHT REV. WILLIAM G. McCLOSKEY,

Fourth Bishop of Louisville.

WILLIAM GEORGE McCLOSKEY was born in Brooklyn, N. Y., November 10, 1883, and made his classical and theological studies at St. Mary's College, Baltimore. He was ordained in New York cathedral October 6, 1852, and began the labors of a missionary as assistant at the church of the Nativity in New York, of which his brother was rector. His merit and ability were, however, known, and within a year or two he was made professor at Mount St. Mary's College, Emmittsburg, and for many years he discharged his duties with such ability that when the American College was founded at Rome by the venerable pontiff Pope Pius IX. he was selected as the first president of that institution. Its organization and successful commencement showed his administrative power. His ability and virtues were soon recognized at Rome, and after the death of Bishop Lavialle he was elected to fill the vacant see. He was consecrated on the 24th of May, 1868, and began his administration with a desire to establish system and order throughout the diocese. His visitations were carefully and strictly made, leading in some cases to discontent and appeals from his judgment; but in a few years the ancient diocese was progressing in all harmony, and in 1884 had 107 churches, with 138 priests. There were 27 academies and 128 parochial schools. During his episcopate the Priests of the Congregation of the Resurrection came to the diocese to assume charge of St. Mary's College, the Franciscan and Carmelite Fathers to labor among the Germans; the Sisters of Mercy, Little Sisters of the Poor, and Franciscan Sisters joined the older communities in their special works of charity and mercy.

DIOCESE OF MANCHESTER.

RIGHT REV. DENIS M. BRADLEY,

First Bishop of Manchester.

DENIS M. BRADLEY was born in Ireland February 25, 1846, and when eight years of age came with his mother to America. Mrs. Bradley settled with her five children at Manchester, in New Hampshire, the State in all the North where Catholicity has had its hardest struggles. To this day no Catholic can hold office in this mountain State.

The boy attended the Catholic schools in the town, and, evincing talent and a desire for higher study, was sent to the College of the Holy Cross, Worcester, Mass. After being graduated at that institution he entered St. Joseph's Provincial Seminary, Troy, N. Y., and was ordained there by Bishop McQuaid, of Rochester, on the 3d of June, 1871. Bishop Bacon, of Portland, to whose diocese the young priest belonged, appointed him to the cathedral, where he remained during the lifetime of that prelate, acting during the last two years as rector of the cathedral and chancellor of the diocese, and continuing to discharge the same duties under Bishop Healy till June 16, 1880, when he was made pastor of St. Joseph's Church, Manchester. N. H. When it was decreed at Rome that New Hampshire should be detached from the diocese of Portland and constituted into a separate diocese, the Rev. Mr. Bradley was recommended for the new see by the bishops of the province, his zeal and services in parochial duties and his experience in diocesan affairs fitting him for the episcopate. He was appointed by Pope Leo XIII., and consecrated June 11, 1884.

The first church in New Hampshire was erected in 1823 by the convert Rev. Virgil H. Barber. By 1833 there was a second church at Dover, but not a priest resident in the whole State.

Even ten years later, and down to 1847, there were but these two churches, though they had priests and Portsmouth was regularly attended. In 1847 a church was begun at Manchester by the Franciscan Father, John B. Daly.

On the establishment of the see of Portland there were only these three churches in the State; but Catholicity then began to gain strength. Mother Mary Francis Warde established at Manchester a convent of the Sisters of Mercy, which soon had under the Sisters an academy, parochial schools, and an orphan asylum. When the diocese of Portland was ten years old New Hampshire had seven churches and as many priests; in 1873 they had grown to eighteen priests and sixteen churches—Manchester alone having three churches, thus taking lead as the Catholic centre of the State.

When Bishop Bradley was installed as Bishop of Manchester, in 1884, he had 42 priests in his diocese and 37 churches or chapels. The Catholic population of the State was about 60,000, and there were 3,500 children in the Catholic schools. The large manufacturing towns contained numbers of Catholic operatives, and there were many Catholic farmers, and the different congregations were easily reached.

Soon after the consecration of Right Rev. Dr. Bradley the alumni of St. Joseph's Provincial Seminary resolved to honor the first bishop appointed from their number, and presented to Bishop Bradley a fine testimonial.

DIOCESE OF MARQUETTE.

RIGHT REV. FREDERIC BARAGA,

First Bishop of Marquette and Saut Ste. Marie.

FREDERIC BARAGA was born on the 29th of June, 1797, in Treffen Castle, Carniola, the home of his noble and wealthy parents. He received his earliest instruction under private tutors, and during his college life distinguished himself by his rapid progress in Illyrian, German, French, Italian, and Latin. After studying law for five years at the University of Vienna he felt himself called to a higher vocation. Entering on a course of theology, he was ordained in 1823. Seven years were spent in zealous work as a priest and in preparing popular devotional works in Sclavonic, which are still highly esteemed. Resolving to devote himself to the Indian missions in America, he landed in New York December 31, 1830, and as soon as navigation opened hastened to the field he had selected in Michigan, where he was to labor till his death. His large property in Europe he resigned to his brothers and sisters, retaining only an annuity of $300, and even that he ultimately renounced. He came to America to face poverty and hardship. When he took up his residence in the Indian country, northern Michigan, especially the Lake Superior district, was an almost unbroken wilderness, known only to the Indian and trapper. The devoted priest found that the religious ideas implanted among the Indians in early times by the Jesuit missionaries were nearly effaced. He soon acquired influence among the Indians and half-breeds, gathered them together, induced them to build cabins, obtained for them simple tools and implements, and encouraged them to work and adopt the habits of civilized people. Having mastered their language, his influence was great, and soon extended to other points. Travelling like the Indians, enduring extraordinary hardships and privations, during his long years of missionary life among the Ottawas and Chippewas Rev. Mr. Baraga was their father, guide, and pastor. Besides establishing the missions of Arbre Croche, Grand Traverse, and Grand River, on Lake Michigan, from 1831 to 1835, and those of Lapointe, Fond du Lac, Bad River, and L'Anse, on Lake.Superior, from 1835 to 1853, he regularly visited the small bands of Indians scattered along the shores and on the islands of both lakes from Grand Haven to Superior City. Amid all these labors, travelling by canoe or in winter on snow-shoes amid the greatest cold of winter, the laborious missionary found time to prepare a series of works in Ottawa and Chippewa—catechisms, prayer-books, and devotional works for his spiritual children, books that he had educated them to use; while for the assistance of clergymen who came to share or succeed in his labors he prepared an invaluable grammar and dictionary of the Otchipwe, or Chippewa language, a work since reprinted in Canada to meet the demand for it among missionaries. The catalogue of North American Linguistics issued by the Smithsonian Institution gives the titles of no fewer than sixteen of Bishop Baraga's works in Indian languages.

When white people began to settle in his district he ministered with his wonted zeal to all their settlements in the upper peninsula. Wherever Rev. Mr. Baraga appeared his humanity, his disinterested zeal and true Christian charity, joined with remarkable abstemiousness and utter disregard of comfort, gained for him the unbounded respect as well as the love of all who came in contact with him.

When, at the instance of Bishop Lefevre, the Holy See in 1853 detached the northern peninsula of Michigan from the diocese of Detroit, forming it into a vicariate-apostolic, the Rev. Mr. Baraga was selected to direct it. He was consecrated Bishop of Amyzonia and Vicar-Apostolic of Upper Michigan on the feast of All Saints in the year 1853. The vicariate embraced the northern peninsula with the adjacent islands, containing at the time six churches, five priests, and five schools. But Bishop Lefevre ceded to him his power, authority, and jurisdiction over five counties in the southern peninsula, and the Bishop of Milwaukee ceded to him jurisdiction over the Apostle islands in Lake Superior, and the Bishop of Dubuque made a similar cession, so that he had in a short time sixteen priests, with fourteen churches and six thousand Catholics, under his care.

His exaltation to the episcopate made no change in his deportment. He remained a missionary to the last. After visiting Rome, Austria, France, and Ireland in the interest of his diocese, he took up his lonely abode at Saut Ste. Marie, where for several years he did all the duties of a pastor among the neighboring Indians, as zealous, patient, and charitable as ever.

On the 9th of January, 1857, the diocese of Saut Ste. Marie, or Marianopolis, was erected, and Bishop Baraga was transferred to the new see. A journey in sleigh and snow-shoes to attend the council in 1862 undermined his constitution. He never recovered from the exposure, having reached Thunder Bay sick and almost frozen. On the 15th of October, 1865, the see was transferred to Marquette, where he took up his residence, making St. Peter's his cathedral. Early in 1866 paralysis, hereditary in the family, showed itself in his hand, but he continued active in discharging his duties, and in September preached sermons at Hancock in three languages. He set out soon after to attend the Plenary Council of Baltimore, and during its sessions was struck down with apoplexy on the steps of the archiepiscopal palace. The assembled bishops in vain urged him to retire and in the home of some of his brethren pass his remaining days in well-earned repose. Bishop Baraga determined to die at his post, and returned to Lake Superior. There he resumed his missionary work, teaching, baptizing, hearing confessions, and visiting persons less sick than himself. But his infirmities increased, and he could leave his room only to hear Mass on Sundays and holidays. Then he spent his time in prayer and meditation. On the eve of Epiphany, 1868, he received a warning of his approaching dissolution, and, strengthened by the sacraments, expired, after a short agony, on the feast of the Holy Name of Jesus, January 19, 1868.

RIGHT REV. IGNATIUS MRAK,

Second Bishop of Marquette and Saut Ste. Marie.

IGNATIUS MRAK was born at Pölland, in Carniola, a province of the Austro-Hungarian Empire, on the 10th of October, 1810, and, after a thorough course of study, was ordained on the 13th of August, 1837. Having spent eight years in mission labor in his own country, he came to the United States in 1845, beginning his labors as an Indian missionary at Arbre Croche, where he became assistant to the Rev. Francis Pierz. In this and two dependent stations there were fifteen hundred Ottawa Indians with their churches and schools. On the 10th of July, 1847, Bishop Lefevre confided to Rev. Mr. Mrak the missions of La Croix, Middletown, Castor Island, and Manistee, containing six hundred souls, which he attended, still residing at Arbre Croche. He soon took up his abode at St. Anthony's Church, La Croix, and continued from it to attend Middletown two years after Bishop Baraga was made vicar-apostolic, in 1853. Then he was stationed at Eagle Town, on Grand Traverse Bay, where his church and school kept the faith of a large district alive. In 1860 he was made vicar-general of the diocese of Saut Ste. Marie, and from Eagle Town attended ten different stations. On the death of Bishop Baraga the Rev. Mr. Mrak and his missions, which had been ceded only to the late bishop, returned to the jurisdiction of the see of Detroit. Rev. Mr. Mrak was, however, soon selected to fill the vacant see, and was consecrated Bishop of Marquette in the cathedral at Cincinnati by Archbishop Purcell, assisted by Bishops Lefevre and Henni, on the 7th of February, 1869. On assuming direction Bishop Mrak found the diocese with 21 churches, 15 priests, and about 22,000 Catholic souls. He governed it ably for several years, but, finding infirmities to increase with years, he resigned in 1878, and was transferred to the see of Antinoe on the 14th of May, 1881. He continued to reside at Marquette, acting as chaplain to the Sisters of St. Joseph in their chapel of the Sacred Heart, but in 1884 removed to Eagle Town. He is regarded as a prelate of great learning and remarkable linguistic attainments.

RIGHT REV. JOHN VERTIN,

Third Bishop of Marquette.

JOHN VERTIN was born on the 17th of July, 1844, at Rudolfswerth, Carniola, and, after making his preparatory and collegiate course in his native country, came to the United States July 7, 1863, when he was eighteen years of age. His father, whose mercantile affairs brought him across the Atlantic, placed him under the care of the great Bishop Baraga. That prelate received the pious youth into his diocese, and sent him to the Salesianum to complete his theological studies. Archbishop Henni conferred minor orders on him in 1865, and on the 31st of August of the next year he was ordained priest by Bishop Baraga in Marquette, being the first ordained in that place, and the last on whom the eminent bishop conferred holy orders.

The young priest was placed in charge of the mission at Houghton, where he remained five years, and he then labored for seven among the Catholics of Negaunee, both difficult missions, as the flock was composed of men of different origin, who spoke English, German, and French. On the resignation of Bishop Mrak the bishops of the province sent to Rome the name of Right Rev. Doctor Vertin as his successor. He was consecrated by Archbishop Heiss, assisted by Bishops Borgess and Spalding, on the 14th of September, 1879, his parents, who had settled at Hancock, living to see the exaltation of their son. The diocese has prospered under his rule, and in 1884 was estimated as containing twenty-nine thousand whites and between one and two thousand Indians. Thirty-two priests labor there, attending forty-two churches and chapels as well as sixty-eight dependent stations. Sisters of St. Joseph, St. Agnes, and of the Immaculate Heart of Mary direct academies, schools, and an orphan asylum. Bishop Vertin has completed St. Peter's Cathedral at Marquette, a fine structure.

DIOCESE OF MOBILE.

RIGHT REV. MICHAEL PORTIER,

First Bishop of Mobile.

MICHAEL PORTIER was born at Montbrison, France, September 7, 1795, and was trained to piety even amid the terrible days of the French Revolution. His early studies did not chill his fervor, and he entered the Theological Seminary at Lyons, and when Bishop Dubourg, of Louisiana, appealed for missionaries, young Portier was one of the first to respond to the call. He accompanied that prelate to America, and landed at Annapolis, Md., September 4, 1817. Having completed his studies under the Sulpitians at Baltimore, he received the diaconate, and was ordained priest by Bishop Dubourg at St. Louis in 1818. In his first year he was nearly carried off by yellow fever, taken while attending the sick, but recovered, and with a few assistants opened a Catholic collegiate institute at New Orleans, and soon after, became vicar-general. The diocese of Louisiana then embraced all the territory west of the Mississippi, and Florida, with the intervening Gulf shore. The Holy See saw the necessity of dividing this immense territory and confiding portions to separate bishops. Mississippi and Alabama were erected into a vicariate-apostolic, and Pope Pius VII., by bull of January 21, 1823, annexed to it Florida. By a subsequent bull of July 14 Mississippi as a vicariate was restored to the Bishop of New Orleans. The new vicariate was thus composed of Alabama and Florida; and for its government the Very Rev. Michael Portier was selected. He was most reluctant to assume such a responsibility, but finally yielded, and was consecrated by Bishop Rosati at St. Louis, November 5, 1826. His jurisdiction included the two old Spanish Catholic cities of St. Augustine, founded in 1565, and Pensacola, in 1696, each with its church and its congregation of the faithful. In Spanish times Florida had been a missionary field, where Dominican, Jesuit, and Franciscan Fathers shed their blood in their heroic efforts to convert the Indians, some perishing by the hands of the Indians, and some by the hands of bigoted and fanatical English invaders. Florida had been, from its settlement in the province of Santo Domingo, subject directly to the Bishop of Santiago de Cuba, and from 1787 to 1793 to the Bishop of St. Christopher of Havana. The Indian missions had vanished, destroyed by the English and their dusky allies; the streets of the little cities, where Catholic processions and pilgrimages had so often passed, with priests and religious, on their way to hermitage and shrine, now seldom beheld the occasional visits of priests. Catholics of other races were coming slowly in, but Bishop Portier had everything to revive and to restore. He was the only clergyman in his vicariate. "I need two or three priests," he wrote, "and dare not ask for them, as I am afraid I cannot now support them. I have neither pectoral cross nor chapel, neither crosier nor mitre." To add to his difficulties, the little church at Mobile was destroyed by fire in October, 1827. Bishop Portier made a visitation of his vicariate as a missionary priest, beginning at Mobile and riding on horseback to Pensacola, Tallahassee, St. Augustine, till his overtaxed system gave way and he was prostrated with fever. As soon as he could secure one priest to attend the western part, and having induced Bishop England to supply St. Augustine for a time, Bishop Portier went to Europe in 1829. He returned at the close of the year with two priests and four ecclesiastics. During his absence the Holy See had erected Mobile into an episcopal see in the province of Santiago de Cuba, and Bishop Portier was transferred to it. The ancient French city, where a parish had been canonically erected July 20, 1703, thus became the residence of a bishop. Dr. Portier soon reached it and began the erection of a little church twenty feet wide by thirty in depth, the modest cathedral in which he was enthroned. His two-roomed frame palace of still more modest dimensions adjoined it. With his little force of priests he began to meet the wants of his flock, collecting congregations and preparing for the erection of churches at Montgomery, Tuscaloosa, Huntsville, Moulton, and Florence.

One of his first steps was to secure property at Spring Hill, near Mobile, where a college was soon under the presidency of Rev. Mathias Loras, welcoming Catholic students. It subsists to the present time, having been for a season directed by the Eudists and by the Priests of Mercy.

In 1832 he obtained a colony of Visitation nuns from Georgetown, who founded a convent and academy that have for more than sixty years drawn blessings on the diocese. Four years afterwards Bishop Portier replaced his poor cathedral by a temporary brick structure, having laid the corner-stone of the cathedral of the Immaculate Conception in 1835. Owing to the poverty of his diocese it was not completed and dedicated till December 8, 1850, his pro-cathedral then becoming an orphan asylum under the Sisters of Charity and Brothers of Christian Instruction. The Sisters opened soon after an academy at St. Augustine. In 1846 the Jesuit Fathers entered the diocese and assumed charge of Spring Hill College.

By 1850 there were churches at Montgomery, Spring Hill, Summerville, Mount Vernon, Fish River, Tuscaloosa, and Pensacola. In this year the eastern part of Florida was detached from the diocese of Mobile and given to the newly-erected see of Savannah.

Bishop Portier labored incessantly in and for his diocese, visiting Europe in its behalf in 1849. In the Provincial Councils of Baltimore and New Orleans, as well as in the First Plenary Synod, his learning and experience commanded the respect of all.

One of his last acts was the establishment of an infirmary at Mobile under the Sisters of Charity. When, after long years of episcopal service, Bishop Portier found himself attacked by a serious malady, he retired to this institution, and, edifying all by the patience and piety with which he supported his long and severe sufferings, he died on the 14th of May, 1859. The whole city joined with the Catholics in their regret and sympathy on the loss sustained by the death of so truly apostolic a prelate.

RIGHT REV. JOHN QUINLAN,

Second Bishop of Mobile.

JOHN QUINLAN was born in Cloyne, County Cork, Ireland, on the 19th of October, 1826, and began his studies in a well-known classical school in Midleton. When he was eighteen he accompanied his widowed mother to the United States, and desiring to give his life to the service of God, applied to Archbishop Purcell, by whom he was placed at Mount St. Mary's, Emmittsburg. He was ordained priest in 1853 by Dr. Purcell, Richard Gilmour, his fellow-student, receiving the holy order, at the same time. After two years' service at Piqua, Ohio, he became assistant to the Rev. James F. Wood, pastor of St. Patrick's Church, Cincinnati. He was soon selected for a position of greater responsibility, that of superior at the theological seminary near Cincinnati known as Mount St. Mary's of the West, where he filled also the chairs of philosophy and theology. When the see of Mobile fell vacant by the death of Bishop Portier, the bishops of the province of New Orleans and Archbishop Purcell recommended his appointment. He was consecrated on the 4th of December, 1859, by Archbishop Blanc in St. Louis' Cathedral, New Orleans. Bishop Quinlan was installed in the cathedral of Mobile on the feast of the Immaculate Conception. In spite of the long and earnest labors of Bishop Portier, the diocese was in by no means a flourishing condition; there were twelve churches and fourteen schools, for which he had but eight secular priests, the Jesuit Fathers of Spring Hill College, eighteen in number, directing that institution and attending several missions in Alabama.

After visiting Rome he proceeded to Ireland, where he obtained in the seminaries of that Catholic island eleven young candidates for holy orders who volunteered to become missionaries in his diocese. Before he could carry out any of the projects for the extension of the faith Civil War swept over the land, imposing new duties and entailing great disasters on his struggling diocese.

After the battle of Shiloh, Bishop Quinlan hastened to the field in a special train and ministered to the spiritual and temporal wants of both armies. Some of his priests were sent as chaplains to the Catholic soldiers in the Confederate armies, sharing all the perils of battle while ministering to the wounded on the field. During the war the churches of Pensacola and Warrington were destroyed and many of the congregations scattered. As soon as peace was restored the Bishop of Mobile began the work of restoration, crippled with debt, and finding few resources in his diocese and little help from without. Besides the ruined churches which he rebuilt, he erected St. Patrick's and St. Mary's churches in Mobile, and established churches at Huntsville, Decatur, Tuscumbia, Florence, Cullman, Birmingham, Eufaula, Whistler, and Three Mile Creek.

He attended the canonization of the martyrs of Japan, China, and Corea on the 29th of June, 1867, and in 1869 attended the Vatican Council in the Eternal City. He also took part in the Provincial Councils of New Orleans. In a later visit to Rome in 1882 he contracted the fatal Campagna fever, and never recovered from its effects, his enfeebled frame yielding readily to an attack of pneumonia. On the last day of the year 1882 he became the guest of Rev. Mr. Massardier, of New Orleans, hoping for relief from a change of air; the improvement was very slight, and in March the pain became great. He blessed his vicar-general, and in his person the clergy and laity of his diocese, and, receiving the last sacraments, with calmness prepared for death. He retained his consciousness, and was absorbed in prayer, repeating invocations of the holy names of Jesus, Mary, Joseph, and petitions for mercy, till he breathed his soul into the hands of his Maker.

One of the last acts of his administration was to invite the ancient order of St. Benedict to assume charge of missions in Alabama. He developed schools as much as possible, establishing Sisters of St. Joseph and Mercy in many of the parishes of his diocese.

RIGHT REV. DOMINIC MANUCY,

Vicar-Apostolic of Brownsville and Third Bishop of Mobile.

DOMINIC MANUCY was born at St. Augustine, Florida, December 20, 1823, of parents both natives of that ancient Catholic territory, his ancestors—Italian and Irish on the father's side and Spanish on the mother's—having settled in Florida soon after the middle of the last century. He was sent to Spring Hill College, and was graduated in that seat of learning. After preparing by study and prayer for the reception of that sublime dignity, he was ordained priest on the feast of the Assumption, 1850, by the venerable Bishop Portier, of Mobile.

He was employed on several of the laborious missions of the diocese of Mobile, as well as at the cathedral. Towards the close of the Civil War he took charge of the mission of Montgomery, where he labored zealously for ten years. The very large diocese of Galveston was divided in 1874, and, besides the new bishopric of San Antonio, a vicariate-apostolic was formed embracing the territory lying along the Rio Grande. The climate and the nature of the country repel immigration, and the district is occupied mainly by a population of Mexican origin living in scattered ranches, who subsist by raising and attending vast herds of cattle. These people are Catholics, whose religion has suffered greatly by the infidel doctrines prevalent in Spanish-America and by contact with degraded and bigoted Americans. Rev. Mr. Manucy was selected, September 18, 1874, to organize this vicariate, and was consecrated Bishop of Dulma in the cathedral of Mobile on the feast of the Immaculate Conception. The new bishop found that the whole system for the maintenance of religion among the rancheros must be adapted to the peculiar character of the country and its inhabitants. The mass of the people have no fixed home or fireside, but lead a nomadic life, following flocks and herds which are seldom their own. The only way to reach them and keep the faith alive is to be constantly on the move among them, enduring a life almost as hard as their own. This the bishop found the Oblate Fathers and a few secular priests courageous enough to undertake.

Aided by the Association for the Propagation of the Faith and the exertions made by himself and his little band of priests, Bishop Manucy succeeded in building nine small churches to serve as lighthouses of the faith in this moral desert. Five young men zealous enough to face the labors of such a mission were ordained by him. He drew in devoted women to undertake schools; the Sisters of the Incarnate Word at Corpus Christi and Brownsville, the Ursuline Nuns at Laredo, and Sisters of Mercy at San Patricio and Refugio have academies, which enable them to maintain free parochial schools for girls, and in some cases for the younger boys. For those more advanced there are only the Oblate college at Brownsville and a boys' school at Laredo. Much could be done in missions and schools, were there any source from which money could be obtained. With all the restrictions arising from scanty means, Bishop Manucy brought the vicariate into the way of spiritual progress. The forty thousand frontier Catholics have twenty-four churches and chapels and twelve priests. It is to be hoped that aid will come to keep the faith alive and extend it. On the 9th of March, 1884, Bishop Manucy received a Papal Brief transferring him to the see of Mobile without relieving him of his duties as vicar-apostolic. He was installed in the cathedral on Passion Sunday. The diocese to which he has so recently been called has difficulties of its own, and the zeal, patience, and ability of the bishop are required to restore it to prosperity and fit it for the future which the rising industries of the State will in time create.

The burden of the diocese, encumbered with great difficulties, was too heavy for Bishop Manucy, and he soon earnestly sought to be relieved from it. The Holy Father, yielding to his entreaties, accepted his resignation and transferred him to the titular see of Maronea. Bishop Manucy waited at Mobile only to transfer the diocese to his successor. He was, however, struck down by a fatal illness, and died piously at Mobile December 4, 1885.*

* For Life of Bishop O'Sullivan, see page 359.

RIGHT REV. JEREMIAH O'SULLIVAN, D.D.,

Fourth Bishop of Mobile.

THE Right Rev. Jeremiah O'Sullivan was born at Kanturk, County Cork, Ireland, about the year 1844, and while a student resolved to devote himself to the service of God. Coming to America at the age of nineteen, he entered St. Charles' College, from which he passed to St. Mary's Seminary, Baltimore. He was ordained by Archbishop Spalding in June, 1868, and was first stationed at Barnesville, Montgomery County, Md. During his nine years' pastorate at Westernport, in that State, he erected a large church, and a convent for the Sisters of St. Joseph, whom he called to his parish to direct the schools. From this field of labor he was summoned to St. Peter's Church, Washington City, where his zeal and ability made him widely known. Having been selected for the see of Mobile, he was consecrated on the 20th of September, 1885, and soon after proceeded to his diocese.

DIOCESE OF MONTEREY AND LOS ANGELES.

RIGHT REV. THADDEUS AMAT,

Second Bishop of Monterey and Los Angeles.

THADDEUS AMAT was born at Barcelona, in Spain, in the year 1811, and, after pursuing his theological studies in Paris, entered the Congregation of the Priests of the Mission, founded by St. Vincent de Paul. Summoned to aid the members of his order in the United States, he was appointed, in 1841, master of novices at Cape Girardeau, and the next year assumed a professor's chair in the theological seminary of the diocese of St. Louis, of which for the next two years he was superior, displaying not only learning as a professor and gifts as a spiritual guide, but ability in the direction of an institution. Accustomed to the country and its needs, he then for several years was president of the preparatory seminary or college of St. Mary's at the Barrens, acting also as pastor of St. Mary's Church, and, with his associates in the college, attending several dependent missions and stations. In 1848 he was appointed superior of the theological seminary of St. Charles Borromeo at Philadelphia, and for four years directed that important institution.

California, before its acquisition by the United States, had formed part of a diocese, with a bishop resident at Monterey, and under Bishop Alemany that city had been made an episcopal see. The influx of population soon required a division of the diocese, and Dr. Alemany was appointed to the see of San Francisco, with the dignity of archbishop. To the see of Monterey, left vacant by his promotion, the learned and pious Lazarist was appointed on the 29th of July, 1853. He was solemnly consecrated on the 12th of March in the following year by his Eminence Cardinal Fransoni in the church of the College of the Propaganda at Rome.

His predecessor had accomplished much, and Bishop Amat found in the part of California assigned to him seventeen priests and twenty-three churches. His zeal was directed, therefore, mainly to completing the work of placing the Holy Sacrifice and the sacraments within the reach of all the faithful in his diocese, and also to endowing his bishopric with religious institutions and schools.

In 1856 he obtained Sisters of Charity from Emmittsburg, who opened an asylum and school at Los Angeles. A few years later they had a flourishing academy and an hospital under their care.

Bishop Amat then visited Europe for the good of the diocese, and returned with priests and Sisters. At this time the see was transferred to Los Angeles, which became his residence. There the Lazarists soon opened St. Vincent's College; and while they were securing Catholics a higher education for their sons, Brothers of the Third Order of St. Francis and Sisters of the Immaculate Heart of Mary assumed the direction of parochial schools at many points. A spinal affection under which Bishop Amat had long suffered intense pain, while it never disturbed his serenity, made assistance necessary, and in 1873 his vicar-general, the Very Rev. Francis Mora, was consecrated as his coadjutor.

Meanwhile Bishop Amat labored to complete his cathedral, which he dedicated to God, under the patronage of St. Bibiana, April 9, 1876. His health failed more rapidly after that time, and he died piously on the 12th of May, 1878, leaving in his diocese much to attest his zeal and labors, not the least having been his efforts to benefit spiritually and temporally the remnant of the Mission Indians.

RIGHT REV. FRANCIS MORA,

Third Bishop of Monterey and Los Angeles.

FRANCIS MORA was born near the city of Vich, in Catalonia, a province of Spain, on the 25th of November, 1827, and was thus by birth a countryman of many of the most energetic among the early missionaries in California, Texas, and Florida. It was therefore natural that a taste for foreign missions should early have been awakened in his heart. Devoting himself in early youth to the service of God in the sanctuary, Francis Mora made his ecclesiastical studies in the episcopal seminary at Vich; but in 1854, when Bishop Amat appealed for recruits for his diocese, the young seminarian offered his services, and, without waiting to receive priestly orders, accompanied him across the Atlantic. He was ordained priest by Bishop Amat at Santa Barbara, California, and was successively rector at St. Juan Bautista, Pajaro vale, and San Luis Obispo. His zeal and ability rendered him one of the chief auxiliaries of the Right Rev. Bishop Amat, who in 186 appointed him rector of the pro-cathedral of Los Angeles and vicar-general of the diocese. When Bishop Amat required the services of a coadjutor, the Rev. Francis Mora was elected to the see of Mossynopolis on the 20th of May, 1873, and was consecrated on the 3d of August. Being thus coadjutor, with the right of succession, he labored for the well-being of the diocese, of which he became bishop May 12, 1878. The diocese then contained a Catholic population of 21,000, three thousand being the surviving descendants of the Indian converts of the early missionaries. There were thirty churches, with two others in course of erection, and three erected in Catholic times, now little more than ruins. His clergy, secular and regular, numbered thirty-eight.

Bishop Mora has done much to infuse new energy into the Catholic body in Lower California and make the church confided to him prosper. In 1884 the children of the true faith of Christ numbered 28,000; the Indians, whose wrongs had to some extent been remedied, had increased; the Lazarist College of St. Vincent at Los Angeles, and that of Our Lady of Sorrows at Mission Santa Barbara, where the Franciscans, deriving hope even in the affliction and ruin of their missions, were renewing their labors, gave promise of great good. Daughters of Charity, Sisters of the Immaculate Heart of Mary vied with each other in works of mercy. Thirty-three secular priests and twelve regulars attended the thirty-four churches, sixteen chapels, and thirty-six stations in the portion of California under his jurisdiction.

In 1884 the diocese of Monterey was the scene of a most consoling celebration. The Rev. Angel Casanova, priest at Monterey, had long desired to restore the ancient church of San Carlos, which contained the remains of Father Juniper Serra, O.S.F., the founder of the great Franciscan missions in Upper California. By a course of careful investigation in the ruined church he discovered the vault containing the remains of the illustrious friar, and at once began the restoration of the mission church. The remains of the venerable founder were properly and piously encased, and on the 28th of August, 1884, the church of San Carlos was rededicated to the service of God with all possible pomp. Bishop Mora officiated on this interesting occasion, the centennial of the venerable Father's death, and, with the Archbishop of San Francisco and other bishops of the province and attendant clergy and laity, offered up the holy sacrifice of the Mass for the repose of the humble and self-denying friar to whom California owed so deep a debt. The diocese, at the close of the year 1884, contained fifty churches and chapels, with forty-five priests.

DIOCESE OF NASHVILLE.

RIGHT REV. RICHARD PIUS MILES,

First Bishop of Nashville.

RICHARD PIUS MILES was born in Prince George's County, Maryland, May 17, 1791; but as the family emigrated to Kentucky when he was only five years old, he grew up in the West. The hereditary faith of the family was seen in the piety of the boy, who at the age of fifteen solicited admission into the order of St. Dominic. He received the white habit October 10, 1806, and, notwithstanding his youth, persevered in the state to which he felt that God had called him. After years of discipline and study he was ordained priest in September, 1816, and entered on a long career of missionary labor in Ohio and Kentucky, especially at Somerset and Zanesville, being one of the most active and prominent priests in establishing Catholicity in those States.

To give teachers for the children of the faithful, and devoted women for works of mercy, Father Miles, with the consent of his superiors, founded a community of Sisters of the Third Order of St. Dominic, drawing up rules suited to the wants of the country. This community now occupies the convent of St. Catharine of Sienna, near Springfield, Ky.

The Fathers of the Third Council of Baltimore recommended the erection of Tennessee into a separate diocese, and proposed Father Miles for the first Bishop of Nashville. He was consecrated in the cathedral of Bardstown, September 16, 1838, by Bishop Rosati, of St. Louis, and proceeded alone to Tennessee—a State in which there was not then a priest, and only two shells, that could not by any stretch of fancy be called churches. The pioneer bishop entered Nashville a stranger, without resources, and sought an humble lodging as a shelter till he could prepare.

for his work. At the very outset he was prostrated by illness, and might have died unattended had not Providence guided a priest to his bedside. On recovering Bishop Miles proceeded to Memphis, where he began his labors as a missionary. He appealed to Ohio to aid him, and obtained some auxiliaries, but there were not many priests who chose to enter so unpromising a district.

In his diocesan city the Dominican bishop collected the Catholics soon after his arrival, and preached a mission; but his words drew only nine persons to receive the Blessed Eucharist. Yet by his assiduous labors he beheld the flock increase, till he was able in 1847 to dedicate his cathedral to the Almighty under the invocation of Our Lady of the Seven Dolors. He also erected a suitable house for himself and his successors, as well as an academy and hospital under the charge of the Sisters of Charity of Nazareth. He introduced a colony of the Sisters of St. Dominic, whom he had founded, into Memphis, where a church had been built. These good religious soon had school and asylum under their charge.

In 1842 Bishop Miles ordained the first priest ever elevated to that dignity in the State of Tennessee.

Bishop Miles was not young when called to assume the duties of the episcopate, and his cares added more years than his previous missionary labors. In 1859 he solicited a coadjutor, and the Right Rev. James Whelan, a friar of his own order, was appointed. A cough which had long annoyed Bishop Miles now showed that the disease had reached a critical point. After reciting his office on February 17, 1860, seated before the fire, Bishop Miles found himself unable to rise. He was conveyed to his bed and medical aid summoned. His case was at once pronounced fatal, and, after receiving the last sacraments from the hands of Bishop Whelan, he calmly expired on the 21st of February.

Considering the condition of Catholicity in the State of Tennessee, where the faithful are few, poor, and scattered, often separated from each other by mountain ranges, the work accomplished by Bishop Miles in organizing and building up the diocese was certainly remarkable.

RIGHT REV. JAMES WHELAN, O.S.D.,

Second Bishop of Nashville.

JAMES WHELAN was born at Kilkenny, Ireland, on the 8th of June, 1823, but spent most of his youth in London and New York, where he received his early training in religion and letters. Even in boyhood he was remarkable for a great love of solitude and for an extraordinary application to books. He seemed set apart for the religious life, and, applying to the venerable Father N. D. Young, was taken by that experienced director to the novitiate of the Dominicans, St. Joseph's, Perry County, Ohio. Here he manifested great talent for sacred studies, and won the affection of all his superiors and brethren by his genial disposition and strict observance of the rule. He was ordained priest on the 2d of August, 1846, and was soon an active and laborious missionary, filling many offices of trust and responsibility in Dominican convents, until at last, in October, 1854, he was elected provincial of the order in Ohio and Kentucky. He served the usual term, four years, with much credit to himself and satisfaction to his brethren. Having been soon after appointed coadjutor to the Bishop of Nashville, he was consecrated Bishop of Marcopolis on the 8th of May, 1859. The declining health of Bishop Miles compelled him to assume at once all the active duties of the episcopate, and on the death of that prelate in the ensuing year he became Bishop of Nashville. The country was already in the midst of the excitement which culminated the next year in fratricidal strife. As a border State Tennessee was torn and distracted for four long years by the almost constant occupation of contending armies, some of the severest battles of the war having been fought on its soil. The afflictions of the diocese confided to his care, with his own utter inability to remedy them, broke the spirit of the bishop, and in 1864 he obtained leave to resign the episcopate and return to the quiet and seclusion of a convent of his order. From that time till his death he lived among his religious brethren, devoting his whole time to theological, historical, and chemical studies, some of the fruits of which are manifested in contributions to the periodical literature of the time. In 1872 he published a work of enduring value: "Catena Aurea; or, A Golden Chain of Evidences demonstrating from 'Analytical Treatment of History' that Papal Infallibility is no Novelty." In a popular form easily grasped this work presented the question of the infallibility of the Pope teaching *ex cathedra*, so that all could understand it and see the fallacy of those who denied it. Dr. Brownson regarded it as one of the best works ever written on the subject.

In 1871 Bishop Whelan took up his residence in Zanesville, and, after a brief illness, expired at the residence of the Dominican Fathers in that city, on the 18th of February, 1878. His remains were conveyed to St. Joseph's and laid beside those of his religious brethren who had ended their career on the missions of Ohio.

RIGHT REV. JOSEPH RADEMACHER,

Fourth Bishop of Nashville.

JOSEPH RADEMACHER was born at Westphalia, in the State of Michigan, on the 3d of December, 1840. He was placed at an early age at St. Vincent's College, under the care of the Benedictine Fathers of the abbey of that name in Westmoreland County, Pennsylvania, and after completing his classical course entered the diocesan seminary of St. Michael's, at Pittsburgh, to prepare for the holy order of priesthood, to which he felt he was called. He was ordained priest on the 2d of August, 1863, by the Right Rev. Dr. J. H. Luers, for the diocese of Fort Wayne. He was placed in charge of the church of Attica, Indiana, and of the dependent missions, and was a laborious missionary there for six years. He was then pastor of the church of St. Paul of the Cross, Columbia City, for eight years. Right Rev. Bishop Dwenger then summoned him to Fort Wayne, and confided to him the church of St. Mary, Mother of God. It was a position of difficulty, but his piety, prudence, and firmness triumphed over all obstacles. During his residence at Fort Wayne he acted as chancellor of the diocese, but he was soon appointed pastor of St. Mary's Church, Lafayette, which, next to the cathedral, had the largest congregation in the diocese. In all these positions the Rev. Mr. Rademacher acquitted himself as a priest of ability, devoted to his flock, earnest, pious, careful of the education of the young. On the 21st of April, 1883, he was appointed Bishop of Nashville, and was consecrated on the 24th of June by his predecessor, who had been promoted to the see of Chicago. Since his enthronement at Nashville Bishop Rademacher has labored earnestly by visitations to learn the wants of his diocese and advance the kingdom of God.

At the close of the year 1884 the diocese contained thirty churches, twenty-six priests, a college, twenty-one academies and schools attended by more than two thousand pupils.

DIOCESE OF NATCHEZ.

RIGHT REV. JOHN J. CHANCHE,

First Bishop of Natchez.

JOHN MARY JOSEPH CHANCHE, the son of John Chanche and Catharine Provost, was born October 4, 1795, in Baltimore, to which his parents had fled from the horrors of St. Domingo. At the age of eleven he was placed in the college opened by the Sulpitians in that city, and soon showed that he was called to the ecclesiastical state. He received the tonsure from Archbishop Carroll when he was only fifteen. After receiving minor orders from Archbishop Neale he was ordained by Archbishop Maréchal, June 5, 1819. Having been received into the community of Saint Sulpice, he was made a professor in St. Mary's College, and continued to discharge his duties, becoming in time vice-president, and in September, 1834, on the elevation of Dr. Eccleston to the episcopate, president of the college, an office for which he possessed marked qualifications.

Dr. Chanche had been proposed for the position of coadjutor at Baltimore, at Boston, and at New York, but steadfastly declined the dignity of bishop. He took an important part in several of the Provincial Councils of Baltimore, his learning, eloquence, and thorough knowledge of all prescribed forms and ceremonies being recognized by all. When the see of Natchez was erected, July 28, 1837, the Rev. Thomas Heyden was appointed bishop, but declined. The Rev. Dr. Chanche was subsequently named, and was induced to accept the bulls issued by Pope Gregory XVI., December 15, 1840. His consecration took place on the 14th of March in the next year, Archbishop Eccleston officiating, assisted by Bishops Fenwick and Hughes. Dr. Chanche proceeded to his diocese alone, and, landing at Natchez, began to organize a diocese in the State of Mississippi. Catholicity was in no flourishing condition, yet some of the early French settlements and missions had been planted on its soil, and in their tragic annals were recorded the deaths of heroic men who laid down their lives while announcing the truths of the Gospel to the white settler and the dark-hued son of the forest. Biloxi, Natchez, Yazoo had been French posts early in the seventeenth century. The secular priests St. Cosme and Foucault, the Jesuit Fathers Du Poisson, Souart, and Senat, had died by Indian hands in Mississippi or on the adjacent river. Even in earlier days eminent Dominican Fathers had labored here in the colony of Tristan de Luna.

During the French occupancy of Louisiana there was a church at Natchez attended by a Capuchin Father, and when Spain acquired the territory a priest was maintained there. Bishop Carroll, unable to send a priest to a point so remote from other settled parts of his diocese, asked Bishop Peñalver, of Louisiana, to continue to supply the isolated church. Subsequently priests were sent from Spain, who remained till 1798, when the United States took possession of Natchez and confiscated the church property to its own use. From that time the mission was served at intervals only, and the church was at last destroyed by fire in December, 1832. A little chapel of the Holy Family soon rose, however, and when Bishop Chanche arrived was the only sign of Catholicity; but it was so small that the faithful met in a hired hall. Rev. Mr. Brogard, the only priest in Mississippi, was there but temporarily, and the bishop was virtually alone. He obtained aid, and, assembling the Catholics, roused their zeal and spirit. In 1842 he laid the corner-stone of his cathedral, and about the same time opened an academy for young ladies, under the direction of accomplished teachers whom he brought from Frederick, Md. His visitations were rather missions to find, collect, and organize the Catholics than visits to parishes, and his labors, like those of the few priests whom he could induce to share his ministry, were those of a missionary priest. For the good of his diocese he visited Havana to secure documents to substantiate the claim of the Catholic Church to its property; but his appeal to the United States for its restitution was unavailing.

The Sisters of Charity came to his diocese early in 1848, and soon had thriving schools and an orphan asylum. Bishop Chanche was earnestly desirous of uniting the Sisters of Charity in America with the order in France, and went to France with the documents which led to the accomplishment of that design. By the year 1852 the diocese, so utterly destitute when he arrived, began to show the results of his zeal. He had a nucleus of a clergy in the eleven priests whom he had gathered around him. Eleven churches had been built, and there were more than thirty places where Catholics gathered at stated times to hear Mass and approach the sacraments.

At the First Plenary Council, in 1852, Bishop Chanche was chief promoter, and after the close of its sessions he went to Frederick to rest awhile at the house of a friend. There he was seized with cholera-morbus, which baffled the skill of physicians. He lingered several days without a murmur, bearing all his sufferings with resignation and serenity till he died, on the 22d of July, 1853. At his own request his body was conveyed to Baltimore and interred in the cathedral cemetery. An able and accomplished man, he had renounced the episcopate in sees where the Church was organized and progressing, in order to devote his energies and life to the hardest struggles in a State where the prospects of Catholicity were feeble indeed.

RIGHT REV. FRANCIS JANSSENS,

Fourth Bishop of Natchez.

FRANCIS JANSSENS was born in Tilburg, North Brabant, Holland, on the 17th of October, 1847. After preliminary classical studies he entered the episcopal seminary at Bois-le-Duc, or Herzogenbusch, but, wishing to devote himself to the missions in the United States, sought entrance into the American College at Louvain, where he was ordained priest on the 21st of December, 1867. Bishop McGill, of Richmond, had visited the institution the preceding year and depicted the wants of his diocese so eloquently that the young seminarian, full of courage, offered his services. He began his labors in the diocese of Richmond in September, 1868, and was soon recognized as a most able and energetic priest, full of resources and prompt at every call. As assistant priest at the cathedral, and from 1870 as rector, attending also missions at Warrenton, Gordonsville, and Culpepper, acting too as secretary and chancellor of the diocese, he endeared himself to all. In 1877 he was made vicar-general of the diocese, and on the translation of Bishop Gibbons to the see of Adramyttum, as coadjutor of Baltimore, the Very Rev. Mr. Janssens became administrator of the diocese of Richmond. When Bishop Keane was installed in the capital of Virginia he retained the able priest as vicar-general of his diocese and pastor of the cathedral. Bishop Chanche had been succeeded at Natchez by the Right Rev. Dr. Van de Velde, who was transferred from Chicago, and the diocese had been afterwards ably directed by Right Rev. William H. Elder for many years; but his appointment as coadjutor to the venerable Archbishop Purcell, of Cincinnati, left the see of Natchez vacant. The Very Rev. Francis Janssens was selected for the position, and he was consecrated in the cathedral of St. Peter at Richmond on the 1st of May, 1881, by Archbishop Gibbons, assisted by Bishops Becker, of Wilmington, and Keane, of Richmond, Bishop Elder preaching the sermon on the occasion. The ceremony was the grandest ecclesiastical function ever seen in Richmond, and attracted the largest gathering known in the history of the Church in the State. After the consecration Bishop Janssens made a most touching address to the members of the hierarchy and to his fellow-clergymen, whom he thanked for all their kindness and brotherly feeling towards him from the day of their first cordial welcome. He then proceeded to Europe, and after visiting his native place, where he was received with a public ovation, and with rapture by the loving mother whom he had left for God's service, he went to Rome, and then, returning to this country, took possession of his diocese.

The ability shown at Richmond augurs a devoted and profitable administration at Natchez. Catholicity has not made in

RT. REV. FRANCIS MORA, D.D.
Born at Vich, Spain, Nov. 25, 1827.
Consecrated Bishop of Mosynopolis, May 20, 1873;
Bishop of Monterey and Los Angeles, May 12, 1878.

RT. REV. FRANCIS JANSSENS, D.D.
Born at Tilburg, Holland, Oct. 17, 1847.
Ordained Dec. 21, 1867; Consecrated Bishop of
Natchez, May 1, 1881.

RT. REV. JOSEPH RADEMACHER, D.D.
Born Westphalia, Mich., Dec. 3, 1840.
Ordained Aug. 2, 1863; Consecrated Bishop of
Nashville, April 21, 1883.

RT. REV. RUPERT SEIDENBUSH, D.D.
Born in Munich, Bavaria, Oct. 20, 1830.
Ordained in June, 1853; Consecrated Bishop of Halia
and Vicar-Apostolic of Northern Minnesota, May
30, 1875.

Mississippi the strides that it has at the Northwest, but under the care and prudence of his predecessors the little grain of mustard-seed found by Bishop Chanche has grown. The Catholic population was in 1884 estimated at not quite 14,000, the yearly baptisms of infants being 736; the parochial and colored schools, chiefly under the care of religious communities, number nearly 2,000 pupils; and this body of Catholics has 53 churches, attended by 30 priests.

DIOCESE OF NATCHITOCHES.

RIGHT REV. AUGUSTUS MARY MARTIN,

First Bishop of Natchitoches.

AUGUSTUS MARY MARTIN was born in Brittany, France, and after a pious education was ordained priest. Though gentle and unassuming, he resolved to seek a foreign mission, and came to the United States in 1842. Having been received into the diocese of New Orleans, he was appointed chaplain to the Ursuline nuns. As soon as he had acquired a knowledge of the mission work he was made pastor of St. Martin's Church, Attakapas; in 1845 he was transferred to St. James' parish, and two years later was entrusted with the charge of St. Joseph's Church, East Baton Rouge, attending also the dependent missions of the Plains and Manchac. In all this parochial work he made himself singularly beloved by the people, and won the respect and esteem of his fellow-priests. His archbishop showed his confidence by making him vicar-forane. The Plenary Council of 1852 recommended the division of the diocese of New Orleans, and a new see was erected at Natchitoches. To this the Rev. Mr. Martin was elected on the 29th of July, 1853, and he received episcopal consecration at the hands of Archbishop Blanc in New Orleans on the last day of November. His diocese comprised the more sparsely settled part of the State, lying north of the thirty-first degree. Natchitoches had been established as a French post as early as 1717, and a priest was stationed there from time to time; not far off was the Spanish mission of San Miguel at Adayes, founded in 1715 by the Venerable Father Anthony Margil de Jesus. In our time a church dedicated to St. Francis was erected at Natchitoches in 1826. The diocese of Natchitoches when organized contained about twenty-five thousand Catholics, with only seven churches and four priests. The only institution was a convent of the Sacred Heart.

As the population gained little by emigration, the great object of Bishop Martin was to give his people churches, priests, and schools to meet their wants. He encouraged and stimulated the erection of churches wherever they could be maintained, and succeeded so that he left more than sixty churches and chapels. For works of education and charity he introduced the Sisters of Mercy and the Daughters of the Cross, an order founded by St. Vincent de Paul.

After governing the diocese for twenty-two years he died piously September 29, 1875.

RIGHT REV. ANTHONY DURIER,

Third Bishop of Natchitoches.

THE Right Rev. Anthony Durier, who succeeded to the mitre of Natchitoches after Archbishop Leray had governed the diocese for nearly six years as administrator, was born at Rouen, France, in the year 1833, of a family which gave many of its members to the priesthood and religious orders, one of them dying as a missionary in China. Anthony was pursuing his theological studies at Lyons when with a fellow-seminarian he responded to an appeal of Archbishop Blanc for priests for Louisiana. He came to the United States in 1855, and completed his theological studies at Mount St. Mary's of the West, where he acquired a familiarity with the English language. After being ordained by Archbishop Purcell in 1856, he was stationed at Chillicothe, but the next year began his labors in New Orleans as assistant priest at the cathedral of that city. From 1859 to his elevation to the episcopate he was the zealous, charitable, and laborious pastor of the Church of the Annunciation. He was consecrated Bishop of Natchitoches in St. Louis' Cathedral, New Orleans, by Archbishop Leray on the 19th of March, 1885.

DIOCESE OF NESQUALLY.

RIGHT REV. AUGUSTINE MAGLOIRE BLANCHET,

First Bishop of Nesqually.

AUGUSTINE MAGLOIRE ALEXANDER BLANCHET was born on the 22d of August, 1797, at Saint Pierre, Rivière du Sud, in the diocese of Quebec, and after a pious youth entered the seminary, and was ordained priest on the 3d of June, 1821. The young priest's earliest missionary labors found their field in the islands of La Magdelaine and Chetican; then he was stationed at Magré, in Cape Breton, in 1822. For sixteen years dating from 1826 he exercised the holy ministry in the diocese of Montreal as parish priest of St. Luc de l'Assomption, St. Charles, Rivière Richelieu, and St. Joseph de Soulanges. His parish was the scene of some of the patriot risings in 1837. He was subsequently appointed by Bishop Bourget one of the canons of the chapter of Montreal. When the Holy See, in 1845, erected the dioceses of Walla Walla and Fort Hall in Oregon, he was appointed to Walla Walla, and was consecrated in the cathedral of Montreal on the 27th of September, 1846. The diocese embraced the territory between the Pacific and White Salmon River above the Cascades, the British possessions, and the Columbia River. The Jesuit Fathers had already begun missions among the Cœurs d'Alénes, Flatheads, and Kalispels, and Protestant missionaries were engaged in attempting to gain converts in other native tribes. Bishop Blanchet set out from Montreal in March, 1847, and reached Fort Walla Walla on the 5th of September, accompanied by four Oblate Fathers and two secular priests. His arrival excited great bitterness at the Protestant missions, and the invitation of the Cayuse chief Tamatowe to the bishop added to the feeling. Before the bishop and his priests could begin any active mission work the Cayuses murdered Dr. Whitman, a Protestant missionary, and his wife; another missionary, the Rev. Mr. Spalding, was saved from a similar fate only by the exertions of one of Bishop Blanchet's priests, Rev. Mr. Brouillet. The bishop, then at Tamatowe's camp, used every effort to rescue the whites held as prisoners by the Indians and to prevent further crime, but, finding himself powerless, retired to St. Paul. Rev. Mr. Brouillet remained, but was soon compelled to leave, and his house was burned, as well as the chapel. The Rev. Mr. Spalding, far from showing any gratitude to the men who saved his life, began at once to charge the Catholic bishop and clergy with complicity in the massacre and to inflame the public mind against them. This course he pursued for years, and though the calumny has been again and again refuted, it is repeated to this day.

Bishop Blanchet in June, 1848, set out for the Umatilla mission, but, being ordered back by the Superintendent of Indian Affairs, established the Dalles mission of St. Peter.

The Cayuse war prevented the progress of settlements, and, the difficulty of restoring missions being great, a change was made. The Sovereign Pontiff on the 31st of May, 1850, erected the see of Nesqually and transferred Bishop Blanchet to it in the following October. He took up his residence at Fort Vancouver, on the Columbia, and there he soon had a modest cathedral, while chapels rose at Olympia and Steilacoom, on the Cowlitz River, and among the Chinooks. In 1853 the diocese of Walla Walla was suppressed, and part of it, including the Dalles and Cayuse territory, was annexed to Nesqually.

Bishop Blanchet took part in the Provincial Council of Oregon and in the Plenary Councils of Baltimore in 1852 and 1866.

When the Territory of Washington was organized in 1853 the diocese of Nesqually was made to include it. Religion was at last making sure but steady progress, when the discovery of gold in California diverted immigrants, and even sent many from Oregon to that tempting field. The Catholic population, of about six thousand, lost severely, and even the number of priests and chapels declined. From 1856 the diocese had Sisters of Charity, who established an academy and hospital at Vancouver, and in time spread to Steilacoom, Walla Walla, St. Ignatius, and Tulalip.

Through all the trials and difficulties that checkered his episcopate from the outset Bishop Blanchet labored on courageously, seeking to do all that could be effected for his flock. In February, 1879, he was relieved of the burden, which had become too great for his years and health, and became titular Bishop of Ibora, taking up his abode at St. Joseph's Hospital, Vancouver. The diocese, when he transferred it to his successor, contained 16 priests, 24 churches and chapels, Indian missions at Fort Colville, Yakima, and Tulalip, colleges at Vancouver and Walla Walla, with the numerous institutions of the Sisters of Charity, and a Catholic population which had grown to nearly twelve thousand.

RIGHT REV. ÆGIDIUS JUNGER,

Second Bishop of Nesqually.

ÆGIDIUS JUNGER was born on the 6th of April, 1833, at Burtscheid, near Aix-la-Chapelle, in the diocese of Cologne, and, after preparing by a pious youth and the study of years, was ordained priest on the 26th of July, 1862. Destined for the American mission, he came to this country October 31, 1862. On reaching the diocese of Nesqually he was stationed at Walla Walla City, and attended the church there with its dependent missions; but from 1864 he was attached to the cathedral of St. Augustine and St. James at Vancouver. There his ability, zeal, and piety made him favorably known. When the aged Bishop Blanchet was at last permitted to resign the see which he had so long filled, the Rev. Mr. Junger was elected Bishop of Nesqually, and was consecrated on the 28th of October, 1879.

Since he has been at the head of the diocese the Territory of

Washington has been brought into closer communication with the East by railroad. Coal-mines have been opened and new towns are arising. Some of the incoming population is Catholic, and the number of the faithful is on the increase. There were in 1884 twenty-seven priests attending thirty churches and sixty-two stations and Indian missions; the number of institutions had grown, the Sisters of the Holy Names of Jesus and Mary having entered the diocese to aid the Sisters of Charity or of Providence in the labors which they have so long and so heroically sustained. Bishop Junger attended the Third Plenary Council of Baltimore in November, 1884.

DIOCESE OF NEWARK.

RIGHT REV. WINAND MICHAEL WIGGER,

Third Bishop of Newark.

WINAND M. WIGGER, who became third Bishop of Newark—Bishop Bayley, the first, having been promoted to the see of Baltimore, and Bishop Corrigan, his successor, having been promoted to the see of Petra as coadjutor of New York—was born in the city of New York on the 9th of December, 1841, his parents, who had emigrated from Westphalia, having settled in that city. He pursued a classical course at St. Francis Xavier's College, under the Fathers of the Society of Jesus, and, resolving to serve God in his sanctuary, entered the Theological Seminary at Seton Hall, South Orange, New Jersey, where he remained some years; but in October, 1862, enrolled his name among the theological students at the college of Brignoli Sale, Genoa, where he completed his divinity course, winning the doctor's cap. He was ordained priest in 1865, and, returning to the diocese of Newark, became assistant priest at the cathedral. On the death of Rev. James D'Arcy he was appointed rector of St. Vincent's Church, Madison, where he remained several years, enjoying the respect and attachment of his flock and of persons of all creeds, his only absence being a temporary removal to Summit for his health. On the promotion of Bishop Corrigan the diocese of Newark was reduced to the counties of Hudson, Passaic, Bergen, Essex, Morris, Union, and Sussex, the rest of the State being formed into the new diocese of Trenton. The Rev. Dr. Wigger, elected to the see of Newark, was consecrated in the cathedral at Newark on the 18th of October, 1881, by Archbishop Corrigan, assisted by Bishop McQuaid, of Rochester, and Bishop Loughlin, of Brooklyn. Under his care the diocese, though small in extent, has advanced in the way of prosperity, containing at the close of the year 1884 a hundred and fifty thousand Catholics, with eighty-eight churches and one hundred and fifty-five priests. It had three colleges, seventeen seminaries for young ladies, twenty thousand Catholic children in the parochial schools, and twelve asylums and hospitals.

DIOCESE OF OGDENSBURG.

RIGHT REV. EDGAR P. WADHAMS,

First Bishop of Ogdensburg.

EDGAR P. WADHAMS, son of Luman Wadhams and Lucy Bostwick, was born on the 21st of May, 1817, in the township of Lewis, Essex County, N. Y., and was graduated at Middlebury College, Vermont. Brought up a Protestant, he resolved to prepare for the ministry, and went through the course of studies at the Protestant Episcopal General Theological Seminary, New York. After receiving deacon's orders in that denomination he became a missionary at Ticonderoga, but there the doubts as to his religious position yielded to the power of reason enlightened by prayer. Retaining his wish to serve in the ministry, he proceeded directly to St. Mary's Seminary, Baltimore, where he was received into the Church by the Rev. Peter Fredet in June, 1846. Entering on the course of sound study, he received the tonsure and minor orders from Archbishop Eccleston, September 2, 1847; deaconship, October 24, 1849, and was ordained priest in St. Mary's Pro-Cathedral, Albany, by Right Rev. John McCloskey on the 15th of January, 1850. He was immediately appointed assistant at the pro-cathedral, and retained the same position in the cathedral of the Immaculate Conception on its dedication in 1853 till he became rector in 1866. Acting also as vicar-general of the diocese, his mission life was one of labor and consolation. When the diocese of Ogdensburg was set off he was appointed to it on the 15th of February, 1872, and was consecrated by Archbishop McCloskey, of New York, assisted by Bishops de Goesbriand and Williams, in the cathedral at Albany, on the feast of St. Pius V.—a pope who took a zealous interest in the progress of the faith in our territory. Bishop Wadhams was

RT. REV. AEGIDIUS JUNGER, D.D.
Born at Bartscheid, Germany, April 6, 833.
Ordained July 26, 1862; Consecrated Bishop of
Nesqualy, Oct. 28, 1879.

RT. REV. EDGAR P. WADHAMS, D.D.
Born at Lewis, N. Y., May 21, 1817.
Ordained Jan. 15, 1850; Consecrated Bishop of
Ogdensburg, May 5, 1872.

RT. REV. WINAND M. WIGGER, D.D.
Born in New York, Dec. 9, 1841.
Ordained June 10, 1865 ; Consecrated Bishop of
Newark, Oct. 18, 1881.

RT. REV. JAMES O'CONNOR, D.D.
Born at Queenstown, Ireland, Sept. 10, 1823.
Ordained 1845 ; Consecrated Bishop of Dibona
and Vicar Apostolic of Nebraska, Aug. 20, 1876.
Transferred to the See of Omaha in 1885.

installed in St. Mary's Cathedral, Ogdensburg, on the 16th of May, 1872. The modern city occupies the site of the Mission of the Presentation, founded in the last century by a zealous Sulpitian, the Abbé Picquet. The diocese has an area of ten thousand five hundred square miles, including the Adirondack Mountains and some of the wildest scenery in the State. The population is scattered, the sixty-three thousand Catholics intermingled among a total of three hundred thousand.

Limited as the resources of Bishop Wadhams have been, he has been seconded in zeal by hard-working clergy and a flock ready to make sacrifices. In this wilderness-diocese of New York State, during his administration, thirty-three churches have arisen where there was never a church before, and churches already existing when he became Bishop of Ogdensburg have been rebuilt or enlarged.

Gradually, under the impulse he has given, provision is made for the education of the rising generation, and there are twenty schools with about fifteen hundred pupils. The Oblate Fathers of the Immaculate Conception, now the great missionary body of Canada, have a house at Plattsburg, the Augustinians at Carthage, the Franciscans at Croghan and Mohawk Hill, and the Missionary Fathers of the Sacred Heart at Watertown. The d'Youville Sisters of Charity (Gray Nuns), Sisters of Charity, of Mercy, and of St. Joseph, with Franciscan Sisters, supply fifty teachers for schools.

DIOCESE OF OMAHA.

RIGHT REV. JAMES O'GORMAN,

First Vicar-Apostolic.

JAMES MICHAEL O'GORMAN was born in the County Limerick, Ireland, in 1809, and entered the Trappist Order at the age of nineteen, renouncing the world, and all preferments even in the Church. He was one of the first sent from Melleray to found a new monastery of Trappists in Iowa. There he showed himself a religious full of the spirit of the Cistercian Order, discharging with zeal the ministry for the benefit of the souls placed under his care. When the Rev. Father Smyth was appointed to the see of Dubuque, Father O'Gorman became prior of New Melleray and governed the monastery with charity and prudence. In 1859 the voice of the Holy Father called him from his cloister to assume the episcopate as Vicar-Apostolic of Nebraska. He was consecrated Bishop of Raphanea on the 8th of May. Everything was to be done in the Territory. There were scattered Catholics, but only one or two churches, three priests, and not a single institution of any kind. A monk of an austere, contemplative order, observing the strictest silence, seemed scarcely fitted for the task; but Bishop O'Gorman displayed all the powers of administration and organization. He induced zealous priests to join his vicariate, and aided them to build up church and school; he introduced Sisters of Mercy and Benedictine nuns, so that academies, schools, hospital, asylum soon attested Catholic life. When he laid down the burden there were twenty priests and as many churches under his care, many stations, and several Indian missions.

While at Cincinnati in the summer of 1874 he was attacked by cholera morbus, and died on the 4th of July, at the age of sixty-five. His remains were conveyed to Nebraska and laid in the cathedral of St. Philomena in the city of Omaha.

RIGHT REV. JAMES O'CONNOR,

First Bishop of Omaha.

WE have seen the career of the Right Rev. Dr. O'Connor, the distinguished Bishop of Pittsburgh, and come now to sketch briefly the career of his able brother. James O'Connor was born in Queenstown, Ireland, on the 10th of September, 1823, and, coming to this country in 1838, finished his preparatory studies in the Seminary of St. Charles Borromeo, Philadelphia, from which he was sent to the Urban College at Rome. Trained there to the soundest philosophy and theology by the eminent professors of the College of the Propaganda, he was ordained in the Eternal City on the feast of the Annunciation in the year 1845. On his return to this country he was for seven years engaged in missionary duties in the diocese of Pittsburgh. In 1857 he was appointed superior of St. Michael's Theological and Preparatory Seminary at Glenwood, near Pittsburgh, and organized the different departments, directing the whole so ably that he was compelled to erect an additional wing in 1862 to accommodate the increased number of students.

Resigning his position in the following year, he was appointed Director of the Seminary of St. Charles Borromeo at Overbrook, near Philadelphia, filling also the chairs of philosophy, moral theology, and ecclesiastical history, until the year 1862, when he visited Europe and on his return became pastor of St. Dominic's Church, Holmesburg. In 1876 he was elected Vicar-Apostolic of Nebraska, and was consecrated titular Bishop of Dibona on the 20th of August. He founded Creighton College in 1879, and confided it to the Fathers of the Society of Jesus, and introduced the Franciscan Fathers, who have two houses of their order. The vicariate, when Bishop O'Connor attended the Plenary Council of Baltimore in 1884, contained more than seventy-five priests, one hundred and fifty churches, and six charitable institutions, six academies, and seventeen parochial schools.

In 1885 the State of Nebraska was made the diocese of Omaha, and Bishop O'Connor was transferred to the new see.

DIOCESE OF PEORIA.

RIGHT REV. JOHN LANCASTER SPALDING,

First Bishop of Peoria.

JOHN LANCASTER SPALDING was born at Lebanon, Ky., on the 2d of June, 1840, "coming," as Bishop Rosecrans well said on the day of his consecration, "from a family of priests who have supported the fabric of our religion in this country, and will maintain its honor, not only among Catholics, but will defend it also among those who are not Catholics." After brilliant studies in America and Europe he was ordained by dispensation on the 19th of December, 1863, and was recognized as a priest of great intellectual ability and high culture, in general literature as well as in the lore of the theologian.

Returning to his native State, he was appointed one of the clergy of the cathedral at Louisville, where he remained till 1870, when he took charge of St. Augustine's Church, which had been opened for colored Catholics. He also acted as secretary and chancellor of the diocese till 1873, when he removed to New York and became one of the priests laboring in the large and important parish of St. Michael. His eloquence and ability led to frequent applications for his services in the pulpit on important occasions, while his zeal and prudence showed his fitness for more responsible duties than had hitherto been assigned to him.

When the diocese of Peoria was formed in Illinois, in 1877, the Rev. Dr. Spalding was selected for the new see, and was consecrated on the feast of St. Philip and St. James, the 1st day of May, in the cathedral of New York, by His Eminence John Cardinal McCloskey, Archbishop of New York, Bishop Rosecrans, of Columbus, preaching on the occasion.

The diocese confided to his care comprised the central portion of the State of Illinois, between the dioceses of Chicago and Alton. There were already seventy-five churches, attended by fifty-one priests, and a Catholic population estimated at forty-five thousand. Fathers of the order of St. Francis, Ladies of the Sacred Heart, Sisters of St. Benedict, St. Dominic, and of St. Francis, were in charge of academies or charitable institutions.

Bishop Spalding developed the resources of his diocese, and new churches with institutions soon rose in various parts, so that by the close of the year 1884 there were in the district under his episcopal charge 159 churches, 109 priests, 8 academies, 41 parochial schools with nearly 7,000 pupils, 5 hospitals, and an orphan asylum. The Catholic population had increased in a remarkable degree, the annual baptisms being 3,574.

Bishop Spalding has co-operated actively in the movement for Catholic colonization, and his own diocese, as well as others further West, show the benefit resulting from the effort to aid immigrants in taking up lands for their new homes where they can enjoy the consolations of their religion.

The project of a great Catholic University in the United States is also one for which Bishop Spalding has labored assiduously, his project being encouraged by the Third Plenary Council of Baltimore, which adopted his plans in 1884, a noble-hearted young Catholic lady, Miss Caldwell, having given $300,000 to begin the great undertaking.

DIOCESE OF PITTSBURGH.

RIGHT REV. MICHAEL O'CONNOR,

First Bishop of Pittsburgh.

LIKE many of the able and energetic bishops of the United States, the Right Rev. Michael O'Connor was a native of Ireland. He was born near Cork September 27, 1810, and, after receiving his earlier training at Queenstown, was sent to France to follow a course for the priesthood, to which he aspired. From his talents and piety he was selected by the Bishop of Cloyne as a student at the Urban College in Rome. The learning and ability displayed in his defence of his theses for the doctor's cap attracted the attention of all. He was ordained priest June 1, 1833, and was appointed to the chair of Holy Scripture in the Propaganda, and vice-rector of the Irish College. After discharging the duties of parish priest at Fermoy, in the diocese of Cloyne, for some time, he came to Philadelphia in 1839 on the invitation of Dr. Kenrick, who desired to secure the services of the learned priest for his seminary of St. Charles Borromeo. Of that institution he soon became president; but while thus absorbed in scholastic duties he did not forego the work of a missionary priest, taking charge of stations, and building a church, which he dedicated to St. Francis Xavier. His veneration for that Apostle of the Indies was an indication of his desire to enter the Society of Jesus—a desire which he never abandoned.

In 1841 he was appointed vicar-general of the western part of the diocese of Philadelphia, and pastor of St. Paul's Church in Pittsburgh. The historian of that portion of the State says that his arrival marked a new era. Schools, churches, a Catholic Institute showed the designs of the active mind. In May, 1843, he went to Rome to solicit permission to enter the Society of Jesus—a step which, as a student of the Propaganda, he could not take without direct sanction from Rome. But when he obtained an audience of the Holy Father he was forbidden to rise till he promised to accept the mitre as first Bishop of Pittsburgh. He was consecrated in St. Agatha's Church, in Rome, on the feast of the Assumption, 1843, by Cardinal Fransoni.

He visited Ireland, and, obtaining some candidates for the priesthood and Sisters of Mercy, reached Pittsburgh in December. The diocese comprised fourteen counties, over which were scattered some twenty-five thousand Catholics, attended by fourteen priests. There were only thirty-three churches and one orphan asylum. The only religious orders were the Priests of the Most Holy Redeemer and the Sisters of Charity. This district had in earlier times been the field of labor of the great missionary Prince Dmitri A. Galitzin, who endeavored to build up Catholic colonies near his church at Loreto. Here in 1847 the Franciscan Brothers, invited by Bishop O'Connor, established a house of their teaching order. The year before the Rev. Boniface Wimmer began a community of the order of St. Benedict. It has grown into a congregation, of which he was in 1884 archabbot. The Benedictines have a great Abbey of St. Vincent's near Latrobe, and several abbeys and many priories, filiations of St. Vincent's, exist in the United States, the missionaries laboring in college or parochial work, from the Atlantic to the Pacific. Bishop O'Connor also obtained a colony of Passionists from Rome in 1852, and these austere religious have increased, and by their missions revived the faith in thousands. Among other aids the bishop also obtained some Sisters of Notre Dame.

The diocese had increased so much that in 1852 the Plenary Council solicited its division, and a new see was erected at Erie. To this Bishop O'Connor was transferred July 29, 1853; but as Dr. Young was reluctant to replace him at Pittsburgh, Bishop O'Connor returned to that see.

His cathedral had been destroyed by fire in 1851, but he had at once begun the erection of a new and finer edifice. This was dedicated with great solemnity on the 24th of June, 1855. But the active zeal of Bishop O'Connor was arrested by softening of the brain, attended with great pain, and he earnestly sought relief from the responsibilities of his bishopric. In May, 1860, Pope Pius IX. permitted him to resign his see, and Dr. O'Connor at once carried out the project of his early years by entering the Society of Jesus. At this time the diocese of Pittsburgh alone contained eighty-six priests and seventy-seven churches, with a seminary, a college, academies, and schools, as well as charitable institutions. The population was estimated at fifty thousand.

In the order which he entered he edified all by his humility and piety. As his health permitted he discharged the ministry in the confessional and the pulpit, and especially in giving retreats to religious communities. He died most piously amid his religious brethren at Woodstock, in Maryland, on the 18th of October, 1872. The historian of the Pittsburgh diocese, Rev. A. A. Lambing, justly styles him "one of the most brilliant lights that has ever shed its lustre on the Church in the United States."

RIGHT REV. MICHAEL DOMENEC,

Second Bishop of Pittsburgh.

MICHAEL DOMENEC was born at Rioz, near Tarragona, in Spain, in 1816, and at an early age corresponded to a vocation to the priesthood. While studying at the Spanish capital the disturbed state of his native country induced him to proceed to France. Continuing his course there under the Priests of the Congregation of the Mission, he joined that family of St. Vincent de Paul, and came to the United States in 1837 with the Very Rev. John Timon. Completing his studies at the seminary of the order at the Barrens, Missouri, he was ordained June 29, 1839. After acting as professor at St. Mary's College he founded St. Vincent's Male Academy at Cape Girardeau in 1842, and was subsequently employed on mission duties in the State of Missouri. In 1845 he was sent to Pennsylvania, and, after some service at Nicetown, erected the church of St. Vincent de Paul in Germantown, of which he was pastor when he was selected as successor to Bishop O'Connor. He was consecrated in the cathedral at Pittsburgh by Archbishop Kenrick, of Baltimore, on the 9th of December, 1860. The progress of religion continued during the administration of Bishop Domenec, several new churches having been erected. The bishop visited Rome in 1862 and again in 1867 to attend the canonizations in those years. In 1875 the diocese of Pittsburgh was regarded as too large for a single bishop, as it contained 115 churches, 160 priests, and, as was believed, 200,000 Catholics. A new see was erected at Allegheny. To this Bishop Domenec was transferred on the 11th of January, 1876, being succeeded in Pittsburgh by Right Rev. Dr. Tuigg. The organization of the new diocese engaged Bishop Domenec's attention, and, ever zealous and active, he doubtless planned many things for its advantage. But the division of the diocese entailed difficulties which he had not foreseen. In order to bring all questions to a decision Dr. Domenec proceeded to Rome in 1877, but, finding the matter a difficult one, he resigned the see of Allegheny on the 29th of July and retired to Barcelona. There he impressed all by his eloquence and zeal. Toward the close of the year he set out for his native city, but at Tarragona was seized with a fatal illness, and expired calmly on the 7th of January, 1878.

RIGHT REV. JOHN TUIGG,

Third Bishop of Pittsburgh.

THE Right Rev. John Tuigg, Bishop of Pittsburgh, is a native of Ireland, born in the County Cork in the year 1820. His divinity studies, begun at the Missionary College of All-Hallows', Drumcondra, were completed at St. Michael's Seminary, Pittsburgh. He was ordained May 14, 1850, and while assistant at the cathedral founded the parish of St. Bridget, beginning to erect the church; but in 1853 he was assigned to the important mission of Altoona, of which he was the first resident pastor.

He acquired a pastoral residence, a cemetery, and enlarged the church. A very fine school-building was the next work, and, in the hands of Sisters of Charity, the parochial school has been a great blessing.

Rev. Mr. Tuigg had charge also of several dependent missions, and, having been appointed vicar-forane of the eastern part of the diocese in 1869, soon required other priests to aid him. He then commenced a new church, which was dedicated in 1875.

Having been appointed to the see of Pittsburgh in the following year, he was consecrated on the 19th of March, 1876, by the Most Rev. James F. Wood, Archbishop of Philadelphia. The diocese committed to his care was no slight burden, but on the resignation of Bishop Domenec the administration of Allegheny was also confided to him. The arduous duties proved too trying even for his vigorous constitution. In December, 1882, he was prostrated by an attack of heart-disease and his life was despaired of; but he rallied, and, though thrice stricken with paralysis, recovered sufficiently to administer the dioceses under his care.

At the close of the year 1884 the united dioceses of Pittsburgh and Allegheny contained 192 priests, 132 churches, and 44 chapels. There were three colleges, six academies, and sixty-five parochial schools attended by nearly twenty thousand pupils. The religious orders were numerous: Benedictine monks, Capuchin and Carmelite friars, Passionists, Redemptorists, Priests of the Holy Ghost and the Immaculate Heart of Mary, Franciscan Brothers, Benedictine and Ursuline nuns, Sisters of Charity, of Mercy, of St. Joseph, of St. Agnes, of St. Francis, of Divine Providence, of the Good Shepherd, Little Sisters of the Poor, School Sisters of Notre Dame, teach the ignorant, minister to the afflicted, or strive to reform the erring.

RT. REV. JOHN L. SPALDING, D.D.
Born at Lebanon, Ky., June 2, 1840.
Ordained Dec. 19, 1863; Consecrated Bishop of
Peoria, May 1, 1877.

RT. REV. RICHARD PHELAN, D.D.
Born in Ireland, Jan. 1, 1825.
Ordained May 4, 1854; Consecrated Bishop of Cebyra
and Coadjutor of Pittsburgh, Aug. 24, 1885.

RT. REV. JOHN TUIGG, D.D.
Born Co. Cork, Ireland, in 1820.
Ordained May 14, 1850; Consecrated Bishop of
Pittsburgh, March 19, 1876.

RT. REV. JAMES A. HEALY, D.D.
Born near Macon, Ga., in 1830.
Consecrated Bishop of Portland, June 2, 1875.

RIGHT REV. RICHARD PHELAN, D.D.,

Bishop of Cèbyra and Coadjutor to the Bishop of Pittsburgh.

THE Right Rev. Richard Phelan, son of Michael Phelan and Mary Keoghan, was born on the 1st day of January, 1825, near the small town of Ballyragget, in the County of Kilkenny, Ireland, the oldest of a family of nine, four of whom devoted themselves to the service of God. After attending schools near his home, and receiving private instruction, he entered St. Kyran's College, Kilkenny, about 1844, and, finding no vacancy in the seminary of his native diocese, accepted an invitation from Bishop O'Connor and was one of six who came to Pittsburgh in January, 1850. He made his divinity course at St. Mary's Theological Seminary, Baltimore, and was ordained priest at Pittsburgh, May 4, 1854, by Bishop O'Connor. He was first stationed in Indiana County, but repaired to Pittsburgh to aid the clergy of that city during the cholera then raging. After three years' service in Pittsburgh Cathedral he was sent to Freeport, where he found heavy debts to meet and a large district to attend. Succeeding Dr. Mullen at St. Peter's Church, Allegheny, he built a new church, costing $150,000, on a more advantageous site, and paid nearly all its cost as well as that of schools. In 1876 this church became the pro-cathedral of the new diocese of Allegheny. In 1881 Dr. Phelan was administrator of the dioceses of Pittsburgh and Allegheny during the absence of Bishop Tuigg, and was next made vicar-general. When Bishop Tuigg was stricken with partial paralysis, and recovery seemed remote, the Very Rev. Dr. Phelan was selected by the Pope as coadjutor. He was consecrated August 2, 1885, at Pittsburgh by Archbishop Ryan, and entered on the discharge of the episcopal duties which Bishop Tuigg's health precluded him from performing. Bishop Phelan continued to reside in Allegheny, St. Peter's again enjoying the presence of one invested with the episcopal dignity.

DIOCESE OF PORTLAND.

RIGHT REV. DAVID W. BACON,

First Bishop of Portland.

DAVID W. BACON was born in the city of New York in the year 1814, and after an academic course he was sent to the Sulpitian Seminary, Montreal, and subsequently entered Mount St. Mary's College, Emmittsburg, where he was distinguished for his brilliant and studious course. After his ordination by Archbishop Eccleston, on the 13th of December, 1838, he returned to the diocese of New York. One of the first positions of the young priest was that of assistant at Utica, but he was soon appointed to organize a new parish in Brooklyn. He acquired an unfinished building begun as a revolt from the Church, and on the foundation reared a church which he dedicated to Our Lady in her Assumption. His flock, at first poor and scanty, gradually increased, many converts being won by the zealous priest. Though gentle, he was firm, and his decision saved the church of St. James from destruction by a mob. During seasons of sickness and epidemics Rev. Mr. Bacon was untiring and fearless. In time he projected a new church to meet the wants of Catholics in the growing city, and, collecting money from house to house, began the church of St. Mary, "Star of the Sea"; but though he nearly completed it, he refused to leave his old parish.

He was, however, summoned to a higher charge, having been appointed to the new see of Portland. The diocese of which it was the spiritual centre comprised the two States of Maine and New Hampshire, where Catholics were few, but prejudice and intolerance intense. A year before a zealous and blameless priest, the Rev. John Bapst, was tarred and feathered, by order of a town meeting, at Ellsworth, and churches in New Hampshire—a State in which to this day no Catholic can hold office—had been attacked and burned.

Bishop Bacon was consecrated in the church of the Immaculate Conception, Portland, April 22, 1855, and courageously undertook to extend Catholicity in the dangerous field assigned to him, in which there were estimated to be thirty thousand Catholics, but only ten priests in the two States attending the humble churches. Yet Catholicity had been the first to plant the altar in Maine, at Boone Island and Mount Desert; and there were in the State Catholic Indians, descendants of the converts of early Jesuit, Capuchin, and Recollect. Bishop Bacon began his work with judgment and zeal. Aided by the friends his course had made in Brooklyn, he was enabled to meet some pressing wants. The Sisters of Mercy came in response to his call for aid, and churches began to arise, while zealous priests came to open new fields. Year by year the progress of the faith could be seen, and after an administration of nearly twenty years he had a fine cathedral, sixty-three churches, fifty-two priests, twenty-three parochial schools, and nearly eighty thousand Catholics. In 1874 his health failed, and, in hopes of regaining strength, he visited Europe with Archbishop McCloskey. On reaching Brest it was necessary to convey him to an hospital. Rallying after a time, he longed to return to America, but reached New York only to expire, at St. Vincent's Hospital, soon after his arrival, November 5, 1874.

RIGHT REV. JAMES AUGUSTINE HEALY,

Second Bishop of Portland.

JAMES AUGUSTINE HEALY was born in 1830 near Macon, Georgia, but was educated in the North, having passed several years in Quaker schools on Long Island and New Jersey. He then entered the college of the Holy Cross at Worcester, Massachusetts, where he was graduated in 1849. Feeling that he was called by God to the ecclesiastical state, he then entered the theological seminary in Montreal directed by the Sulpitians, and completed his course in the institution at Paris directed by the same association of learned priests.

On returning to the diocese of Boston, to which he had become attached, he was stationed at the cathedral, where he acted for many years as chancellor and secretary. He then became pastor of St. James' Church, Boston, holding the position for nine years, winning the respect of his fellow-priests and the attachment of the flock confided to him. From this position he was summoned by the voice of the Holy Father to assume the burden of the episcopate. He was consecrated Bishop of Portland on the 2d of June, 1875.

During his nine years' administration more than thirty new churches were erected, and the clergy rose from fifty-two to eighty-nine. The immigration of Catholics from Europe was more than equalled by the influx of Canadians, who settled in the factory-towns and drew priests of their own language from the neighboring Dominion. To meet the wants of his people Bishop Healy introduced Sisters of Charity, Sisters of the Congregation of Notre Dame, as well as Sisters of the Holy Names of Jesus and Mary from Canada, and also Marianite Sisters of the Holy Cross and Sisters of the Good Shepherd.

In 1884 the Holy See erected the State of New Hampshire into a diocese, of which Manchester became the episcopal see, Bishop Healy retaining the less promising field of Maine, which now constitutes the diocese of Portland. After the division the diocese of Portland had 51 priests, 55 churches, and 11 chapels, with 3 academies and 12 parochial schools, 3 of them for Indian children, with more than 3,000 pupils under Catholic training. Sisters of Mercy, of Charity, of the Good Shepherd, and of the Congregation of Notre Dame acted as teachers and conducted asylums. The annual baptisms were 2,690.

DIOCESE OF PROVIDENCE.

RIGHT REV. THOMAS F. HENDRICKEN,

First Bishop of Providence.

PROVIDENCE was for a time the residence of the Bishop of Hartford, but, a division being made in the diocese, the Rhode Island capital became an episcopal see. Right Rev. Thomas F. Hendricken, the first Bishop of Providence, was born in the cathedral parish of the city of Kilkenny, Ireland, on the 5th of May, 1827, his parents being John Hendricken and Anne Maher. After preliminary studies in McDonald's Academy, Kilkenny, he entered St. Kyran's College in that city, and showed such ability that he was selected as one of the few to enter the great theological seminary at Maynooth in 1847. He was ordained at All-Hallows' College, Dublin, April 29, 1853, by the Right Rev. Bernard O'Reilly, of Hartford, to whom he had offered his services. His earliest missions in America were at the cathedral in Providence, at St. Joseph's, in the same city, at Woonsocket and Newport. On the 17th of January, 1854, he was appointed pastor of St. Joseph's, West Winsted, Conn., and on the 5th of July in the ensuing year was stationed at Waterbury, in the same State. This became a permanent field of labor, and for seventeen years he was the zealous pastor of Waterbury and of the missions dependent on it.

What he accomplished in this parish commended him to a higher appointment, and on the division of the diocese of Hartford he was selected as Bishop of Providence. The district placed under his charge comprised the State of Rhode Island, together with Bristol, Barnstable, and part of Plymouth County in Massachusetts, and the islands of Martha's Vineyard and Nantucket.

Bishop Hendricken was consecrated bishop on the 28th of April, 1872, and proceeded to organize his diocese.

During the Revolutionary war the chaplains of the French army and navy officiated in Rhode Island. The famous convert, Rev. John Thayer, had visited Newport as early as 1791, and ministered to the Catholics there, and they were occasionally visited in later years; but it was not till 1828 that Rev. Robert D. Woodley, purchasing an old school-house, opened the first church in that city. In the same year a lot was given for a church in Providence. From such small beginnings the faith grew, and when Bishop Hendricken assumed the direction of his diocese Providence had ten churches, that of St. Peter and St. Paul becoming his pro-cathedral, and there were thirty-three churches outside the limits of his episcopal city. The Catholic body had grown to the imposing strength of 125,000, and there were institutions directed by Brothers of the Christian Schools, Sisters of Mercy, and Sisters of Charity. Yet there was work to be done, and the bishop zealously undertook it. Canadian-French had settled in the factory-towns, and Portuguese in the fishing-villages on the coast, once the nursery of hardy New England seamen. These needed priests able to address them in their own language. Ladies of the Sacred Heart and Ursuline nuns established academies of a higher grade than any yet in the diocese, Sisters of the Holy Names and of the Holy Cross increased the number of teachers, while the Little Sisters of the Poor opened a Home for the Aged. Nearly a hundred priests were laboring in 1884 in this diocese, and there were fifty-five churches; parochial schools are numerous, and the attendance reaches nearly ten thousand, the whole Catholic population being estimated at 156,000, the baptisms in Rhode Island in 1883 being 3,602, and in Massachusetts 2,500. A large and imposing cathedral, worthy of the diocese, was nearly completed in 1884.

DIOCESE OF RICHMOND.

RIGHT REV. PATRICK KELLY,

First Bishop of Richmond.

VIRGINIA had, as a colony, closed her doors against the Catholic. Lord Baltimore was not permitted to land, and when his son founded a home for Catholics in Maryland the fanaticism in the older colony left traces of its bitterness in the penal laws on her statute-book. There were few Catholics in Virginia at the period of our Revolution, and few emigrants of the ancient faith ventured to settle. Yet, small as the body was, there were malcontents, chiefly at Norfolk, where a plot was formed to bring in a Jansenist bishop from Holland. About 1820 they succeeded in persuading the Sovereign Pontiff that the Catholics of Virginia were neglected, and that, as they were able and willing to maintain a bishop, the State ought to be formed into a separate diocese.

The see of Richmond was erected in 1820, and the Rev. Patrick Kelly, President of Birchfield College, was selected as first bishop. He was consecrated at Kilkenny on the 24th of August, 1820, by the Most Rev. Archbishop Troy, of Dublin, and in January of the next year reached Norfolk. He found but seven churches in the whole State, four of them attended by priests living in Maryland. The resources of the Catholics proved to have been grossly exaggerated, and the learned bishop opened a school at Norfolk in order to maintain himself, the congregation being unable to support him. He struggled manfully to afford the scattered Catholics the consolations of their religion, but the difficulty of travel and communication at that period made it no easy task to reach them. After a year's arduous service Bishop Kelly's health failed, and in July, 1822, he was translated to the united sees of Waterford and Lismore, which he held till his death, October 8, 1829, leaving a reputation for piety and earnest zeal in his episcopal functions.

RIGHT REV. RICHARD VINCENT WHELAN,

Second Bishop of Richmond and First Bishop of Wheeling.

AFTER the departure of Bishop Kelly the administration of the diocese of Richmond was committed to the Archbishop of Baltimore and his successors in that see, nor was it till twenty years later that the Catholic body in Virginia had grown so large as to require a resident bishop.

Right Rev. Richard Vincent Whelan, selected as the second Bishop of Richmond, was born in Baltimore on the 28th of January, 1809. After some years spent at Mount St. Mary's College, Emmittsburg, he was sent to Paris, where he pursued studies for the priesthood under the disciples of the Venerable Mr. Olier. He was ordained in 1832 and was soon after sent to Virginia; he traversed a large part of the State, finding scattered Catholics, but meeting great courtesy from the people at large. Martinsburg became his central mission, whence he attended Harper's Ferry, trudging to and from it on foot. He also made missionary excursions to Winchester and Bath. To aid him in his work he obtained three Sisters of Charity, who founded a house at Martinsburg. When, in 1838, Archbishop Eccleston found that Virginia had a Catholic population of nine thousand, and eight churches, he requested the Holy See to fill the long-vacant see of Richmond. The zealous pastor of Martinsburg was selected, and he was consecrated in the cathedral of Baltimore on the 21st of March, 1841. He began a theological seminary in order to create a supply of priests, opened an asylum at Richmond under the Sisters of Charity, and a school at Norfolk which he committed to other members of that community.

Bishop Whelan visited his diocese and became fully aware of

the condition and prospects of his flock. Catholics were increasing so much in numbers in Western Virginia that in 1846 he resolved to take up his residence at Wheeling. Here he found more abundant work; but as the distance from Richmond was great, he felt that it was necessary to have a bishop in each city. The Fathers of the Seventh Council of Baltimore, adopting his view, petitioned the Holy See for a division of the diocese. The see of Wheeling was erected by a bull of July 23, 1850, and Bishop Whelan was transferred to it. When he fixed his residence in the western city its Catholic population did not exceed six hundred, and they had one small church. Outside the city there was one other church in the new diocese. Yet Bishop Whelan resolved to erect a cathedral, and, purchasing one fine house for a convent-school and another for a site of his projected church, took it down to lay the corner-stone. By the time it was ready for use there were two priests attached to the cathedral, a large school taught by six seminarians, and an academy under Visitation nuns. The rest of his diocese was not neglected. He traversed mountain and stream to visit his flock, preaching in churches, court-houses, administering confirmation, encouraging his hard-working priests. His activity and courage were great, and even advancing age could not diminish them. On one of his visitations he was prostrated by illness, and had not a charitable family taken him in and nursed him the Bishop of Wheeling might have died uncared for.

In 1853 the Sisters of St. Joseph opened an hospital; in 1866 a college was begun at Wheeling, and at Parkersburg a Visitation academy and a high-school for boys were opened. The Sisters of St. Joseph also enlarged their work, establishing academies at Charleston and Grafton.

Bishop Whelan lived to see forty-eight churches and twenty-nine priests where he had found two churches and four priests. He died piously at St. Agnes' Hospital, Wheeling, July 7, 1874.

RIGHT REV. JOHN McGILL,

Third Bishop of Richmond.

JOHN MCGILL was born in Philadelphia, November 4, 1809, his parents, James McGill and Lavinia Dougherty, natives of Ireland, having settled and married there. Bardstown became the home of the family in 1818, and two years after John entered St. Joseph's College at its opening. His father, liberally educated himself, wished his son to enjoy every advantage. He was graduated in due time with distinguished honor. He studied law, and fame and wealth seemed certain, but he threw all aside to enter the seminary, where he was trained to the spirit and learning befitting a priest by the venerable Bishop David, by whom he was ordained June 13, 1835. As pastor of St. Peter's, Lexington, and assistant at St. Louis' Church, Louisville, his ministry was marked by success. In 1838 he was sent to Europe to accompany the venerable Bishop Flaget on his return to Kentucky. Then he resumed his duties in the parish, and as editor of the *Catholic Advocate* made a decided impression on the public mind in his clear and convincing articles. When a league of Protestant ministers was formed to denounce Catholicity in a series of sermons, Dr. McGill answered them so ably as to put them on the defensive and finally compel them to retire from the field. He then published a criticism on some statements in Macaulay's "England" in reply to Rev. James Craik. This was followed by a translation of Audin's "Life of Calvin."

Bishop Spalding made the learned and able clergyman his vicar-general, and in 1850 he was appointed to the see of Richmond. He was consecrated by Archbishop Kenrick, of St. Louis, on the 10th of November, in St. Joseph's Church, Bardstown, where he had made his First Communion, received the tonsure and holy orders. His aged parents were present to receive his episcopal blessing.

In Virginia Bishop McGill found a warm welcome and acquired the esteem of all. He zealously undertook the direction of the diocese, acting in concert with his clergy, and adding to the means for preserving the faith of the people. His diocese comprised eastern Virginia and the valley formed by the Blue Ridge and Allegheny Mountains as far as Monroe County, where it crossed the valley and followed the Blue Ridge as the line dividing it from the diocese of Wheeling. There were but ten churches in it and only eight priests. The Sisters of Charity from Emmittsburg had two institutions in the diocese, combining orphan asylum and school. Under his administration churches were erected and dedicated at Norfolk, Fortress Monroe, Richmond, Fredericksburg, Warrenton, and at Fairfax Station. His diocese was the great battle-ground of the civil war, and the Catholic churches fared ill at the hands of both armies. The church at Bath was destroyed by fire while used as quarters by Confederate soldiers. The United States troops stabled their horses in the church at Winchester and utterly wrecked it. Bishop McGill had therefore a heavy charge, but he formed a little seminary, and after the war introduced the Visitation and the Benedictine nuns, who gave Richmond fine academies, and Sisters of the Holy Cross, who established a similar institution in Alexandria. He had fourteen parochial schools—a large number for a Catholic population of not more than seventeen thousand.

Bishop McGill visited Rome at the definition of the Immaculate Conception in 1852, and to attend the General Council of the Vatican. While Bishop of Richmond he published "The True Church" and "Faith the Victory." His health failed in 1871, and he made a farewell visit to his relatives in Kentucky. Upon his return he gradually grew worse, and, after great suffering, expired Sunday, January 14, 1872.

RIGHT REV. JOHN J. KEANE,

Fifth Bishop of Richmond.

JOHN J. KEANE was born at Ballyshannon, County Donegal, Ireland, on the 12th of September, 1839, and came with his family to the United States when he was seven years old. He received his early education in Baltimore, and, after a classical course at St. Charles' College, entered St. Mary's Seminary, Baltimore, and was ordained in 1866. He was immediately appointed assistant pastor of St. Patrick's Church in the city of Washington, and labored in that position with such zeal and earnestness that he was selected in 1878 to fill the see of Richmond. He was consecrated on the 25th of August in that year. The State in which the first Catholic altar in our land was reared by the sons of St. Dominic, ere the sixteenth century had reached its zenith, had not been favorable to the growth of the Church of the living God. In colonial days it had degraded the children of the faith to the level of the negro slave; in 1878 only twenty-two churches were to be found in the Old Dominion where Divine Worship was offered to the Most High.

Bishop Keane has taken an active part in the organization of Catholic societies throughout the country. He was one of the leading members of the Third Plenary Council of Baltimore in 1884. In 1885 his diocese contained thirty-five churches, with twenty-seven priests, four academies, thirty-two parochial schools with more than two thousand pupils.

RT. REV. T. F. HENDRICKEN, D.D.
Born in Kilkenny, Ireland, May 5, 1827.
Ordained April 29, 1853; Consecrated Bishop of
Providence, April 28, 1872.

RT. REV. BERNARD J. McQUAID, D.D.
Born in the City of New York, Dec. 15, 1823.
Ordained July 16, 1848; Consecrated Bishop of
Rochester, July 12, 1868.

RT. REV. JOHN J. KEANE, D.D.
Born at Ballyshannon, Ireland, Sept. 12, 1839.
Ordained in 1866; Consecrated Bishop of
Richmond, Aug. 25, 1878.

RT. REV. J. C. NERAZ, D.D.
Born at Anse, France, Jan. 12, 1828.
Ordained Feb. 19, 1853; Consecrated Bishop of
San Antonio, May 8, 1881.

DIOCESE OF ROCHESTER.

RIGHT REV. BERNARD J. McQUAID,

First Bishop of Rochester.

BERNARD JOSEPH McQUAID was born in the city of New York, and, after preliminary studies at one of the schools there, was sent to Chambly, and subsequently to the College of Montreal, directed by the priests of the Association of St. Sulpice. He was one of the students of St. Joseph's Theological Seminary at Fordham after its establishment by Bishop Hughes, and was ordained on the 18th of January, 1848. His first appointment was that of pastor of the church of St. Vincent de Paul at Madison, New Jersey; the congregation of St. Mary's, Morristown, being also under his charge. He showed himself an active and energetic missionary in the care of a large district, and when the diocese of Newark was formed, in 1853, Rev. Mr. McQuaid was selected by Bishop Bayley as pastor of St. Patrick's Cathedral. His influence was soon apparent, and when Seton Hall College was opened, in 1856, at Madison, he was appointed president; but, after organizing that institution, resumed his position at the cathedral till 1859, when he resumed the presidency. In Newark he organized a Young Men's Catholic Association, which erected the Catholic Institute in New Street—a fine building, with library, reading-room, and halls for innocent diversions. This Institute rendered such service to the young men that it received the warmest encomiums from the city authorities and the best class of the people. In 1866 he became vicar-general of the diocese, and in that capacity, as in that of superior of a college and theological seminary, and of pastor of important parishes, attracted such attention that when the diocese of Rochester was formed, in 1868, he was selected as the first bishop, and was consecrated on the 12th of July. The diocese comprised the counties of Monroe, Livingston, Wayne, Ontario, Seneca, Cayuga, Yates, and Tompkins, and contained sixty churches, with thirty-eight priests. Rochester had a house of Redemptorist Fathers, academies under the Ladies of the Sacred Heart and Sisters of Mercy, a hospital and asylum for girls under Sisters of Charity, one for boys under Sisters of St. Joseph, and a German asylum under School Sisters of Notre Dame. Parochial schools existed in several parishes. After organizing his diocese and ascertaining its wants, Bishop McQuaid labored to create churches, and especially schools, wherever Catholics could maintain them. He showed the injustice of the public-school system, which, while professing to be neutral, really imposes Protestant ideas, prejudices, and forms on Catholic pupils, imbuing them with what must sap their religious faith.

In 1870 Bishop McQuaid, always earnest in bringing up zealous young clergymen for his diocese, founded St. Andrew's Preparatory Seminary to foster vocations to the priesthood in the district committed to his care. It opened with seven students, but they were so well chosen that six entered the theological seminary at Troy.

Bishop McQuaid has taken part in the deliberations of a provincial, a national, and an œcumenical council, evincing at New York, Baltimore, and Rome learning, great experience in ecclesiastical affairs, and a thorough knowledge of the position of the Catholics in this country, and the dangers to which the faith of the rising generation is exposed. By his clear and forcible arguments he obtained for Catholic inmates of eleemosynary and penal institutions in his diocese the opportunity of exercising the right to worship God according to the dictates of their conscience, which the constitution of the State of New York guarantees to the meanest of her citizens.

DIOCESE OF SAN ANTONIO.

RIGHT REV. ANTHONY DOMINIC PELLICER,

First Bishop of San Antonio.

ANTHONY DOMINIC PELLICER was born in St. Augustine, Florida, in the year 1825; he was descended from the brave leader of the Minorcans of New Smyrna who in the last century revolted against the tyranny of Turnbull and marched to St. Augustine, where they revived Catholicity. Anthony Dominic, with his cousin, Dominic Manucy, made a college course at Spring Hill College, near Mobile, and both devoted themselves to God's service. After his ordination, about 1850, Rev. Mr. Pellicer was sent to St. Peter's Church, Montgomery, Alabama, where he spent several years, visiting Wetumpka, Tuskigee, Whitecreek, and Lowndesborough, and about 1856 beginning a church at Camden, and subsequently organizing a congregation at Selma. In 1865 he was recalled to Mobile, and became one of the active priests attached to the cathedral, and was in the council of the bishop, who in 1867 made him vicar-general.

During the Civil War he was post-chaplain and was unremitting in his attention to the sick and wounded. His zeal and devotedness struck those who were strangers to the faith, and as many as three hundred sought his guidance.

When the see of San Antonio was erected the Very Rev. Dr. Pellicer was elected the first bishop, and was consecrated at Mobile on the feast of the Immaculate Conception in the year 1875. His episcopal city dated back to the early Spanish days, and several time-honored churches attested the zeal and labors of the Franciscan Fathers who, under the guidance of the Venerable Antonio Margil, planted Christianity in Texas. The diocese of San Antonio, as erected September 3, 1874, comprised the portion of the State of Texas lying between the Colorado and Nueces rivers. In it there were forty thousand Catholics, who had several churches and chapels, attended by thirty-five priests. At San Antonio there was a college under the Brothers of Mary, an academy directed by Ursuline nuns, a hospital and an orphan asylum in charge of Sisters of the Incarnate Word; there were in the diocese eighteen parochial schools under the care of Sisters of the Incarnate Word, Sisters of Mercy, Sisters of the Immaculate Conception, and Sisters of Divine Providence.

Bishop Pellicer soon made a visitation of his diocese, travelling in a wagon or riding on horseback, often sleeping on the open prairie. He thus acquired a practical knowledge of every parish in his diocese, and began his labors to supply every want that he had detected. Under his impulse new churches arose at many places, with schools, and to carry on the work he obtained many zealous priests. His labor was so incessant that his health gave way. He died piously at San Antonio on the 14th of April, 1880.

RIGHT REV. J. C. NERAZ,

Second Bishop of San Antonio.

J. C. NERAZ was born on the 12th of January, 1828, at Ause, in the Department of the Rhone, France, and, after acquiring the rudiments, entered the diocesan seminary of St. Jodard; his philosophical course he followed at the Alix branch of the Great Seminary of Lyons, and completed his theology under the Sulpitians at Lyons. Resolving to devote himself to foreign missions, he came to the United States in 1852, and was ordained subdeacon by Bishop Odin on the 28th of September, receiving the holy order of priesthood on the 19th of February in the succeeding year.

The young priest was assigned to the mission of Nacogdoches, in eastern Texas, which embraced all the northeastern part of the State as far as Red River. After ten years' labors in this arduous field he was transferred in 1864 to Liberty County, in southern Texas, where he remained two years. In 1866 he was made assistant at San Antonio, but in September, 1868, was removed to Laredo. There he completed the convent which had long previously been commenced, and erected the present church. In 1873 he was recalled to San Antonio to become pastor of the church of San Fernando. When the diocese of San Antonio was established the zealous priest was appointed vicar-general by Bishop Pellicer. On the death of that prelate he became administrator of the diocese, and, having been chosen to succeed him, was consecrated bishop on the 8th of May, 1881. He attended the Third Plenary Council of Baltimore in 1884.

During his administration as bishop the Priests of the Holy Cross have opened St. Edward's Academy, in Travis County, and the Sisters of the Incarnate Word an academy at Hallettsville, in Lavaca County. The diocese contained at the commencement of the year 1885 forty-seven priests and fifty churches.

DIOCESE OF SAVANNAH.

RIGHT REV. FRANCIS XAVIER GARTLAND,

First Bishop of Savannah.

FRANCIS XAVIER GARTLAND was born in Dublin in 1805, but, coming to this country in his youth, entered Mount St. Mary's, Emmittsburg, and was ordained priest by Right Rev. Dr. Conwell, Bishop of Philadelphia, in 1832. The Rev. John Hughes, the future great Archbishop of New York, had just erected St. John's Church, and the young priest was appointed his assistant. When Dr. Hughes was made coadjutor of New York, Rev. Mr. Gartland became pastor of St. John's. His zeal and eloquence endeared him to his congregation, and his virtues won him the esteem of his bishop and his fellow-priests. From the year 1845 he acted also as vicar-general of the diocese, and when the Holy See, on the recommendation of the Seventh Council of Baltimore, formed a new diocese with the episcopal see at Savannah, the Very Rev. Dr. Gartland was selected as the first bishop. He was consecrated in his own church at Philadelphia, on the 10th of September, 1850, by the Most Rev. Archbishop Eccleston.

The diocese of Savannah, as constituted by the bull of erection, comprised the State of Georgia with East Florida. For the five thousand scattered Catholics there were eight churches in Georgia and five in Florida, Savannah, Augusta, and Locust Grove being the cradles of Catholicity in the former State. There were no institutions except a convent of the Sisters of Our Lady of Mercy at Savannah, and an asylum with a school at Augusta.

The Church was feeble in Georgia; for though Oglethorpe planted the colony as a refuge for the afflicted and persecuted, he was a slave to unmanly bigotry, and, by its fundamental law, Georgia was forbidden to receive a Catholic within its borders. Dr. Gartland, after acquainting himself with the state of his diocese, visited Europe to obtain aid for it. Then he devoted himself zealously to give his actual flock and the increase which he felt would surely come every advantage for practising their religion. He made several visitations, enlarged the church of St. John the Baptist, which he selected as his cathedral, erected churches at Jekyll Island, St. John's Beach, Palatka, and Mandarin, and was preparing to establish one at Dalton. In 1853 the Sisters of Our Lady of Mercy began a convent and academy at Augusta. The next year the yellow fever descended on the fair city of Savannah, and Dr. Gartland showed the people of Georgia what a Catholic bishop was. When others fled he went from house to house, visiting the sick by day or night, shrinking from none of the terrible forms of death, till he was himself prostrated by the disease, and died on the 20th of September, 1854.

RIGHT REV. JOHN BARRY,

Second Bishop of Savannah.

JOHN BARRY was born in Wexford, Ireland, in 1799, and while in a seminary volunteered to become a missionary in the diocese of Charleston. Completing his studies under Bishop England, he was ordained by that great prelate September 24, 1825. After one or two temporary missions he became pastor of the church of the Holy Trinity at Augusta, in 1827, with about one-third of Georgia for his parish. Twelve years after he was made vicar-general for that State, and in 1844 for the whole diocese. Recalled at that time to Charleston, he assisted in the cathedral, was superior of the seminary, and was commissioned to attend all vacant stations in the diocese. The historian of the Church in the Carolinas and Georgia says: "He labored on every mission, in every church, and in nearly every town in the three States at one time or another. He was known to every man, woman, and child either personally or by reputation." He was full of activity and zeal, creating asylum and school, caring for the young and the helpless. During the visitations of the cholera and yellow fever he was unremitting in his care. In 1844 he was theologian to Bishop Reynolds in the council held at Baltimore. When the diocese of Savannah was established he remained at Augusta, and became Bishop Gartland's vicar-general in 1853, and on the bishop's death hastened to Savannah to replace him in attending the sick. After governing the diocese for two years as administrator he reluctantly accepted the mitre, and was consecrated by Archbishop Kenrick in the cathedral of Baltimore August 2, 1857. But his constant and unremitting labors had broken the strong constitution and the buoyant spirit. He went to Europe in 1859, hoping to derive benefit from a change of climate, but at Paris he sought admission into the hospital of the Brothers of St. John of God, and there expired on the 19th of November, 1859, edifying all by his patience and piety. His body lay in the Cemetery of Père La Chaise till 1869, when Bishop Persico conveyed it to Savannah and laid it beside that of his predecessor.

RIGHT REV. AUGUSTINE VEROT,

Third Bishop of Savannah and First of St. Augustine.

AUGUSTINE VEROT was born at Le Puys, France, in May, 1804, and, after passing through a grammar-school, entered the seminary of St. Sulpice, Paris, at the age of sixteen. After making a course of philosophy and theology, with Lacordaire and Dupanloup as fellow-students, he was ordained by Archbishop de Quelen September 20, 1828. Having been admitted into the society of St. Sulpice, he was sent to Baltimore in 1830, and was for several years professor in St. Mary's College and in the seminary. In

1853 he was pastor at Ellicott's Mills, but his learning and prudence were so well recognized that Archbishop Hughes desired him to become superior of the provincial seminary which he had established at Troy.

Florida, which had belonged successively to the dioceses of Santiago de Cuba, St. Christopher, New Orleans, Mobile, Charleston, and Savannah, was formed into a vicariate-apostolic, and Dr. Verot was selected, December 11, 1857, as the first to govern it. He was consecrated titular Bishop of Danabe on the 25th of April in the ensuing year. The vicariate comprised all the State of Florida lying east of the Apalachicola River. When the vicariate was established there were only three priests within its limits, two at St. Augustine and one at Jacksonville, the other churches and chapels being deprived of resident pastors. Bishop Verot was installed June 3, 1858, and, regarding the education of the young as his most urgent duty, introduced the Brothers of the Christian Schools and Sisters of Mercy; he completed the church at Palatka, enlarged that at Fernandina, and took steps to erect churches at Mandarin, Orange Spring, and Tampa Bay. He revived the memory of early martyrs of the faith in Florida and endeavored to regain the Church property. His impulse was felt in all parts of Florida. But the State was not to be his sole charge. On the death of Dr. Barry he was, in July, 1861, transferred to Savannah, but retained the direction of Florida as vicar-apostolic. The period during which he wore the mitre of Savannah includes that of the Civil War. In that terrible period the bishop had much tribulation and much to stimulate his zeal. St. Mary's Church in Camden County and the elegant church at Dalton were destroyed by fire, but the church at Atlanta was spared amid the general desolation. Notwithstanding the difficulties of the times, the church of the Holy Trinity at Savannah was completed and dedicated, and when peace was restored a church was erected at Albany. The Ursuline convent at Columbia having been destroyed during the war, a colony of the nuns established a school at Macon, and the Sisters of Mercy from St. Augustine opened a house at Columbus. At Jacksonville, Florida, the church and parochial residence fell victims to the flames.

Dr. Verot directed the diocese of Savannah and the vicariate of Florida till the erection of the see of St. Augustine, in 1870, when, at his own desire, he was transferred to it. In 1876 his health failed, but he remained cheerful, and no immediate danger was suspected; but after saying Mass on the 10th of June he expired so suddenly that there was no opportunity to administer Extreme Unction or recite the prayers for the dying.

Bishop Verot spoke and wrote well, and prepared one of the best catechisms in use in the country.

RIGHT REV. IGNATIUS PERSICO,

Fourth Bishop of Savannah.

IGNATIUS PERSICO was born in Naples on the 30th of January, 1823, of a noble Sorrentine family, and received in baptism the name of Camillus William Mary Peter. After completing his classical course in the college of the Jesuit Fathers at Naples young Persico renounced all worldly prospects that lay open to him through the influence of his family with the government, and in April, 1839, entered the order of Minor Capuchins, desiring to devote himself to the foreign missions. His course of study was most thorough, embracing the whole range of secular and sacred lore. He made his vows in January, 1844, and was ordained by dispensation January 25, 1846. He then proceeded to Rome to enter the missionary college of the order and pass the examination at the Propaganda. Having been made apostolic missionary, he was sent to the vicariate-apostolic of Patna. For some years he visited the remotest parts of that extensive vicariate, reaching the frontiers on every side, including Nepaul, Sickim, and Chinese Tartary. In 1852 he was chosen companion to Bishop Hartman, apostolic visitor in the East Indies. The pretensions of the Archbishop of Goa seriously embarrassing all the vicars-apostolic in India, Father Persico was unanimously selected to proceed to Rome as commissary. He obtained the celebrated bull *Plene nostis*, and then, with the approval of the Holy See, went to England to advocate before the English government the interests of the Catholic population in India. His mission had most satisfactory results, and the position of Catholics was completely changed, not only in regard to the vicars-apostolic and military chaplains, but also in regard to the erection of churches, asylums, schools, and other institutions, Catholics being placed on the same footing as Protestants. Having been chosen coadjutor to the vicar-apostolic of Bombay March 8, 1854, he was consecrated Bishop of Gratianopolis, and soon after was made apostolic visitor of the Agra vicariate, which he visited, and, being made vicar-apostolic, governed it with great fruit. His administration was most laborious and eventful, his cure extending to Cashmere, Cabul, Afghanistan, and Thibet. He established schools and orphanages, created new missions, and formed villages of native Christians till the Sepoy war swept all away, leaving nothing but ruins and slaughtered missionaries and Christians. Bishop Persico was confined for months in the fort of Agra, subjected to every hardship and privation. On his release he served as chaplain to the British army, doing much to save unfortunate people. After the war he sailed for Europe to solicit means to restore the Church in his vicariate to its former condition, but was shipwrecked and escaped almost miraculously. Having succeeded in his mission, he returned to the vicariate, and his energy and zeal were soon rewarded by consoling results. The changed condition of India after the war required another delegation to England to secure Catholic interests, but his constant labors and journeys had enfeebled Bishop Persico so much that the climate of India menaced his life. Having resigned the vicariate, he was advised, at the centenary of St. Peter in 1867, to try the climate of the United States, and spent two years at Charleston as an active missionary. He attended the Provincial Council of Baltimore and the Vatican Council, and on the 20th of March, 1870, was elected to the see of Savannah. For three years he directed the diocese, but, as his former symptoms reappeared, he was compelled, against his will, to resign the see. He was then sent by the Holy See to Canada to adjust some delicate questions there, and subsequently to Malabar, where he obtained the submission of the Chaldean Patriarch Auder. In 1878 he was appointed bishop of the united dioceses of Aquino, Pontecorvo, and Sora; here, having officiated as bishop in three continents, Dr. Persico labors as earnestly as ever, adding to his episcopal duties those of consultor of the Propaganda and apostolic visitor of the Chinese College in Naples.

RT. REV. WILLIAM H. GROSS, D.D.,

Fifth Bishop of Savannah,

was transferred in 1885 to the archiepiscopal see of Oregon.

RT. REV. THOMAS A. BECKER, D.D.,

Sixth Bishop of Savannah,

was transferred to this see from that of Wilmington, under which a sketch of his life will be found.

DIOCESE OF SCRANTON.

RIGHT REV. WILLIAM O'HARA,

First Bishop of Scranton.

THE first Bishop of Scranton, Right Rev. William O'Hara, is a native of the County Derry, Ireland, and came to this country with his parents in 1820. They made Philadelphia their home, and sent their son to a select school till he was ready to enter Georgetown College. From the early age of sixteen he felt himself called to serve God in his sanctuary, and, having attracted the notice of Bishop Kenrick, he was sent to Rome. There he remained eleven years, pursuing a most thorough course in the Urban College of the Propaganda. After his ordination in 1843 he was for thirteen years pastor of St. Patrick's Church; he was also for many years rector and professor in the theological seminary. In 1860 he was appointed by Bishop Wood vicar-general. When the diocese of Scranton was set off, in 1868, this learned and experienced priest was elected the first bishop, and was consecrated on the 12th of July. The district placed under his episcopal care comprises Luzerne, Lackawanna, Bradford, Susquehanna, Wayne, Tioga, Sullivan, Lycoming, Pike, and Monroe counties. He found most of the churches in a very primitive condition, but by his untiring zeal the diocese has attained a flourishing condition, with fine places of worship, zealous priests, and large congregations. He found fifty churches, twenty-eight priests, and one religious community, the Sisters of the Immaculate Heart of Mary. In 1884 he could report seventy churches with sixty-six priests, and sixteen parochial schools, Sisters of Mercy and Sisters of Christian Charity having come to aid in education. Bishop O'Hara had to contend with a long and obstinate litigation begun by a priest whom he attempted to remove from a church whose interests had been grossly neglected and mismanaged. Though the courts finally decided in the bishop's favor, it gave him great anxiety and entailed heavy losses.

DIOCESE OF SPRINGFIELD.

RIGHT REV. P. T. O'REILLY,

First Bishop of Springfield.

THE Right Rev. P. T. O'Reilly is a descendant of the old Breffny tribe, and was born in Cavan, Ireland, on the 24th of December, 1833. He came to this country when a child, and, as he had an uncle in Boston, a chemist in affluent circumstances, he was brought up in that city. Evincing a desire to become a priest, he was sent to St. Charles' College, Maryland, and from it passed in due course to St. Mary's Seminary, Baltimore. He was ordained priest in the cathedral of the Holy Cross, Boston, on the feast of the Assumption in the year 1857, by Bishop Bacon, of Portland, who officiated in consequence of the illness of Bishop Fitzpatrick. After spending five years as assistant to the Rev. John Boyce at Worcester, he was appointed to organize St. Joseph's parish, Boston, of which he became the first pastor, and remained so till January, 1864, when he was chosen to succeed Rev. Mr. Boyce as pastor of St. John's Church, Worcester.

The diocese of Springfield, established June, 1870, comprises the counties of Berkshire, Franklin, Hampshire, Hampden, and Worcester, and at that time contained fifty-four churches built or in course of erection, and forty priests, not including the Fathers of the Society of Jesus attached to the fine college of the Holy Cross at Worcester. There were a few schools, directed by Sisters of Mercy and Sisters of Notre Dame. Rev. Mr. O'Reilly was elected Bishop of Springfield June 28, 1870, and was consecrated in St. Michael's Church, which became his cathedral, on the 25th of September by Archbishop McCloskey, of New York. The diocese has prospered under his prudent zeal, and at the commencement of the year 1885 there were one hundred and thirty-three priests engaged in its limits, the churches numbering ninety and the parochial schools twenty-one, Sisters of St. Joseph, Sisters of St. Anne, and Sisters of Charity, as well as Gray Nuns from Canada and Brothers of the Christian Schools, co-operating with the clergy.

RT. REV. WILLIAM O'HARA, D.D.
Born Co. Derry, Ireland.
Ordained in 1843; Consecrated Bishop of
Scranton, July 12, 1868.

RT. REV. JOHN MOORE, D.D.
Born at Castletown Delvin, Ireland, June 27, 1835.
Ordained in 1860; Consecrated Bishop of
St. Augustine, May 13, 1877.

RT. REV. P. T. O'REILLY, D.D.
Born Cavan, Ireland, Dec. 24, 1833.
Ordained Aug. 16, 1857; Consecrated Bishop of
Springfield, Sept. 25, 1870.

RT. REV. JOHN IRELAND, D.D.
Born at Burnchurch, Ireland, Sept. 11, 1838.
Ordained Dec. 21, 1861; Consecrated Bishop of Maronea and Coadjutor of St. Paul, Dec. 21, 1875; Bishop of St. Paul, 1884.

DIOCESE OF ST. AUGUSTINE.

RIGHT REV. JOHN MOORE,

Second Bishop of St. Augustine.

JOHN MOORE was born in Castletown Devlin, County Westmeath, Ireland, on the 27th of June, 1835. Arriving in Charleston, S. C., in October, 1848, he began his classical studies in the Collegiate Institute and in the seminary of St. John the Baptist. In July, 1851, he was sent to the college of Courbrée, where he remained four years, commencing his philosophical studies. After pursuing a theological course in the Urban College of the Propaganda he was raised to the dignity of the priesthood by Mgr. Luigi Busso in 1860. Returning to his own diocese, he was for five years assistant at St. Finbar's Cathedral, Charleston, witnessing its destruction during the war; he was then for twelve years pastor of St. Patrick's Church in that city, and for six years vicar-general of the diocese. While still pastor of St. Patrick's Church, Charleston, the Very Rev. Mr. Moore was appointed by the Holy See to succeed Dr. Verot; he was consecrated Bishop of St. Augustine by the Right Rev. Dr. Lynch in St. John's Pro-cathedral on Sunday, May 13, 1877, the Right Rev. James Gibbons, then Bishop of Richmond, delivering the sermon. He was duly installed in his diocese on the 20th.

Florida is the oldest State in the Union, dating from its first permanent settlement, St. Augustine having been founded September 8, 1565. The records of the parish church, preserved in Havana and Florida, exist, and cover nearly three centuries, extending from 1594 to the present time. From the first settlement of St. Augustine there was a parish church, besides various chapels in or near the city, and before the close of the sixteenth century the Franciscan Fathers established a convent there, which gave missionaries to the Indian tribes from Albemarle Sound to Pensacola. Many of the missionaries lost their lives at the hands of the Indians or the English of the neighboring provinces.

The parishes and missions of Florida were subject to the bishops of Santiago de Cuba; nor was the supervision merely nominal, several of the bishops making regular visitations of Florida, and not without danger, one of them, while on his way to Florida, falling into the hands of pirates, from whom he was with difficulty ransomed. During the last century bishops-auxiliary were appointed to the Bishop of Santiago, and, as these were charged exclusively with the affairs of Florida, they resided in St. Augustine. The most eminent of these was the zealous Bishop San Buenaventura Tejada, who established schools in St. Augustine, and, having been translated to a see in Mexico, died from the hardships he underwent in making a visitation of the missions in Texas. Among others who lived in Florida as auxiliary bishops were Dr. Pedro Ponze de Carrasco, Dr. Ricino, a native of Havana, and Right Rev. Cyril de Barcelona, of the Capuchin Order, who became auxiliar to the Bishop of Havana when that see was erected and Florida assigned to it. Florida was again under that jurisdiction when it became part of the United States, after having for a time been included in the bishopric of Louisiana. When a bishop was placed in St. Augustine in our time, the Catholic property had been almost all swept away from the Church; the "Casa Episcopal," the house and grounds occupied and owned by the auxiliar bishops, had been given by the United States government to the Episcopalians; the ancient convent of the Franciscans is still held by the government as barracks.

Bishop Moore has done much to advance the interests of religion in this ancient vineyard, and has stimulated the Catholic colonization under which settlements have been formed, with every prospect of success. He attended the Third Plenary Council of Baltimore, and after its close visited the Thresholds of the Apostles.

DIOCESE OF ST. PAUL.

RIGHT REV. JOSEPH CRÉTIN,

First Bishop of St. Paul.

The Right Rev. Joseph Crétin, first Bishop of St. Paul, was born at Lyons, in France, in the year 1800, and had studied for the priesthood in order to devote himself to foreign missions. Soon after his ordination Bishop Loras, of Dubuque, appealed for zealous priests to aid him to create a Catholicity in Iowa, and Rev. Mr. Crétin offered his services. Accompanied by another volunteer, Bishop Loras and his young coadjutor reached his diocese in April, 1839. Rev. Mr. Crétin was at once attached to St. Raphael's Cathedral, and was soon appointed vicar-general of the diocese, laboring zealously in attending distant and scattered bodies of Catholics. In 1843 he began a mission among the Winnebagoes, and revived the early missions among them until he was expelled in 1848 by the United States government, which had constantly thwarted his Christian work of civilization. He then resumed his duties at the cathedral of Dubuque; but when the diocese of St. Paul, embracing the Territory of Minnesota, was erected in 1850, the Very Rev. Mr. Crétin was appointed bishop. Having accepted the appointment, he visited France to appeal to the zeal of his countrymen to contribute to the arduous work before him. He was consecrated at Belley January 26, 1851, and set out for his diocese, where he was welcomed by the pioneer priest, Rev. Mr. Ravoux. The first report of the diocese showed only seven churches, ten priests, and one school. The bishop began a seminary, planned a cathedral, opened schools, brought in Sisters of St. Joseph, who created academies, asylums, hospitals, schools. The Brothers of the Holy Family were next to aid him; but the Benedictine prior Wittman founded at St. Cloud a house to grow in time to a great abbey and college. Bishop Crétin revived his old mission among the Winnebagoes, and recalled the Chippewas to the faith. Of Catholic emigration he was an active and persistent advocate, and saw its beneficial results. Gauged by time, his administration was a short one, but by results, and it was most successful. He died of apoplexy February 22, 1857.

RIGHT REV. THOMAS L. GRACE, O.S.D.,

Second Bishop of St. Paul.

THOMAS L. GRACE was born in Charleston, South Carolina, on the 16th of November, 1814. Evincing in childhood a strong inclination to minister at God's altar, he commenced his studies in the seminary of his native city when he had attained the age of fifteen. But the next year he entered the convent of St. Rose in Kentucky, assuming as a novice the white habit of St. Dominic. After years of retirement, prayer, and study he was sent to Rome, and for seven years pursued a most thorough theological course at the Minerva. He was ordained priest at Rome December 21, 1839. Returning to this country five years later, he was engaged in missionary duties in Kentucky and Tennessee for many years. Memphis was the chief theatre of his labors; he erected the church of St. Peter and St. Paul, one of the finest in that city, as well as the convent of St. Agnes and an orphan asylum. During his long pastorship of thirteen years Father Grace had endeared himself to all the people of Memphis, and his appointment to the see of St. Paul in 1859 came with a sense of personal loss to them. He was consecrated in the cathedral of St. Louis by Archbishop Kenrick on the 24th of July, 1859, and two days after set out with a delegation of the clergy of the diocese who had come to escort him to St. Paul, which he reached by steamer, there being no lines of railroad.

The labor before Bishop Grace was immense, giving him incessant occupation, but, without discouragement, he devoted himself with wonderful zeal. Northern Minnesota was set off as a vicariate in 1875, and in that same year the bishop obtained a coadjutor in the person of the Right Rev. John Ireland. Dakota, which had also been subject to Bishop Grace, was placed under the care of a vicar-apostolic in 1879. Five years afterwards the diocese of St. Paul, thus curtailed, contained one hundred and fifty-three priests and more than two hundred churches, with hospitals, asylums, protectories, academies, and schools. Mere statistics give little idea of the real work of a bishop in looking after the neglected Catholics, exciting faith, guiding the clergy, stimulating them in their arduous labors, watching over the rising generation. In July, 1884, Bishop Grace celebrated the silver jubilee of his episcopate, the city tendering him a most heartfelt ovation. Then, to the regret of all, he resigned the see of St. Paul and became titular Bishop of Mennith.

RIGHT REV. JOHN IRELAND,

Third Bishop of St. Paul.

THE third Bishop of St. Paul, Right Rev. John Ireland, was born at Burnchurch, County Kilkenny, Ireland, on the 11th of September, 1838, and came with his parents to America when he was eleven years old. After temporary residence at Burlington, Vermont, and Chicago, Illinois, his father, Richard Ireland, settled in St. Paul and became a builder. While a pupil in the cathedral school young Ireland attracted the attention of Dr. Crétin, who discerned in the talented boy a vocation to the priesthood. He was sent by the bishop to Meximeux, France, where he went through the Preparatory Seminary, and entered the Grand Seminary at Hyères for his theological course. Returning to Minnesota in 1861, he was ordained by Bishop Grace on the 21st of December. The young priest was soon on his way to the front as chaplain of the Fifth Minnesota regiment, and for fifteen months he served, fearlessly confronting all dangers, so as to excite the admiration and reverence of those most prejudiced against his faith. When his health yielded to the constant and laborious duty on the field, he was recalled to St. Paul and became pastor of the cathedral. Here his zeal, activity, and energy made him a marked man. The building up of the State by immigration, the study of its early history, the cause of temperance, all found in him an active advocate, while no one was more exact and devoted in his priestly duties. On the 12th of February, 1875, he was appointed, by the Pope, Bishop of Maronea and Vicar-Apostolic of Nebraska. To prevent his diocese from losing so able a man, Dr. Grace went to Rome and pleaded so successfully that the bishop-elect was made his coadjutor; as such he was consecrated on the anniversary of his ordination, December 21, 1875. His work as an advocate of temperance became more general. He entered warmly into projects for forming Catholic colonies in Minnesota, engaging capitalists in the East in the good work, and obtaining most consoling results, so that some districts are permanently Catholic, with schools under Catholic direction. It is a sign of the general appreciation with which he is regarded that he has been for several years president of the State Historical Society of Minnesota. He attended the Plenary Council of Baltimore in 1884, and on his return to his diocese presided in New York at a meeting to organize a Catholic Historical Society for the United States. In the establishment of a Catholic University he has also been a most active worker.

DIOCESE OF TRENTON.

RIGHT REV. MICHAEL J. O'FARRELL,

First Bishop of Trenton.

MICHAEL J. O'FARRELL was born in Limerick, Ireland, on the 2d of December, 1832, of a family which had given many zealous priests. After preliminary studies he entered the college of All-Hallows in 1848, and during his theological course proceeded to St. Sulpice, Paris, where he completed his studies under the able disciples of Olier. After receiving ordination in Ireland on the 18th of August, 1855, he returned to Paris and was received into the community of St. Sulpice. On the conclusion of his novitiate he was appointed professor of dogmatic theology at Paris, and he subsequently held a professorship in their seminary in Montreal. He was made pastor of St. Patrick's Church in that city, and showed as great zeal and ability in parochial work as he had displayed learning in the professor's chair. In July, 1869, he became assistant at St. Peter's Church, New York, and in 1872 pastor of Rondout. But when the Rev. William Quinn was transferred to the cathedral the Rev. Dr. O'Farrell became pastor of New York's oldest church. During his administration he erected a noble school-house, fitted with every requisite, and was consoled by seeing it filled with children. In 1881 the Holy See divided the diocese of Newark, and fourteen counties of New Jersey, embracing all the seaboard, were formed into the diocese of Trenton. Having been elected first bishop, Dr. O'Farrell was consecrated on All Saints' day in St. Patrick's Cathedral, New York, by his Eminence Cardinal McCloskey, assisted by Archbishop Corrigan and Bishop Loughlin. He made the church of St. Mary his cathedral, and prepared to establish institutions to develop religion in the southern part of New Jersey. The progress did not fail to excite hostility, and in 1883 St. John's, the oldest of the churches in Trenton, was set on fire. Bishop O'Farrell has issued pastorals of remarkable vigor and ability, and has stimulated the erection of many churches and institutions. He labored successfully to obtain for Catholics in prisons and reformatories a deliverance from the horrible and unchristian persecution by which they were deprived of their own worship and forced to attend services which they abhorred. He was one of the most learned and eloquent of the Fathers of the Third Plenary Council of Baltimore.

MOST REV. J. J. LYNCH.
Born near Cloves, Ireland, Feb. 6, 1816.

Entered the Congregation of the Mission at St. Lazare, Paris, 1839; came to U. S. in 1846 and began missionary work in Texas; Superior of St. Mary's Seminary, St. Louis, Mo.; Consecrated Bishop of Echines and Coadjutor to the Bishop of Toronto, Nov. 20, 1859; received Archbishop's Pallium, March 25, 1870.

MOST REV. C. O'BRIEN.
Born in Rustico, P. E. Island, May 4, 1843.

Entered Propaganda College, Rome, Dec. 5, 1864; Ordained April 8, 1871; Professor in St. Dunstan's College, Prince Edward Island; in charge of Cathedral Parish, Charlottetown; Indian River Parish, 1874; Consecrated Archbishop of Halifax, Jan. 21, 1883.

RT. REV. EDWARD C. FABRE.
Born in Montreal, Feb. 28, 1827.

Ordained Feb. 23, 1850; Chaplain of the Cathedral, Montreal; Vicar at Sorel, 1852; Chaplain at Montreal, 1854; Canon, 1855; elected Bishop of Gratianopolis and Coadjutor of Montreal, May 1, 1873; Bishop of Montreal, May 11, 1876.

MOST REV. ALEXANDER A. TACHE.
Born in St. Patrice, P. Q., Canada, July 23, 1823.

Ordained Oct. 12, 1845; elected Bishop, June 14, 1850; Consecrated Nov. 23, 1851; created Archbishop of St. Boniface, Province of Manitoba, Canada, Sept. 22, 1871.

DIOCESE OF VINCENNES.

RIGHT REV. SIMON GABRIEL BRUTÉ,

First Bishop of Vincennes.

SIMON WILLIAM GABRIEL BRUTÉ DE RÉMUR was born March 20, 1779, at Rennes, France, where his family had long held an influential position. Losing his father at an early age, he was formed for the career before him by his mother, a woman of judgment and piety. The famous Abbé Carron prepared him for his First Communion in 1791, when the terrible Revolution was already in progress, and young Bruté witnessed and recorded some of the most heartrending persecutions and slaughters of priests and religious. A diligent student, with a mind that grasped at all knowledge and a happy memory, he made rapid progress, and, escaping by address the law of conscription, began the study of medicine in 1796, and completed it at Paris in 1803, taking the highest prize over more than a thousand fellow-students. But, with success before him, he resolved to become a priest, and, after being trained to ecclesiastical life by the Sulpitians, was ordained in 1808. Declining a professorship in the seminary at Rennes, and a canonry, he offered his services to Bishop Flaget and came to Baltimore in the summer of 1810. After two years spent as professor in St. Mary's Seminary he was sent to Mount St. Mary's College, Emmittsburg, and for many years was connected with that institution, training, under God, numbers of excellent priests. When the see of Vincennes was established in 1834 Dr. Bruté was chosen to become its first occupant. He was consecrated in the cathedral of St. Louis October 28, 1834, and was soon after installed by Bishop Flaget.

He began his labors with one priest, Rev. S. P. Lalumiere. Vincennes was originally a French post, established about 1730, and had a series of priests till the overthrow of the French rule in Canada and the American Revolution isolated it. Then it had received occasional visits, but the people had lost much of the knowledge of their faith and their early fervor while deprived of the sacraments. At other and less important French posts the decline had been still greater. All these Catholics were to be visited, marriages rehabilitated, baptisms performed, the youth to be instructed and prepared for First Communion and Confirmation. Illinois was subject to his authority, and there a similar state of affairs existed. Besides those of French descent, there were English-speaking immigrants, more earnest, and bands of Indians who still remembered the teachings of the Black Gowns of other days. The studious professor, retained by duty amidst books for so many years, showed all the fresh vigor and activity of a young missionary. His visitations unfolded to him the condition of his diocese, and the utter impossibility of finding within its limits means to meet its wants. A visit to Europe gained some zealous priests and means to establish a seminary, asylum, and school at Vincennes, and aid in erecting plain chapels in places where they were most needed. He was pastor of his cathedral, director of his seminary, teacher in the school; and this, with the strain on his system in his episcopal visits, soon told upon his constitution. On his way to the Council of Baltimore in 1837 he took a heavy cold which ended in consumption; but he never thought of rest, and continued his labors and visits, refusing all indulgence, taking the worst for himself on all occasions. At last he yielded to the disease and prepared serenely to die, his active mind engaged in prayer or in thoughts of his flock. After receiving the Viaticum he directed the Commendation of a Departing Soul to be recited, and surrendered his soul to his Maker on the 26th of June, 1839.

RIGHT REV. CELESTINE RENÉ LAWRENCE G. DE LA HAILANDIÈRE,

Second Bishop of Vincennes.

THE second Bishop of Vincennes was born at Combourg, in Brittany, May 2, 1798, and was baptized the same day by a priest who was concealed in the house. He was educated by a good clergyman at Rennes, and studied law to fit himself for the magistracy. At a mission given by the Fathers of the Faith he resolved, at the age of twenty-four, to renounce the world, although he had been appointed to a judicial position, which he accepted only in obedience to his father's command, but soon resigned. He entered the seminary at Rennes and was ordained at Paris, May 28, 1825. His career won him the esteem of his bishop, who, when Dr. Bruté asked him to name a priest worthy to be his vicar-general and coadjutor, selected the Abbé de la Hailandière. After aiding Bishop Bruté to obtain some good priests and candidates he came to America with him in 1836, and began his labors in Indiana. Two years subsequently he was sent to Europe in the interest of the diocese, and while busily engaged at Paris received information of Dr. Bruté's death and his own appointment as Bishop of Axiern and coadjutor. He was consecrated in the Chapel of the Sacred Heart, Paris, August 18, 1839, by Bishop Forbin Janson, and used every exertion to obtain needed aid for his diocese. He sent over vestments and plate for churches, Eudists to found a college, Brothers of the Holy Cross, Sisters of Providence. Then he came himself to labor in his diocese. One of his first acts was to hold a retreat for his clergy, which was followed by a diocesan synod in 1844. He was a man of projects and action, and his energy made him unpopular with some; seeing this, he endeavored to resign his see in 1845, but on visiting Rome was so encouraged by Pope Gregory XVI. that he resumed his labors for his diocese and returned to it. But the troubles had not ceased. Discouraged completely, he again urged the Holy Father to accept his resignation, and was permitted in 1847 to lay down the burden that had become too heavy. He died on an estate at Triandin belonging to the family, May 1, 1882. By his own desire his remains were brought to the diocese he had loved so well, and laid beside the bodies of the other bishops of Vincennes who had gone to their rest.

RIGHT REV. JOHN STEPHEN BAZIN,

Third Bishop of Vincennes.

JOHN STEPHEN BAZIN was born in the diocese of Lyons in 1796, and entering the priesthood in France, came to the diocese of Mobile as a missionary in 1830. The city of Mobile was the theatre of his labors for seventeen years. He exercised the ministry with great zeal, and devoted himself especially to the education and spiritual instruction of the young. He was made vicar-general of the diocese by Bishop Portier, who sent him in 1846 to France to obtain Fathers of the Society of Jesus to assume the direction of the college at Spring Hill. On the recommendation of the Sixth Provincial Council of Baltimore he was appointed Bishop of Vincennes. He was consecrated in the Vincennes cathedral on the 24th of October, 1847, by Bishop Portier, of Mobile. He issued a pastoral letter, in which he said to his clergy: "Having been inured for many years to the labors of a missionary life, we feel ready, in spite of our advanced age, to share with you all the hardships of the ministry. We are ambitious of no distinction. We expect to find in each of you a friend."

But he was almost immediately stricken down by illness, and expired on the 23d of April, 1848.

RT. REV. P. McINTYRE.
Born in St. Peters, P. E. Island, June 29, 1818.

Ordained 1843; seventeen years in charge of mission of SS. Simon and Jude, at Tignish; succeeded the late Bishop McDonald, 1860; founded St. Joseph's Convent, 1864; presented city of Charlottetown a fully equipped hospital, 1879; erected twenty-nine churches, 1860-1885.

RT. REV. JOSEPH T. DUHAMEL.
Born in Contrecœur, P. Q., Nov. 6, 1841.

Educated at the College of Ottawa; Ordained Dec. 19, 1863, and appointed Curate at Buckingham, P. Q.; Pastor of St. Eugene, Prescott, P. Q.; Consecrated Bishop of Ottawa, Canada, Oct. 28, 1874; appointed "Assistant to the Pontifical Throne," 1882.

RT. REV. JAMES V. CLEARY.
Born in Dungarvan, Ireland, Sept. 18, 1828.

Educated at Rome, in the Royal College of Maynooth, and the University of Salonica; Professor in St. John's College, Waterford, Ireland, 1854; President of the College, 1873; Bishop of Kingston, Canada, 1879; Consecrated at Rome, Nov. 21, 1880.

RT. REV. J. P. F. L. LANGEVIN.
Born in Quebec, Sept. 22, 1821.

Ordained Sept. 12, 1844; Assistant at Notre Dame de Beauport, 1849; Director of the Laval Normal School, 1858; first Bishop of new Diocese of St. Germain de Rimouski, Jan 15, 1867; Consecrated in Cathedral of Quebec, May 1, 1867.

RIGHT REV. JAMES M. MAURICE DE LONG D'AUSSAC DE SAINT-PALAIS,

Fourth Bishop of Vincennes.

MAURICE DE SAINT-PALAIS, of an old family of knightly fame, was born at La Salvetat, in the diocese of Montpelier, November 15, 1811. He made a brilliant course of studies, and was about to enter on a career of honors when the insecurity of human grandeur made him resolve to serve a Master who knows no vicissitude. He was ordained priest in his twenty-fifth year by Archbishop de Quelen, of Paris, and, won by the virtues and sanctity of Bishop Bruté, offered his services to him. He came to Vincennes in 1836 and was sent to a new district, where he built St. Mary's Church, attending stations in two adjacent counties, fertile in resources, and neglecting none, German or Indian, in his district. At Chicago, though malcontents burned his wretched shanty, he built another St. Mary's Church. Logansport was his next mission, then Madison. Bishop Bazin during his brief administration made the Abbé de Saint-Palais his vicar-general, and on his death-bed constituted him administrator of the diocese. He was soon after elected bishop, and was consecrated by Bishop Miles, of Nashville, on the 14th of January, 1849. He began with 35 priests, 50 churches, and 30,000 souls; but what his predecessors had merely sketched out Bishop de Saint-Palais effected in his long and able episcopate of twenty-eight years. He left 151 churches, 117 priests, 90,000 souls, an abbey of Fathers of the Order of St. Benedict, 2 convents of Reformed and 1 of Conventual Franciscans, Brothers of the Sacred Heart, Sisters of St. Francis, Benedictine nuns, Ursulines, Sisters of the Good Shepherd, Little Sisters of the Poor, Sisters of St. Joseph.

On the morning of June 28, 1877, while at St. Mary's of the Woods, he was stricken with paralysis, and all efforts to save him failed. He prepared calmly for death, and, holding his rosary in the left hand he was still able to use, expired peacefully in the afternoon. His body was removed to Vincennes and laid beside Bishops Bruté and Bazin.

RIGHT REV. FRANCIS SILAS CHATARD,

Fifth Bishop of Vincennes.

FRANCIS SILAS CHATARD was born in Baltimore, Md., December 13, 1834, his grandfather, an able physician, having been one of the many French residents who escaped the hands of the negroes and made a home in the United States. His father was also an able and successful physician, eminence in the profession seeming hereditary. The future bishop was educated at Mount St. Mary's, where he was graduated in June, 1853. Adopting the profession in which so many of his family excelled, he became a physician, but in 1857 resolved to study for the priesthood. Having been accepted by Archbishop Kenrick, he was sent to the Urban College, and after a full six years' course won the cap of Doctor of Divinity in August, 1863. Three months afterwards he was appointed vice-rector of the American College at Rome, and on the consecration of Dr. McCloskey as Bishop of Louisville Dr. Chatard became rector, and for ten years presided over that institution, rendering great service not only to those under his immediate charge, but to the American bishops during the Vatican Council. Pope Pius IX. valued his services to religion so highly that he presented to him a gold medal of exquisite workmanship. In consequence of failing health he visited the United States in 1878 to collect for the American College, and soon after his return to Rome was appointed Bishop of Vincennes. He was consecrated on the 12th day of May, 1878, and, repairing to his diocese, made Indianapolis his residence, retaining, however, the title of Bishop of Vincennes. He soon after held the second Diocesan Synod, and a third in November, 1880. He also took part in the Fourth Council of Cincinnati, and in the Third Plenary Council of Baltimore in 1884.

RT. REV. M. J. O'FARRELL, D.D.
Born in Limerick, Ireland, Dec. 2, 1832.
Ordained Aug. 18, 1855; Consecrated Bishop of
Trenton, Nov. 1, 1881.

RT. REV. JOHN J. KAIN, D.D.
Born in Martinsburg, Va., May 31, 1841.
Ordained July 2, 1866; Consecrated Bishop of
Wheeling, May 23, 1875.

RT. REV. FRANCIS S. CHATARD, D.D.
Born in Baltimore, Dec. 13, 1834.
Ordained in 1862; Consecrated Bishop of Vincennes,
May 12, 1878.

RT. REV. THOMAS A. BECKER, D.D.
Born at Pittsburg, Pa., Dec., 1832.
Ordained June 18, 1859; Consecrated Bishop of
Wilmington, Aug. 16, 1868.

DIOCESE OF WHEELING.

RIGHT REV. JOHN J. KAIN,

Bishop of Wheeling.

JOHN J. KAIN was born in Martinsburg, Berkeley Co., West Virginia, on the 31st of May, 1841, the only son of Jeremiah and Ellen Murphy Kain, who emigrated from the neighborhood of Macroom, in the county of Cork, Ireland, and married in this country. Their son first attended the academy then directed by the present Bishop of Wilmington, and, seeking to serve God in his sanctuary, obtained admission to the Preparatory Seminary of St. Charles, where, after a five years' course, he was graduated in 1862. His philosophical and theological studies he pursued in St. Mary's College, Baltimore; and he was ordained by Archbishop Spalding on the 2d of July, 1866. His field of priestly labor embraced the valley of Virginia from the Potomac to Mount Jackson, and centred at Harper's Ferry. Its extent may be seen in the fact that for a considerable time he had charge of the Catholics living in eight counties of West Virginia and four in Virginia. He then obtained an assistant to share his arduous labors. During his administration of this large district he repaired the churches at Harper's Ferry and Martinsburg, which had been greatly injured during the Civil War, and rebuilt those which had been destroyed at Winchester and Berkeley Springs. On the 21st of February, 1875, this laborious priest was elected Bishop of Wheeling, and was consecrated by Archbishop Bayley on the 23d of May, his aged mother, who had attained the age of fourscore, witnessing the exaltation of her son.

At the beginning of the year 1885 the diocese of Wheeling contained thirty-four priests, who attended sixty-two churches, eight chapels, and forty stations. The Catholic white population was estimated at about twenty thousand. There were thirty-four academies and schools, a hospital and asylum under the care of Visitation nuns and Sisters of St. Joseph.

DIOCESE OF WILMINGTON.

RIGHT REV. THOMAS A. BECKER,

First Bishop of Wilmington.

THE future Catholic Bishop of Wilmington was born in Pittsburgh, Pennsylvania, of Protestant parents, December 20, 1832. After spending some time in the Allegheny Institute he entered the Western University, and completed his studies at the University of Virginia.

His mind turned to the great religious question, and, corresponding to the grace of God, he was received into the Church by Bishop McGill. He went to Rome in 1854 to study for the priesthood in the Urban College of the Propaganda, and after receiving the doctorate in theology was ordained by Cardinal Patrizi in the Basilica of St. John Lateran on the 18th of June, 1859.

On his return to Virginia he was assigned to the mission embracing Martinsburg, Winchester, Berkeley Springs, and the adjacent counties. These were attended until the church of Martinsburg was seized by the United States military authorities, who converted it into barracks. He was then sent to Baltimore, where Archbishop Kenrick selected him as one of the faculty of Mount St. Mary's. Under Archbishop Spalding he was one of the clergy of the Baltimore cathedral. Previous to the assembling of the Second Plenary Council the Rev. Mr. Becker was one of the theologians engaged in preparing the matters for the action of the prelates, and during the sessions of the council he was one of the secretaries.

His ability and learning displayed in such varied offices marked him as one to be placed in an important rank. On the

RT. REV. J. WALSH.
Born in Mooncoin, Ireland, May 24, 1830.
Ordained Nov. 1, 1854; Bishop of Diocese of Sandwich, Toronto, Nov. 10, 1867; removed episcopal residence to London, Canada, 1868; celebrated silver jubilee of his priesthood, Nov. 10, 1879; laid corner stone St. Peter's Cathedral, May 23, 1881.

RT. REV. V. GRANDIN.
Born in Laval, France, Feb. 8, 1829.
Entered noviciate of Oblate Fathers of Mary Immaculate, Dec. 28, 1851; Ordained April 23, 1854; appointed Titular-Bishop of Satala and Coadjutor to Bishop Tache, of St. Boniface, and Consecrated Nov. 3, 1859; appointed first Bishop of new See of St. Albert, and took possession April 7, 1872.

RT. REV. DOMINIC RACINE.
Born in St. Ambrose, Canada, Jan. 24, 1828.
Educated at the Seminary of Quebec; graduated 1848; Ordained March 12, 1853; elected Bishop of Chicoutimi, Canada, May, 1878; Consecrated Aug. 4; took possession of his See two days later.

RT. REV. L. F. LAFLECHE.
Born in Ste Anne de la Perade, P. Q., Sept. 4, 1818.
Studied the classics and theology at the Seminary of Nicolet, 1831-'43; Ordained Jan. 6, 1844; Consecrated Titular-Bishop of Anthedon and Coadjutor to the Bishop of Three Rivers, Feb. 25, 1867; raised to the dignity of Bishop of Three Rivers, June 3, 1870.

erection of the see of Wilmington he was elected bishop, and received consecration at the hands of Archbishop Spalding on the 16th of August, 1868.

The diocese of Wilmington, over which he was called to preside, embraces the State of Delaware with the counties of Maryland and Virginia on the eastern shore of the Chesapeake. It contains about fifteen thousand Catholics, who have twenty-nine churches, attended by twenty-four priests.

VICARIATE-APOSTOLIC OF COLORADO.

RIGHT REV. JOSEPH PROJECTUS MACHEBŒUF,

First Vicar-Apostolic of Colorado.

JOSEPH PROJECTUS MACHEBŒUF was born at Riom, in the diocese of Clermont, France, on the 11th of August, 1812, and was in childhood a pupil of the Brothers of the Christian Schools; after being graduated in the college of his native city he entered the Sulpitian seminary at Montferran, where he mastered philosophy, theology, and other branches of ecclesiastical learning. After receiving ordination in the Advent of 1836, he was employed in the ministry in France for three years, but, preferring to become a missionary, volunteered with Rev. Mr. Lamy, now Archbishop of Santa Fé, to accompany Bishop Purcell to his diocese. On the 1st of January, 1840, he was appointed pastor at Sandusky, Ohio, where French priests had reared a chapel in the last century. Here he remained eleven years, developing the church and institutions. Having been invited to New Mexico by Bishop Lamy, then vicar-apostolic of that Territory, he reached it by a laborious route through New Orleans and Texas. As vicar-general he labored earnestly in that old Catholic field till 1860, when Bishop Lamy sent him to Colorado, where a new population was gathering. Beginning as vicar-general for that Territory, Rev. Mr. Machebœuf may be said to have created all that the Church has there to-day. He built the first church in Denver, and attended Catholics wherever they gathered, till other priests came to assume local direction of the churches that grew up. So rapidly did Catholicity develop in the Territory that in 1868 there were seventeen churches or chapels. Denver had a convent of

RT. REV. J. CAMERON.
Born in St. Andrews, N. S. Feb. 16, 1827.
Ordained July 26, 1853; appointed Titular-Bishop of Titopolis and Coadjutor to the Bishop of Arichat, Canada, March 11, 1870; Consecrated at Rome, May, 1870; Administrator of the Diocese of Arichat, Jan. 14, 1877, and translated to that See a few months later.

RT. REV. F. CONRAD.
Born in Auro, Switzerland, Nov. 2, 1833.
Ordained Sept. 14, 1856. Proceeded to America, April 27, 1873, under orders from his Abbot to found the Benedictine Monastery of New Engleberg, at Conception, Mo., which was erected into an abbey, April 5, 1881. Assigned as its first Abbot. Dec. 11, 1885.

RT. REV. J. J. CARBERY.
Born in Mullingar, Ireland, April 30, 1823.
Entered Dominican Order, Nov., 1841; elected Provincial of Ireland, 1876; Assistant to the Father-General, 1880; elected Bishop of Hamilton, Canada, Sept. 6, 1883; Consecrated in Rome, Nov. 11, 1883; took possession of See, April 2, 1884.

RT. REV. NARCISSE Z. LORRAIN.
Born in St. Martin, June 13, 1842.
Ordained Aug. 4, 1867; first resident Missionary Priest, Redford, N. Y., Aug. 14, 1869; Assistant Parish Priest, St. Henry, 1879; Vicar-General, Diocese of Montreal, Aug. 5, 1880; Bishop of Cythera and Vicar-Apostolic of Pontiac, July 14, 1882.

Sisters of Loretto, with an academy and a school for boys. Pope Pius IX. in that year constituted the vicariate-apostolic of Colorado, extending over the Territory of that name, and also over Utah. Right Rev. Dr. Machebœuf, having been appointed titular Bishop of Epiphania, was consecrated August 16, 1868, in St. Peter's Cathedral. He has lived to see Denver a city of seventy-five thousand inhabitants, with six Catholic churches, with convents, academy, hospital, asylum, House of the Good Shepherd, and several parochial schools. There are fifty-one priests in the vicariate, officiating in ninety-six churches and chapels, and the Catholic population in 1884 was nearly fifty thousand.

VICARIATE-APOSTOLIC OF DAKOTA.

RIGHT REV. MARTIN MARTY, O.S.B.,
First Vicar-Apostolic of Dakota.

MARTIN MARTY was born at Schwyz, in Switzerland, on the 12th of January, 1834, and, entering in youth the great Benedictine abbey of Einsiedlen, made his profession on the 20th of May, 1855. The young monk had already pursued his theological studies with such zeal and talent that the next year he was ordained, on the 14th of September. A colony of monks from Einsiedlen was sent to Indiana in 1854, and founded St. Meinrad's. Dom Marty arrived in 1860 to share the labors of the sons of St. Benedict, and when the priory was established five years later he was made the first superior. The little community prospered, receiving postulants who persevered, and the mission work increasing. Pope Pius IX. in 1870 erected St. Meinrad's into an abbey, constituting the Fathers connected with it into the "Helveto-American Congregation," and Right Rev. Martin Marty was made mitred abbot. The corner-stone of a new monastery was laid May 22, 1872. Abbot Marty presided for several years, perfecting the institutions under his care, and extending the missions, erecting churches, and fostering education. But he had always desired to undertake missions among the Indians, and at last he went with some Fathers to Dakota. The work there gave such promising hopes that he resigned his dignity of abbot to devote himself to it. In 1879 the Territory of Dakota was formed into a vicariate-apostolic and confided to the care of the zealous Benedictine, who was consecrated Bishop of Tiberias on the 1st of February, 1880. When Bishop Marty attended the Plenary Council, four years later, there were nearly ninety churches and fifty priests in his vicariate, with seven Indian missions attended by his clergy, Benedictine, Ursuline, and Presentation nuns, with Sisters of the Holy Cross and Youville Sisters of Charity aiding in the good work.

RT. REV. DOMINIC MANUCY, D.D.
Born in St. Augustine, Florida, Dec. 20, 1823.
Ordained Aug. 15, 1850 ; Consecrated Bishop of
Dulma and Vicar-Apostolic of Brownsville, Dec. 8,
1874; Bishop of Mobile, 1884-5; Bishop of Maronea,
1885. Died Dec. 4, 1885.

RT. REV. MARTIN MARTY, D.D.
Born at Schivy, Switzerland, Jan. 12, 1834.
Ordained Sept. 14, 1856; Consecrated Bishop of
Tiberias and Vicar-Apostolic of Dakota, Feb. 1, 1880.

RT. REV. J. P. MACHEBOEUF, D.D.
Born at Riom, France, Aug. 11, 1812.
Ordained in 1836; Consecrated Bishop of Epiphania
and Vicar Apostolic of Colorado, Aug. 16, 1868.

RT. REV. A. J. GLORIEUX, D.D.
Born at Dodignies, Belgium, Feb. 1, 1844.
Ordained Aug. 17, 1867 ; Consecrated Bishop and
Vicar-Apostolic of Idaho, April, 1885.

VICARIATE-APOSTOLIC OF IDAHO.

RIGHT REV. LOUIS LOOTENS,

First Vicar-Apostolic.

LOUIS LOOTENS was born at Bruges, in Belgium, about 1825, and after being ordained in Europe, about 1851, came to the California mission some six or seven years afterwards. His first labors were at St. Patrick's Church, Sonora; but in 1859 he assumed charge of St. Vincent's Church at Petaluma and St. Raphael's Church in Marin County. Here he labored for several years with great zeal, erecting a neat church at San Rafael, and enlarging the academy buildings at a cost of five thousand dollars.

When it was determined to erect the Territories of Idaho and Montana into a vicariate-apostolic, Rev. Mr. Lootens was elected on the 3d of March, 1868, and was consecrated Bishop of Castabala on the 9th of August. It was within the limits of the vicariate thus created that Father P. J. De Smet, S.J., had erected the cross at the Flathead village in 1840. At this time there were missions among the Flatheads, Pend-d'oreilles, Cœur d'Alènes, and Nez Percés, with schools and hospitals under Sisters of Providence, Sisters of Charity, and Sisters of the Holy Names. There were also churches at Idaho City, Placerville, Centreville, Pioneer, and Silver City. Under the impulse of Bishop Lootens churches rose at Granite and Deer Lodge. The growth of the vicariate was, however, slow, and the difficulties very great, while the resources were most precarious. The vicar-apostolic labored for some years till his severe mission duties incapacitated him.

and he resigned his office July 19, 1876, and it was more than eight years before a successor was appointed, the vicariate being administered by the archbishops of Oregon. Bishop Lootens has since lived in truly apostolic poverty—a poor return for the zealous labors of his early manhood on the American missions.

RIGHT REV. A. J. GLORIEUX,

Second Vicar-Apostolic.

A. J. GLORIEUX was born on the first of February, 1844, at Dottignies, in the Belgian province of West Flanders, being the son of Auguste and Lucy (Vanderghinste) Glorieux. After a college course of six years at Courtrai he entered the American College at Louvain to study for the priesthood, with the view of devoting himself to the missions in this country. On completing his divinity studies he was ordained in Mechlin by His Eminence Engelbert Cardinal Sterckx on the 17th of August, 1867. Before the close of the year he was in Oregon to begin the mission work. He was first appointed to Roseburg, in Douglas County, attending several dependent stations. From this charge he was transferred to Oregon City and then to St. Paul, in French prairie, the cradle of Catholicity in Oregon. In 1871 he was made president of St. Michael's College, Portland, and discharged the duties of his position so ably that in 1884 he was appointed vicar-apostolic of Idaho, the Catholic interests in that Territory having since the retirement of Bishop Lootens been under the care of the Archbishop of Oregon as administrator. The total Catholic population in 1884 was estimated at 2,300, eight hundred being Nez Percé and Cœur d'Alène Indians. Bishop Glorieux was consecrated in Baltimore, in April, 1885.

RIGHT REV. J. F. JAMOT.
Bishop of Peterborough, Canada.

RIGHT REV. J. SWEENEY.
Bishop of St. John, N. B.

RIGHT REV. A. EDELBROCK.
Abbot of the Benedictine Monastery,
Collegeville, Minn.

RIGHT REV. F. MUNDWILER.
Abbot of the Benedictine Monastery,
St. Meinrads, Ind.

VICARIATE-APOSTOLIC OF NORTHERN MINNESOTA.

RIGHT REV. RUPERT SEIDENBUSH, O.S.B.,

First Vicar-Apostolic.

RUPERT SEIDENBUSH was born on the 30th of October, 1830, at Munich, in Bavaria, and came to America in 1851. On the 6th of January in the following year he made his profession as a monk of the Order of St. Benedict, in St. Vincent's Abbey, Westmoreland County, Pennsylvania. He was ordained priest on the 22d of June, 1853. He was employed on missionary duty in Newark, New Jersey, and in other parts of the country, and when the monastery of St. Louis on the Lake, now called St. John's, was erected into an abbey in 1867 he was appointed first abbot. While at the head of that religious house he was chosen to organize the newly-created vicariate-apostolic of Northern Minnesota, and was consecrated titular Bishop of Halia on the 30th of May, 1875. Under his care religion has progressed. Northern Minnesota, with a Catholic population of about 32,000 Catholics, had at the opening of the year 1885 sixty priests, eighty-six churches and chapels, an abbey, eight convents, a college, an academy, and several schools, as well as Indian missions.

VICARIATE-APOSTOLIC OF ARIZONA.

RIGHT REV. P. BOURGADE, D.D.

BISHOP BOURGADE as second vicar-apostolic of Arizona now directs the Church in the district first evangelized by the famous German Jesuit Kühn, and other Fathers of his order, whose labor the sons of St. Francis continued. He was born in the Department of Puy-de-Dôme, France, October 17, 1845, and after proceeding from the school of the Christian Brothers entered the College of Billom. There the young man felt called to the priesthood, and, entering the *Grand Séminaire*, was trained for the awful responsibility of the ministry by the Sulpitians. As his fifth year of severe study was drawing to a close, the present Archbishop Salpointe of Santa Fé, who had just been appointed vicar-apostolic of Arizona, visited France to receive episcopal consecration, and appeal to the candidates for the priesthood for volunteers to aid him in the work to which he had been assigned, there being only two priests in his district.

Young Bourgade at once felt impelled to go, his confessor approved his inclination, and, having already received deacon's orders, he set out with Bishop Salpointe, and reached Tucson in June, 1870.

Having been ordained priest on the last day of November, he began his mission work at Yuma, in May, 1870, but in the summer of 1873 his health was so shattered that he returned to France to recruit. In 1875 he was again in the vicariate, and was assigned by the bishop to the mission of San Elzeario, Texas, and after six years' hard labor there was sent to Silver City, Colorado, the vicariate of Arizona comprising not only the Territory of that name, but parts of the adjacent State and Territory.

While here zealously laboring for the salvation of souls he was, on the 23d of January, 1885, appointed Vicar-Apostolic of Arizona, and was consecrated titular Bishop of Taumaco by Archbishop Lamy, in the cathedral at Santa Fé, May 1, 1885.

www.ingramcontent.com/pod-product-compliance
Lightning Source LLC
Chambersburg PA
CBHW032031220426
43664CB00006B/442